THE WEIR GROUP

The Weir Group

A CENTENARY HISTORY

W. J. Reader

with a final chapter by
the Right Hon. Viscount Weir CBE, LLD

Research by Elizabeth McClure Thomson

WEIDENFELD AND NICOLSON
5 Winsley Street London W1

ISBN 0 297 00463 8

Printed in Great Britain
by Ebenezer Baylis and Son Limited
The Trinity Press, Worcester, and London

Contents

CONTENTS

Illustrations

The 'Hybrid'

Mr N. M. Niven

The Air Horse

The Skeeter

Early 'Quality' house

Land-based sea-water distillation plant

The Guernsey sea-water distillation plant

The sea-water distillation plant at Aden

The *Fairtry* fish factory vessel

The board of directors (1961–2)

The second Viscount Weir

A Weir Pacific stainless steel Class 150 gate valve

A seven-roomed house constructed according to the advanced Multicom system

The Ashford Common pumping station of the London Metropolitan Water Board

Large pump casting

A galley designed for the Boeing 747 'jumbo-jet'

Three one hundred thousand gallon per minute de-watering pumps

A boiler feed pump

Large cooling tower circulating water pumps

The board (and Secretary) of The Weir Group Limited, March 1971

Preface

This History was commissioned by the Weir Group to mark the centenary of the foundation of G. & J. Weir Limited of Glasgow. The research for it was done by Mrs Thomson but I am alone responsible for the writing of the book and for the way in which the source material has been handled. Mrs Thomson and I have both had full access to all the Company's records and the Company has exercised no form of censorship over what has been said or not said, though naturally I have listened to views expressed while the writing was going on.

The treatment of current, or near-current, affairs in a company history must be different from the treatment of affairs in the more distant past, not only because confidential information cannot freely be disclosed but also because the reporter of recent events has not the historian's advantage of knowing the end of the story, and is therefore in no position to form an historical judgement. Accordingly I am extremely grateful to Lord Weir for supplying an account of the last ten years or so – very important years – of Weirs' history.

Lord Weir has been unfailingly helpful throughout the progress of the work, and so also has Mr N. M. Niven, who after he retired from the Board of Weir Holdings agreed to act as my main link with the Company – a responsibility which he has discharged with informative and genial assiduity. Mr H. Waugh, still fully occupied at Cathcart, has nevertheless gone to great trouble on my behalf, and the statistical appendix, especially, bears witness to my indebtedness to him.

It also bears witness to my debt to Mr J.D.Gillies, who undertook very heavy work in the analysis of Weirs' inward orders. He has also put at my disposal his knowledge of aeronautical history, of technical matters generally and of Weirs' business. I am extremely grateful to him.

In all my dealings with the Weir Group, at all levels, I have met with the utmost helpfulness and kindness. I hope this book does justice, though written by an Englishman, to the record of a business described by its present Chairman as 'Scottish based and under Scottish direction'. I hope it may also serve to throw light on a wider subject – the course of Scottish industrial history, particularly in Clydeside shipbuilding and engineering, over the last hundred years.

W.J.R. London, June 1970

1

The Inventions of a Ship's Engineer 1870–95

'To my generation of naval men,' wrote a naval historian in 1968, 'the name of G. & J.Weir will always recall the peculiar wheeze followed by a loud thump on change of stroke of the boiler feed water pumps.' Captain Roskill and his generation of naval men left the sea in the years following the Second World War. This book will show why they and the generation before them were so familiar with the wheeze-and-thump of Weir pumps, and the name of G. & J.Weir will appear at the beginning of the book and will remain prominent in it to the end.

The Weir Group, as it stands at its centenary, is more than an alliance of pumpmakers. It is broadly-based on different aspects of engineering, with interests in steel casting, in sea-water distillation, in aircraft equipment, and in building, though it still has a heavy commitment to pumping machinery and equipment associated with it. The purpose of this history is to explain how, over the course of a century, technical and commercial logic have interacted with each other and with the force of human personality to bring into being the Weir Group of 1971.

The Group's origins run back to the British shipbuilding industry of the 1870s, when the balance of new construction was swinging from sailing ships to steamers. The tonnage of steamers built in the United Kingdom for the first time overtook the tonnage (though not the number) of sailing ships in 1870 itself, when 433 steamers of 225,700 tons were built, against 541 sailing ships of 117,000 tons. Then for a few years there was a sharp fall in the sailing tonnage built, but in 1875 and 1876 it was once again greater than the tonnage built for steam. In 1877 the steamers went ahead again, and stayed there.[1]

This final triumph of steam was a matter chiefly of the relative costs of steam against sail. So long as the price to be paid for a steamer's advantages – mainly speed and punctuality – remained very high, sailing ships were competitive for most commercial purposes, especially on long voyages. The purposes of warships made rather different demands, which for the moment we may disregard.

The costs associated with steam propulsion were influenced, in the main, partly by the space taken up by machinery and partly by the rate of coal consumption, which in turn affected costs partly through the prices paid for the coal itself and partly through the space which had to be allowed for bunkers. The matter of bunker space was not very important for ships on short voyages, which could take in fresh coal frequently, but it was critical for ocean-going ships. There was no prospect of steamers superseding sailing ships on long voyages, except in special circumstances, until coal consumption had been brought low enough to allow a pay-load which made costs competitive. In the seventies it became possible to reduce the costs of coal consumption very considerably, and it can hardly be accidental that these were the years in which the building of steamships finally overtook the building of sailing ships in the United Kingdom.

The decisive influence was the development of compound engines, in which the steam was expanded in two or more stages, at high pressure and low pressure, so that much more useful work was got out of it than in the simple-expansion engines previously used at sea. Coal consumption was cut by 50 per cent or more, and that gave steamers a competitive advantage over sailing ships even for the longest voyages, especially since the opening of the Suez Canal in 1869 had just provided a much shorter route, which particularly favoured steam power, to the East and Australasia.[2] Sailing ships, nevertheless, long remained economic, even if diminishingly so. As late as 1894 about a quarter of British merchant tonnage (3,500,000 tons out of 13,200,000) was under sail, and the next largest merchant fleet – the American – had a greater tonnage under sail than in steam (1,400,000 tons sail, 600,000 tons steam).[3]

Compound engines finally established themselves about the mid- or late seventies, after development lasting twenty years or more, and they were in general use by the mid-eighties. Over the same period of thirty years, necessarily, marine boilers were also developed, principally for higher working pressures. Simple-expansion engines had worked at 20-25 lb per square inch, but compound engines required pressures ranging from 60 to 110 lb or more.[4] Amongst the technical problems which these advances raised, one in particular is of direct concern to us: corrosion and scaling on the heating surfaces.

This problem had always been present, particularly in boilers fed directly with sea water, but the higher working pressures went, the more urgent it became. There was not only the matter of fuel economy to consider, but safety as well, because a badly scaled and corroded high pressure boiler was only too likely to burst. 'With the higher pressures now adopted,' said a speaker before the Institution of Mechanical Engineers in 1891, reviewing the progress of marine engineering in the previous decade, 'the danger arising from overheating is much more serious, and the necessity is absolute of maintaining the heating surfaces free from deposit.'[5]

Boiler corrosion, accordingly, attracted a great deal of attention in the seventies. In 1874 the Admiralty appointed a committee to go into the whole subject, and four years later it finished its task, having examined 170 witnesses, whose evidence, with many appendices, was published in three large reports. Meanwhile in 1876 a boiler explosion in HMS *Thunderer* killed forty men, and although it had nothing to do with corrosion it was nevertheless a dreadful warning. With such matters as these before him, as well as the experience of

3

his daily work, a marine engineer in the late seventies, with his eye on advancement and profit, might well feel that the problem of boiler corrosion would offer a rewarding field for any inventive talent he might happen to possess.

One such engineer was a Scotsman called James Weir (1843*–1920). He was the second of three brothers, grandsons of John Bishop and Elizabeth, illegitimate daughter of Robert Burns. This couple's daughter Jean (1811–99) married James Weir the elder. He died in 1850 or thereabouts, being then barely forty, leaving his widow rather poorly off. Her eldest son George (1833–1910) became a ship's engineer, and at the time of his father's death, when he was about seventeen, he was probably an apprentice. His younger brothers, James and Thomas, would have been about seven and five respectively.[6]

Both the younger brothers became engineers like the eldest, and like many other Scots with their way to make and not much money to do it on. Thomas lived from 1845 to 1929, and pursued a prosperous career in China. James started work in 1858, aged about fifteen, in the offices of Hamilton & Grandison, consulting engineers in Glasgow. Later (probably in 1860) he moved to another Glasgow firm and became an engineering apprentice. To raise the fees his mother, a resolute woman, turned to needlework and dressmaking, which she considered would provide the five shillings a week for three years that was required. It may well be that by this time she was also getting help from her eldest son, in his late twenties and presumably well launched on his career.

The firm to which James Weir was apprenticed was no doubt chosen, long before the days when a university degree was considered at all appropriate to a career in engineering, as being likely to give him the best possible professional training. It was the firm of Randolph, Elder & Co., later (1868) John Elder & Co., and later still Fairfield Engineering & Shipbuilding Co. It was new, having been founded at Govan

---

* There is doubt about the year of James Weir's birth, which is sometimes said to have been 1839, 1841 or 1842 (16 Sep.), but the date shown appears to be the most likely.

in 1852, and Weir served his apprenticeship under both the original partners. John Elder (1824–69), the younger of them, was pioneering the development of compound engines, so that any apprentice of his was at the leading edge of marine engineering in the fifties and sixties. Charles Randolph (1809–1878), who left the firm in 1868, was at the centre of Glasgow's increasingly rich and powerful business aristocracy. He was a close associate of Charles Tennant (1823–1906), Asquith's father-in-law (1894), and Randolph, like Tennant, had interests in chemicals, explosives and mining, as well as in shipbuilding.[7]

To have been an apprentice with Randolph & Elder must have been an advantage to Weir in the connections it gave him as well as the training. While he was with the firm he patented a marine governor, and the firm's principals allowed him, while still in his apprenticeship, to go to Smith Bros & Co., Canning Street, Glasgow, to supervise the construction of his invention. The gesture seems to have been intended as a compliment, not a dismissal, and presumably Weir could depend on his old firm's goodwill when he set up in business for himself. His governor, which had considerable success, was first fitted to SS *Garland*, owned by Camerons (later Alexander Laird) of Glasgow, and the original model was exhibited at a *conversazione* of the Institution of Engineers and Shipbuilders in Scotland.

Weir's apprenticeship, according to a note on his application to be examined as a second-class engineer, lasted four years, apparently from 1861 to 1865. He first went to sea in the 130 h.p. Sligo steamer *Liverpool*, but after a little less than two months, on 31 August 1865, he joined the Bibby Line steamer *Arabian* in which he remained until 1870. She was a four-masted iron vessel of 1,994 tons gross, with square sails forward and fore-and-aft sails aft. She was driven by a screw and is variously described as being of 200 or 450 h.p. She plied between Liverpool and the Eastern Mediterranean. Weir shipped first as third engineer, qualified as a second-class engineer in November 1866, and in March 1867 was promoted to second engineer of the *Arabian*. He became a first-class engineer in June 1868.[8]

Weir left the *Arabian* in August 1870 for a post as first engineer of another Bibby Line ship, the *Oporto*. He served in her for about ten months (11 August 1870 to 1 June 1871) and then joined the *Princess Royal*, 449 tons register and 170 h.p., owned by John Langlands of Glasgow. The ship's papers show the second engineer to have been George Weir, aged thirty-seven, who must have been James's elder brother, but it seems doubtful whether the brothers sailed together, because George is not shown as having signed off at the end of the voyage. Perhaps he was ill, and James came in at short notice to take his place. Whatever happened, James Weir did not stay in the *Princess Royal* for long. He signed off at Marseilles, along with most of the crew (nearly all Frenchmen), on 19 June 1871, ten days after joining, having presumably only agreed to make this one trip.

James Weir held one more sea appointment, under very curious circumstances. In May 1874, after nearly three years ashore, he signed on as first engineer of the *Queen Anne*, owned by R. & J. Craig of Glasgow, a steamer of 1737 tons register and 350 nominal h.p. She was bound for the East, via Suez, on what appears to have been a tramping voyage expected to last twelve months. Her master was a Londoner, and she carried four engineers.

Weir was on the *Queen Anne*'s books for just six days (9 to 15 May 1874). Then, according to the ship's papers, he deserted. In doing so he seems to have been following the example of his predecessor as first engineer, who signed on a day earlier, did not join the ship and was left behind at Glasgow. Presumably Weir was prevailed upon to take his place, but he also evidently found something about the ship which he could not put up with. Probably both engineers quarrelled with the master, but why we shall never know.

If this episode is disregarded, we may say that James Weir left the sea after his voyage to Marseilles in the *Princess Royal* in June 1871. While he was a ship's engineer he had taken out patents for improvements to steam machinery, and by 1871, with six years' sea service behind him, and presumably some savings, he seems to have decided that he could risk setting up on land as a superintendent engineer for shipowners. In 1871 or 1872 – no record of the exact date survives – he went into partnership with his brother George, and the firm of G. & J. Weir came into existence, first in Liverpool and then in Glasgow.

Weirs were established in Glasgow, at 71 Hydepark Street, in 1873, and in 1874 James Weir married Mary Richmond (1848–1931). There is a tradition that she had a good deal to do with the firm's move from Liverpool to Glasgow, and it may be that she could reinforce her persuasiveness with money. She was the daughter of a blacksmith, William Douglas, and the widow of a bonnet-maker of Kilmarnock. He contracted with the War Office for soldiers' headgear, and there is no reason to think that he left her poorly off, so that she may very well have been able to contribute to the new firm's finances, which would almost certainly have come from within the family. She brought James Weir a stepson, John Ritchie Richmond (1869–1963), who was to become a leading figure in the Weir business.

In 1874 James Weir patented an invention of some importance, the *hydrokineter*, which continued in use for about sixty years. Professor (later Sir) Alfred Ewing (1855–1935), who held the Chair of Mechanism and Applied Mechanics at Cambridge from 1890 to 1903, thus describes it in a standard textbook of the nineties: 'Weir's *hydrokineter* for large marine boilers is [an] apparatus in which the principle of the injector is made use of, with the object of promoting circulation of the water during the time steam is being raised. It consists of a series of nozzles, with water-inlets between them, through which water is drawn by means of a central jet of steam supplied from a donkey boiler.'[9] Weirs had no plant of their own, and the hydrokineter was made for them by Miller & Pearce of Hydepark Street, Glasgow. It was a device for reducing the cost of getting up steam, and cost, as we have seen, was of critical importance to the progress of steam navigation. The hydrokineter's influence, however, could scarcely be more than marginal, since it did not improve the performance of the boiler once steam was up.

With the hydrokineter on the market and contributing both to the firm's profits and reputation, Weir applied himself to the central problem: boiler corrosion.

In 1880 he took out a patent for his most important invention; a device for heating feed water to the boiler. It represented a basic contribution to the science of heat engines as well as bestowing practical operating advantages. The concept was to utilize steam extracted from the engine, at some intermediate point between its inlet and exhaust, to heat the feed water before it entered the boiler.

To achieve the maximum efficiency from any heat engine its cycle of operations should be so arranged that all the heat is supplied at the maximum temperature of the working fluid. In a steam engine cycle all the heat is originally supplied in the boiler, and before the incoming feed water can be vaporized into steam its temperature must be raised in the boiler to the boiling point. This part of the heat supply is, therefore, substantially below the maximum temperature of the cycle (i.e. the temperature of the steam issuing from the boiler) and an inherent thermodynamic loss results.

This loss can be significantly reduced if the temperature of the boiler feed supply can be raised above the lowest cycle temperature (the temperature at which the engine exhaust is condensed in the condenser) by a lower cost heat supply than exists in the boiler. James Weir achieved this objective by using steam which had already done some work by expanding through the engine and which, therefore, represented just such a low cost heat source – since the heat in this steam would not ultimately be wasted by condensing it in the condenser but would all be returned to the cycle. His invention is known as regenerative feed heating. It is applied to the most modern steam plants even to the present day in order to achieve economy of operation.

The invention was linked, at the time, to the most up-to-date practice in marine engineering as the partially expanded heating steam could be extracted between the cylinders of a compound engine. As triple- and quadruple-expansion engines were developed, and turbines after them, it was readily adaptable to multi-stage regenerative feed heating by heating the feed water in stages with steam extracted from successive stages of expansion through the engine.

The earliest application of this principle embodied the heating of the feed water by 'direct contact' with the steam in a closed vessel thus causing the feed water to boil with results which Ewing, in the nineties, describes as follows:

> Besides increasing the efficiency of the boiler by utilising what would otherwise be waste heat, a feed water heater has the advantage that by raising the temperature of the water it removes air, and also, in the case of hard water, causes lime and other substances held in solution to be deposited in the heater instead of being carried into the boiler.[10]

Feed heating thus gave practical advantages by reducing one of the main difficulties – corrosion and scaling – in the way of designing high-pressure boilers. Weir, as might be expected, was not the only inventor working in this potentially lucrative field. Contemporary comment on marine engineering, in the eighties and nineties, refers to other systems of feed heating, some more or less on the same principles as Weir used and others 'which heat the feed in a series of pipes within the boiler' but Weir can nevertheless claim to be the inventor of regenerative feed heating, and thereby produced a system for economizing on the running costs of steam machinery, afloat and ashore, which has never been surpassed.[11]

His other major inventions were two: pumping gear suitable for hot feed water and an evaporator for distilling sea water to provide uncontaminated feed water for the boiler, to make up the continual loss at pipe joints and packings. Older practice had been either to carry fresh water in tanks which took up pay-load space or to use sea water untreated, which was very dangerous in high-pressure boilers. Other inventors worked on evaporators, too, but neither they nor the other feed-heater inventors seem to have combined their inventions into a system in the same manner as Weir, which may be one reason why his work outlasted all the rest.

The Weir Steam Valve

Main Valve to be pulled in this Direction when Auxiliary Valve X is at Top End of Stroke

Main Valve to be pulled in this Direction when Auxiliary Valve X is at Bottom End of Stroke

Main Valve to be pulled in this Direction when Auxiliary Valve X is at Top end of Stroke

Main Valve to be pulled in this Direction when Auxiliary Valve X is at Bottom End of Stroke

Auxiliary Valve X

X

Auxiliary Valve X

Steam

Exhaust

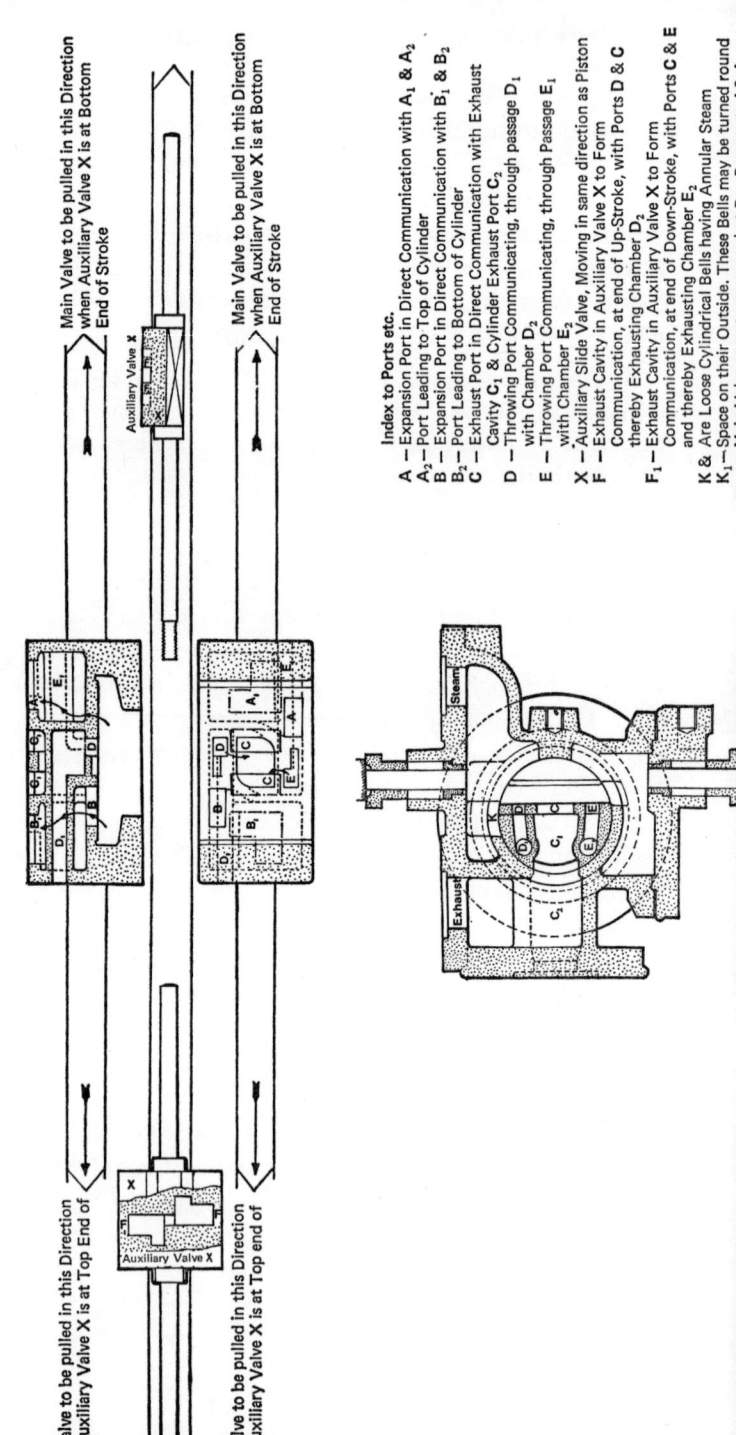

Index to Ports etc.

A — Expansion Port in Direct Communication with A_1 & A_2

A_2— Port Leading to Top of Cylinder

B — Expansion Port in Direct Communication with B_1 & B_2

B_2— Port Leading to Bottom of Cylinder

C — Exhaust Port in Direct Communication with Exhaust Cavity C_1 & Cylinder Exhaust Port C_2

D — Throwing Port Communicating, through passage D_1 with Chamber D_2

E — Throwing Port Communicating, through Passage E_1 with Chamber E_2

X — Auxiliary Slide Valve, Moving in same direction as Piston

F — Exhaust Cavity in Auxiliary Valve X to Form Communication, at end of Up-Stroke, with Ports D & C thereby Exhausting Chamber D_2

F_1 — Exhaust Cavity in Auxiliary Valve X to Form Communication, at end of Down-Stroke, with Ports C & E and thereby Exhausting Chamber E_2

K & Are Loose Cylindrical Bells having Annular Steam

K_1— Space on their Outside. These Bells may be turned round Main Valve so as to open or shut By -Pass ports J & J_1

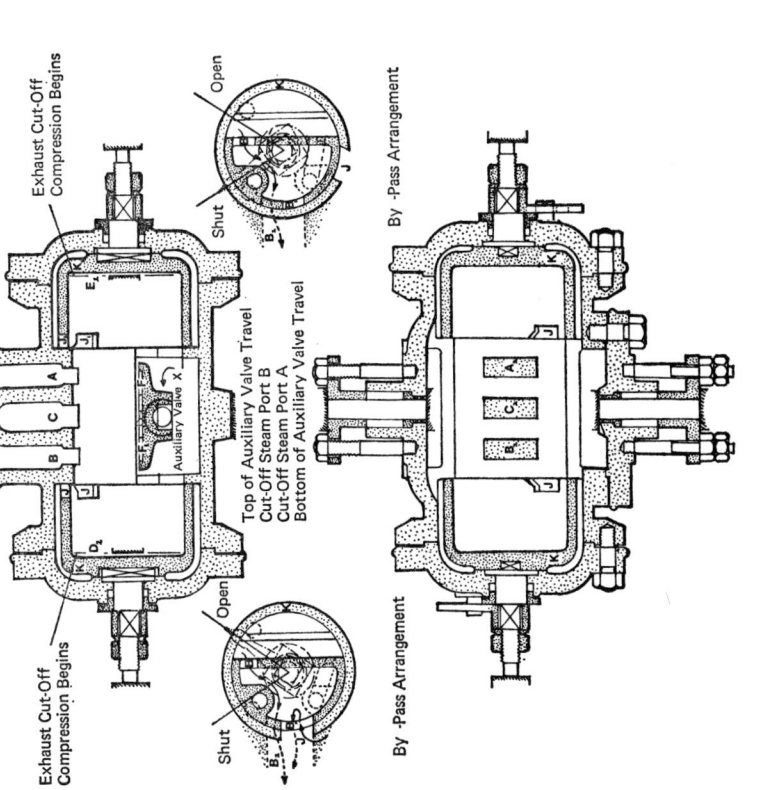

Exhaust Cut-Off
Compression Begins

Exhaust Cut-Off
Compression Begins

Open

Shut

Open

Shut

Top of Auxiliary Valve Travel
Cut-Off Steam Port B
Cut-Off Steam Port A
Bottom of Auxiliary Valve Travel

Auxiliary Valve

By-Pass Arrangement

By-Pass Arrangement

In the public mind – at any rate, the mind of the sea-going public – Weirs' name came to be associated particularly with their feed pumps. They worked independently of the main engines, from which earlier feed pumps had been driven, and they relied on an arrangement of valves devised by James Weir which was covered, in principle, by a patent for the Weir steam valve chest taken out in 1881. Over many years the characteristic wheeze-and-thump of their operation became a familiar noise in every ocean of the world.

In pumping machinery Weirs found more than one rival already established. John & Henry Gwynne made centrifugal pumps, particularly the *Invincible* for fast warships, mail steamers, yachts and launches. In 1841 an American engineer, Henry Rossiter Worthington (1817–80), had taken out a patent for an auxiliary steam pump designed to get canal boats started in the morning, after a night's halt. By the eighties the firm founded on his inventions was probably the leading maker of boiler feed pumps. A vertical marine pump designed by Worthingtons 'to suit the views of the Admiralty' could deal with boiler feeding up to 250 lb pressure, and in 1893 it was said to be 'supplied in numerous sizes to very many naval and mercantile vessels throughout the world'.[12] Worthingtons and other American firms were formidable rivals, determined especially to hold their home market against interlopers, and against Worthingtons in particular Weirs competed strenuously and sometimes acrimoniously until competition was replaced by association in 1969.

'With the eighties,' says a historian of marine engineering,[13] 'a new epoch in the history of the steamship was inaugurated.' For this there were two main reasons – the greater use of steel in construction, and the adoption of triple-expansion engines. In 1880 40 steel steamers were built in the United Kingdom, of 34,800 tons altogether, against 396 iron steamers of 309,800 tons. In 1889 the figures were reversed – 445 steel steamers of 518,100 tons against 113 iron steamers of 35,400 tons. By 1900 the change had gone much further: 84 iron steamers of 5700 tons, against 508 steel ones of 690,400 tons.[14] At the same time triple-expansion engines, and quadruple-expansion engines after them, were taking over propulsion, so that 'the ships of 1900 were as superior to those of 1880, as those of 1880 were to those of 1860.' The largest ship in the world in 1882 (except the derelict *Great Eastern*) was the Inman liner *City of Rome*, 560 ft long, 8141 gross tons, 11,890 hp from a compound engine. In 1902 the German *Kaiser Wilhelm II*, 19,361 tons gross, was 678 ft long and developed 43,000 hp from four sets of quadruple-expansion engines driving twin screws.[15]

The progress of the eighties was led by British shipbuilders and builders of marine engines. About 1884 there were 138 steamers afloat of more than 4000 tons gross, and only ten had been built outside the United Kingdom. Moreover of these 138 ships, more than half had been built on the Clyde. British shipbuilders led the world, and the Clyde firms led British shipbuilders.[16] If ever there was a time and place to set up in any business connected with marine steam engineering, the time was the early eighties and the place was the Clyde. The tonnage of ships built there rose, with wide fluctuations, from 300,000 tons in 1884 to 757,000 tons in 1913, and in that year more shipping was built on the Clyde than in the whole of Germany.[17] This was the flowing tide on which, between 1880 and 1886, James Weir launched his three major inventions: his feed heater, his feed pump, and his evaporator.

1886 itself, in the midst of the period conventionally known as the Great Depression (roughly from the mid-seventies to the mid-nineties), was a very bad year for Clyde shipbuilding. Tonnage built, 172,440, was never so low again until building almost ceased in the depths of the 1930s. Nevertheless it was in 1886 that George and James Weir felt themselves sufficiently secure to begin setting up a factory of their own, so that they would no longer have to rely on contracting out for the manufacture of their gear. The site they chose was at Cathcart, a village on the southern outskirts of Glasgow.

There can be little doubt that a very strong reason for thus launching out on their own was Weirs' need to have machinery specially designed for their own requirements. They first set up a machine shop, a brass foundry and a smithy, and their fourteen original employees were chiefly engaged on millwright's work and on the building of machine tools for the factory that was to be. On these tools James Weir worked in collaboration with the firm of G. & A. Harvey. Together they designed machinery for boring and tapping and for boring and facing. They also produced a valve seat machine, made necessary by the multiple valve arrangement, patented in 1884, which was a feature of James Weir's feed pump.

This concern for machine tools no doubt explains why the Weir partners, looking for someone to manage their growing works, turned to one of the leading firms in the machine tool industry: John Lang & Sons of Johnstone, whose speciality was lathes.[18] James Weir asked John Lang for one of his five sons, and the one who came was the fourth, C.R.Lang (1863–1941). In 1886 he finished three years as a Whitworth scholar in the establishment at South Kensington which in 1907 was transformed into Imperial College of Science and Technology. Lang was therefore something of a rarity: an academically trained engineer. He joined Weirs as Works Manager in 1887, and became a partner in the firm, so presumably either he or his family contributed to its capital.

In 1889 James Weir brought his stepson, John Richmond, into the business. His interests were artistic and literary (he published an edition of Thomas Chatterton's poems) and he had no technical training. In 1889 he was reading law at Glasgow University, and it may be supposed that he would have preferred to take his degree. But James Weir decided that he was needed in the business, roughly in the capacity of office manager, and James Weir was not lightly defied, least of all in his own family. Moreover the business offered Richmond excellent prospects and anything like an equivalent opening elsewhere would have been hard to find. So into Weirs John Richmond went, and applied himself to the firm's affairs for the greater part of the succeeding sixty years.

By the early nineties, then, George and James Weir had laid

the foundations of their firm's success. Feed heating was indispensable to the up-to-date marine engines of the day, and Weirs were coming to be recognized as leaders in that field. They had their own factory. They had a young works manager, trained in the best practice of the time, to run it. Richmond was there to look after the firm's administration. James Weir's elder son, William Douglas Weir (1877–1959) was apprenticed to the business in 1893, with a view to joining the management as soon as he was trained. No records of the firm's finances survive, but there is good reason to suppose that profits were excellent, and that they were mostly reinvested in the expansion of the business.

In 1895 the partnership of G. & J.Weir was replaced by a private company, G. & J.Weir Limited. This was very much in the fashion of the day, for although limited liability had been fairly easy to arrange since the sixties, it did not become widespread until towards the end of the century. The reasons for turning a successful family partnership into a company often arose from the need to find fresh capital, and this may have been Weirs' case, though we have no direct evidence. There was certainly no intention of alienating the ownership or control of the business, which again was typical practice of the day. When a partnership was turned into a company the former partners, transformed into directors, were usually the largest shareholders, and this was certainly so in Weirs.

George Weir, however, took the opportunity to retire to Australia, where he died in 1910. He was a devout Plymouth Brother, less forceful, less ruthless than his younger brother, and by the time the company was formed he was sixty-two, which no doubt seemed to him a reasonable age for retirement. After he left, nevertheless, the business remained firmly in the hands of Weirs and Langs. Some employees became shareholders, but wider dissipation of ownership was prevented by a requirement, common enough in the articles of private companies, that any shareholder who wished to sell should offer his holding, at a price to be determined by the Board, to shareholders remaining.

The new company stood poised for expansion. 'The evaporator,' said Sir Henry Oram, Engineer-in-Chief of the Fleet, in 1911, 'by making it possible to use only fresh water in the boilers, cleared the way for further rises of pressure. These rises of pressure and the demands for reduction in weight and space allowed for machinery finally led to the introduction of the water-tube boiler, the satisfactory use of which at sea had been made possible by the introduction of the evaporator.'[19] And whose evaporator? The Admiralty had several patterns to choose from, and they chose James Weir's, with a feed pump for water-tube boilers designed by him as well. All this at a time when the demand for new construction, for the British Navy and for every other navy in the world, was rising very fast.

2

The Expanding Market
1895–1914

In 1887 Queen Victoria reviewed the British Fleet at Spithead. It was the largest fleet in the world and a very expensive one, since rapid technical progress meant continually replacing ships long before they wore out. Yet the fleet at Spithead, torpedo-boats apart, included only thirty-five fighting ships of any consequence, of which nine were unarmoured.[1] The Navy estimates for 1887–8 amounted to £13,200,000.[2]

In the early nineties the pace of naval expansion and improvement quickened. Battleships' main armament became steadily heavier, and consequently their armour plate. Quick-firing guns came in, made possible by the invention of 'smokeless powder' ('cordite' in the British service). Mines and torpedoes, heavily deplored by British admirals, became practical, and younger officers found themselves in command of new kinds of warship, torpedo-craft and submarines. The general design of ships, including their engines and auxiliary machinery, advanced very fast.

Broadly, it is fair to say that one vessel of each generation of battleships was capable of dealing with an entire battle-fleet of the generation before, and the generations succeeded each other within ten years or less. And at the same time as the armoured monsters were successively outfacing each other, there was continuous development, at the other end of the scale of size, in torpedo-craft and submarines, each of which presented a growing threat to capital ships.

British naval activity, up to the turn of the century, was directed chiefly at the possibility of war with France. Hostility towards the French was part of the national habit of mind, and the French, who cherished similar feelings towards the British, were the only nation with a fleet which entered into anything like serious rivalry with the Royal Navy. Hence the concentration of British sea power in the English Channel and the Mediterranean, and the anxiety with which French developments in naval technology were followed.

In 1898 the Germans gave public notice that they intended to develop formidable sea power. They had 7 battleships, 2 large cruisers and 7 smaller ones. In April 1898 a Navy Law announced that within six years they would build 12 new battleships, 10 new large cruisers, and 23 smaller ones.[3] A fleet on this scale could add nothing to German power on the Continent, which was already overwhelming. It might be directed against the French, but it was much more likely to be aimed at Great Britain, and in Great Britain it was certainly thought to be. Moreover the Navy Law of 1898 was only a start. By 1914 the Germans had 33 battleships and 7 battle-cruisers, with 7 battleships and 3 battle-cruisers building. Therefore from 1898 on, and increasingly as the years went by, British naval building was devoted to outclassing the Germans rather than the French, although it was not until after the *Entente Cordiale* of 1904, and uncertainly even then, that the British began to look on the French as possible allies rather than probable enemies.[4]

The German Empire was not the only rising sea power of the early twentieth century. In Asia, from the mid-nineties on, the Japanese were developing a large and powerful fleet. It showed its quality in the total defeat of the Russians at Tsushima in May 1905. After that, Japanese naval building still went on. The British had no cause for alarm, since their relations with Japan were founded on the Anglo-Japanese alliance of 1902, which represented a good bargain for both parties. The Americans, on the other hand, began to be seriously alarmed. In March 1908 one of William Weir's correspondents in the States reported the arrival of 16 American battleships in the Pacific to face the Japanese, and he went on to draw the correct conclusion: that shipbuilding would be brisk on the Atlantic coast to replace them.[5] By 1914 the Americans had 33 battleships, with 4 building. The Japanese had 17, with one building, as well as 4 battle-cruisers building.

Where Great Powers led, smaller powers would follow, pursuing their own rivalries and gratifying their own self-esteem. All through the twenty years or so before 1914 navies were being built up throughout the world: in Europe, in Asia (in December 1909 Glasgow Corporation were planning a banquet for the members of the Chinese Imperial Naval Commission[6]), and especially in South America, where the prestige of the various republics was held to depend partly on the size and costliness of the warships they ordered. In 1911 the Brazilians ordered from Armstrongs the largest battleship in the world at that time. After many curious adventures, she finally went to sea as HMS *Agincourt*. The officers' quarters were uncommonly luxurious, but it was doubtful whether she could fire all her fourteen twelve-inch guns at once without breaking her back.[7]

This world-wide building covered every class of naval vessel – capital ships, cruisers, torpedo craft, submarines – and raised every kind of problem in naval architecture and marine engineering. The shipbuilders of the world were very happy to take orders from all comers, and their governments encouraged them to do so, because thereby foreigners, as well as domestic taxpayers, contributed to the development of a powerful armaments industry. There were not, however, many countries with a shipbuilding industry which could cover the full range of types required.

The building of smaller vessels was fairly widespread, at any rate in Europe. When it came to battleships and cruisers the only firms of importance in the international market were in Great Britain, Germany, America and, to a lesser degree, France. Therefore orders for heavy ships – and orders for lighter craft were likely to follow them – were bound to go to a narrowish circle of competitors, some of whom restricted their competition with each other by agreement. In all countries capable of it, shipbuilding for export prospered, nowhere more so than on the Clyde.

British shipbuilders did a thriving trade with the Japanese. They modelled their navy, with British help, closely on the Royal Navy, and they chose British firms to build such vessels and equipment as they could not build for themselves. In this dependent position the Japanese had no intention of remaining longer than they could help, and by 1914 they had reached a point where they could build their own capital ships. This did not prevent them – any more than German shipbuilding competence prevented the Germans – from buying British equipment when it suited them to do so, or from making licensing agreements with British firms. The British firms accepted, as they had to, the Japanese drive towards technical omnicompetence and profited handsomely from it on the way.

As well as this flourishing trade in warships there was a large, though fluctuating, demand for merchant ships. At the most prestigious and, no doubt, lucrative end of the scale, this was the classic period of rivalry on the North Atlantic, especially between British and German lines. This rivalry produced, on the German side, ships like *Kaiser Wilhelm II*, *Imperator*, *Vaterland* and *Bismarck*: on the British, *Mauretania*, *Lusitania*, the disastrous *Titanic* and *Olympic*. The proud names mean steadily less as time goes on, but in their day they symbolized wealth, engineering mastery and the international standing not merely of their owners, but of the countries to which their owners belonged.

Many more passenger liners were built for the other great trade routes, and besides them cargo vessels of all kinds. Most of these ships, as well as most of the warships, were built in the United Kingdom, and the world's shipbuilding figures from 1906 to 1912 illustrate both British predominance and the very wide swings in demand to which the shipbuilding industry, as a whole, was liable:

World Shipbuilding (millions of gross tons) 1906–12[8]

	UK	Others		UK	Others
1906	1·8	1·1	1910	1·1	0·8
1907	1·6	1·2	1911	1·8	0·8
1908	0·9	0·9	1912	1·7	1·2
1909	1·0	0·6			

In the world in which Weirs formed their company, then, the demand for warships, large and growing, was important not only for its volume but also because it forced technical development, making for rapid obsolescence. The demand from commercial shipowners, though greater in volume and very valuable, was technically rather sleepy, except at the top of the scale among Atlantic liners, mail steamers and cross-channel steamers on the one hand and in specialized craft such as fast steam yachts, on the other. Naval rivalry, like aero-space rivalry later on, set the pace, and at the same time it offered some insurance against the periodical failure of civilian demand. In 1903, for instance, William Weir remarked, in a letter to his Uncle Tom in China: 'Things in a business way are very quiet here now, in fact were it not for the warships we . . . would be very slack indeed.'[9] Later on, in the difficult years 1908–9, there is little doubt that Weirs were greatly helped by naval work both British and foreign.

Weirs' position in the shipbuilding industry was that of suppliers of auxiliary machinery. The advantage of this position was that no matter who got the order for building a ship – British builder or foreign, on the Clyde or in Bremen – Weirs might still hope to sell their gear if the shipbuilder or his client specified it. On the other hand, without an order from the shipbuilders Weirs could do no business at all. Weir gear was never cheap, and shipbuilders were sometimes tempted to cut their prices by saving on auxiliary machinery.

It was of the utmost importance, therefore, for Weirs to cultivate the good opinion of buyers of ships as well as of shipbuilders. Much the biggest buyer of ships in the world was the British Admiralty, and at the Admiralty the branch responsible for ships' machinery was the Engineer-in-Chief's Branch.

The strength of Weirs' competitive position – it became a very strong position indeed – depended on a close relationship with the officers of the E.-in-C.'s Branch, from the E.-in-C. himself downwards. This relationship, founded on technical excellence, was built up painstakingly and with great success over twenty years or so before the Great War. Its main architect was James Weir's elder son William. He joined Weirs' Board in 1898, at the age of twenty-one, and in 1902 became Managing Director.

Weirs' first introduction to the Admiralty seems to have come by way of a decision, taken in the early nineties, to test water-tube boilers against the cylindrical boilers then in use. As a result of these tests the Engineer-in-Chief chose a boiler designed by Julien Belleville, a French engineer, and it was put into two cruisers, *Powerful* and *Terrible*, in 1896. Belleville had experimented with water-tube boilers as far back as 1856, and the basis of the design favoured by the E.-in-C. had been tested in 1872, so that the Admiralty can hardly be accused of undue haste in the matter.[10]

The essential difference between the old cylindrical 'fire-tube' type of boiler and the water-tube boiler is that in the former the hot gases resulting from the combustion of fuel, flow through relatively large diameter tube(s), which are surrounded by water, whereas in a water-tube boiler the water flows through a large number of relatively small diameter tubes around which the combustion gases flow.

Many advantages accrue from this inversion of the juxtaposition of water and flue gas:

1. By careful arrangement of the tubes vigorous circulation of water through them can be promoted. This improves the rate at which heat can be transferred to the water. A reduction in the total heat transfer surface required results.

2. The amount of water within the boiler can be significantly reduced thus decreasing the time necessary to raise steam and the rate at which steam generation can be increased or decreased whilst steaming, both of vital importance in the operation of a warship. The bulk of the boiler is reduced.

3. The containment of the water which has to stand full boiler pressure takes the form of separate water and steam drums interconnected by the water tubes, all of which are respectively of much smaller diameter than the shell and fire tubes of the 'fire-tube' type of boiler. Considerable savings in material weight can thus be made.

These advantages were particularly important in warships, notably in the more rapid raising of steam and the reduction in size and weight for a given capacity of boiler. The subject was explored thoroughly and acrimoniously before the Institution of Naval Architects in 1897, when the Engineer-in-Chief, in person, reported trials in *Powerful* and *Terrible*, and a rear-admiral spoke from the executive officer's point of view.[11] Boiler design, nevertheless, remained a matter of fierce technical controversy well into the twenties and in 1909 a marine engineer of Liverpool (Arthur J.Maginiss), addressing the Institution of Mechanical Engineers, said flatly '. . . up to the present this class of boiler has not succeeded.'[12] Nevertheless they came into use in every navy in the world before 1914, whatever commercial shipowners might have thought, and in 1938 a historian of marine engineering commented: 'no one to-day questions the wisdom and courage of those responsible for the change [to water-tube boilers].'[13]

Weirs' interest in the matter arose from the fact that the Belleville boiler worked at 300lb pressure, and in the feed line pressure rose to 400–450lb. These figures were much higher than the Engineer-in-Chief had been accustomed to, and although he accepted the boiler itself he was not satisfied with the feed pumps supplied from France with it. Feed pumps were already well known to be Weirs' speciality and James Weir, at the request, it is said, of the Engineer-in-Chief himself, turned his mind to the problem. He succeeded in designing a high-pressure pump which pleased the E.-in-C. much better than the French model.

The Engineer-in-Chief who risked his professional reputation to get water-tube boilers into the Royal Navy was Sir John Durston (1846–1917). In spite of the Engineer-in-Chief's

KCB, conferred in 1897, and the rank of Engineer Vice-Admiral, retired, granted in 1906, the standing of the engineering branch in the Navy remained low. Junior engineer officers' names were not entered in the Navy List until 1870, and long after that executive officers were unwilling to admit that engineers were people whom gentlemen might properly associate with. A letter writer in *Engineering* in 1901 observed that a naval engineer was 'in everybody's watch but in nobody's mess', and compared the pay of young naval engineers – 6s. 6d. a day – with the pay of young naval surgeons, who got twice that rate.[14]

It was made very clear, in fact, that naval engineer officers were engineers employed by the navy – tradesmen, really – who were naval officers only by courtesy, and precious little of that. It may have been for this reason that the staff of the engineering branch of the Admiralty took to William Weir and his firm. Weir and the engineer officers were in the same profession – or trade – and their relationship, based on shared technical competence, was not complicated by considerations of naval tradition. Moreover Weir was a Scot, and so were some of the naval engineers, and to the Scot English notions of social precedence are apt to look a little ridiculous.

The engineering branch of the Admiralty grew with the growing navy. Between 1902 and 1914 it almost doubled in numbers. The staff, however, remained remarkably stable, moving upwards rather than out. Thus the successive Engineers-in-Chief who followed Durston (Sir Henry Oram, E.-in-C. 1907–17 and Sir George Goodwin, 1917–22) both came from within the branch, and lower down the scale the same names recur from year to year, including at least one future E.-in-C. – Engineer Lieutenant H.A.Brown, who was at the Admiralty in 1914 and retired as E.-in-C. in 1936.

Weirs, therefore, could rely on continuity in the organization they were dealing with. Engineer officers put in spells of sea service to qualify for promotion, but they then commonly returned to the Admiralty in higher appointments.

Weirs' own management, in the twenty years before the

Great War, was equally stable. James Weir became Chairman of the company on its foundation, and for a time in the middle nineties he was very busy with his own design of water-tube boiler, for which he took out a patent in 1894 (3724), two more in 1896 (4995 and 28961) and another in 1898 (12308). His work is referred to, fairly respectfully, in Rowan's *Practical Physics of the Steam Boiler* (1903), and a boiler-making subsidiary (Weir Boilers Limited) was formed. The established boiler firms, however, made it clear that they would not welcome what they regarded as poaching, and Weirs, no doubt, were too prosperous in their own specialities to welcome the idea of a fight. Weir Boilers was wound up in 1908.[15]

About the turn of the century, when he was approaching sixty, James Weir began gradually to withdraw from active business. He made lengthy, leisurely tours abroad, and in 1903 he bought an estate at Over Courance, Dumfriesshire, where he built a house to his own design and developed an interest in agricultural improvement, which he pursued with the originality of mind formerly applied to problems of marine engineering. Within the firm his technical advice was still sought, and the tone of surviving letters makes it clear that he was held in considerable awe by his juniors. But he made it evident that his retirement was not a sham by selling his shares in the business to his elder son William. William was not at first in a position to buy the shares from his father, so the old man lent him the money, which over the years was duly paid back.

With James Weir's retirement the management of Weirs' business passed to the next generation. C.R.Lang in the works and J.R.Richmond in the office we have already met. On the sales side there was James Latta, a Director from 1912, who was related to the Douglas's, Mrs James Weir's family. He was a large, handsome man with a Kaiser Wilhelm moustache and a heavy, astrakhan-collared overcoat: evidently very much the dashing salesman. He travelled incessantly in Europe, Japan and North America, and indeed during most of the twenty years before the Great War he almost certainly spent more time abroad than at home.

William Weir seems always to have been regarded as his father's designated successor, and as early as 1901 he was described as 'head of the constructive department', with Richmond alongside him as 'chief of the administrative department'.[16] He probably regarded himself as first among equals, but his appointment as Managing Director (1902) emphasized his primacy, and by 1912 he was Chairman, though there is no record of the exact date when he took over the position from his father.

He was small and neat, very lively in appearance and manner. He had an engaging disposition which combined with strength and honesty of purpose to carry him through the storms of a long public career without making personal enemies among his numerous opponents. In later life he was regarded with respect by many eminent men, including H.G.Wells, Ernest Bevin and Winston Churchill. One of his closest personal friends was the first Lord Trenchard.[17]

Before 1914, however, he was a Glasgow businessman, trained in engineering and principally concerned to advance the interests of his firm. Public affairs came later. His business letters of this period have survived in quantity, although most other records of the firm's progress have disappeared. It is mainly through William Weir's eyes, therefore, that we are enabled to see the development of the business, and there is an obvious danger of exaggerating his importance at the expense of Lang, Richmond and Latta. There seems to be no reason to doubt, however, that in general they accepted his leadership, and that both inside and outside the firm he was regarded as its executive head and chief representative.

In 1903 James George Weir (b. 1886), William's young brother, started an apprenticeship to the business. It culminated, in 1906, with a period in Germany, beginning with three months in the foundry belonging to Norddeutsche Maschinen und Armaturen Fabrik, Bremen, mainly to learn German. 'I may say,' wrote William Weir, recommending James to the German management, 'that he is a very smart young chap, and a very good workman indeed, and would be no loss to you in the foundry.' The Germans did their best to impress the young man with their technical efficiency, but when the foundry manager ('he and I have long yarns every day') claimed $1\frac{1}{2}$ per cent as their percentage overall of bad castings, James commented: 'I can scarcely believe it, as I have seen during the short time I have been here as fine a selection of scabs, bursts, blow-ups, run-outs, etc. as ever took place at Holm Foundry.'[18]

From the foundry at Bremen J.G.Weir went on to Freiburg Academy, where he got a place in the Chemical Laboratory ('I know some men who have not been so lucky'). Outside the laboratory he took a mixed course of mathematics, physics, chemistry and metallurgy which, he told his brother, 'looks a good deal but the whole lot scarcely aggregate the amount of time spent in the Lab.'[19] From Freiburg, his practical and academic technical education complete, J.G.Weir returned to take his place in the business at Cathcart. He joined the Board in 1909.

Adventurous, ingenious and gay, sometimes pugnacious, not at all attracted to routine, and passionately interested in the dangerous new sport of flying, James made a contribution all his own to the management of Weirs. His elder contemporaries, there is no doubt, sometimes found his exuberance alarming. 'My brother, Mr James G.Weir,' wrote William Weir in 1912, evidently with relief, 'has been induced to give up aeroplaning.'[20] How wrong he was! Mr James G.Weir was still 'aeroplaning', in theory if not in practice, in 1969.

With the entry of J.G.Weir the second generation of Weirs' management was complete. Latta left, as we shall have occasion to observe, towards the end of the Great War. The two Weirs, Richmond and Lang remained substantially in control throughout the twenties and thirties, although about 1930 younger men – a third generation – began to come forward. C.R.Lang died in 1941 but William and James Weir, and Richmond, remained on the Board until well after the Second World War. Lang and Richmond had come into the management of the business in the late eighties, William Weir in 1898, and James nine or ten years later. There was thus personal continuity in the direction of Weirs' affairs for some sixty-five years – almost two-thirds of the hundred years covered in this book.

During the twenty years before the Great War Weirs' management was predominantly young, or in early middle age. Leaving James Weir out of account, the oldest member of it was Charles Lang who in 1900 was thirty-seven, with Richmond thirty-one and William Weir twenty-three. The company was then making sales invoiced at about £200,000 a year, and profits of about £26,000 gross. Both figures rose steeply, though not without setbacks, over the following fourteen years, and in the last year of peace Weirs' invoiced sales reached about £750,000, yielding profits of £204,000.

During the pre-war years Weirs' trade developed and altered in a manner to be examined in the rest of this chapter. Its main foundation at all times, however, was pumping machinery, particularly up to about 1908. In the years 1898–1908, indeed, about 80 per cent by value of the orders coming in were for direct-acting pumps, and the remainder divided roughly as follows:[21]

Heaters	10%	Condensers	2%
Evaporators	5%	Sundries	3%

The greater part of Weirs' output went into ships, but there was a rapidly rising demand for various uses on land. An examination of Weirs' order books in four sample years before the Great War illustrates these points. It also shows the great increase in Weirs' business generally, and particularly in that part of it derived from naval work, both British and foreign, which in 1913 was twenty times as great, by value, as in 1898:

	1898 £	%	1903 £	%	1908 £	%	1913 £	%
Admiralty (a)	21,848	19	59,268	47	50,321	25	417,490	61
Generating plant			4827	4	2809	2	52,698	8
Other land plant	7833	6	13,889	11	38,009	18	51,083	7
Marine (b)	86,719	75	48,461	38	110,761	55	158,992	24
		100		100		100		100
	116,400		126,445		201,900		680,263	
Index (1898 = 100)	100		108		174		577	

Notes: (a) includes work for British and foreign navies

(b) i.e.: work for all ships other than warships

The base for this expansion was the works at Cathcart. From 1898 onward they were reorganized and enlarged on principles developed in America and Germany, where engineering practice was drawing ahead. Already by the turn of the century management and men in British engineering were widely known for a habit of mind which took no delight in innovation, whether in technology or in labour relations. In particular, there was little or no enthusiasm on the management side, and positive hostility on the side of labour, towards the system of work-study associated with the name of the American engineer Frederick W. Taylor.[22]

Weirs were exceptional, and recognized to be so, in their attitude to these matters. In 1901 a writer in *Engineering*, opening a description of the works at Cathcart, remarked:

At the present time, when so much is being written on the subject of foreign competition, and when foreign workshop practice is being compared with methods obtaining in this country, especially in the direction of standardisation, the use of automatic and semi-automatic tools, and the adoption of the premium system of labour payment, it is interesting to indicate that there are cases in this country where these important adjuncts to efficient work and contented employés are as extensively adopted as in any foreign establishments.[23]

Later in the same year, after a visit to America, William Weir found himself obliged to made a disturbing admission: 'I have had to give up one of my strongest prejudices ... that a Scotch mechanic of the best class can always do a job in the same time as an American mechanic of the best class. This I find is not the case. The capability of the American for working hard is really astonishing and makes one enquire very seriously as to what the reason is.'[24] The reason may have been connected with greater willingness to try out new ideas.

Weirs' business, the writer in *Engineering* pointed out, lent itself fairly readily to standardization. 'Excepting the main castings of the steam and water ends,' he said, 'the other various parts of the pumps can be standardized to a large extent.' He went on to say that over fourteen years – that is, presumably, since starting at Cathcart – the firm had supplied feed pumps for boilers totalling 16,500,000 i.h.p. and for about 4200 vessels. 'Standardization,' he concluded, 'has become a valuable element in the economy of the works.'

It was certainly a selling point with the Admiralty. If the E.-in-C.'s branch could see that Weirs got the contract for pumps for a whole class of ships, rather than individual ships, William Weir could offer attractive prices. He could also point out how much faster repairs and replacements could be carried out with standardized parts than without. In July 1903 a steam cylinder broke in one of the new pumps for HMS *Carnarvon*. It was impossible to supply a new pump at short notice, but a new cylinder was sent off by passenger train from Glasgow to Deptford, London, where it was required, and within about twenty-four hours of the breakdown the pump was under steam again.[25] Weir took care to inform the Admiralty of this 'little incident', as he called it.

In buying machine tools, a matter to which William Weir gave great attention, particularly in the early years of the century, Weirs went to a wide variety of suppliers. William Weir and Richmond, personally, held a considerable interest[26] in the Glasgow firm of G. & A. Harvey which, under James Weir's direction, had supplied much of Cathcart's original equipment (page 14). Through Charles Lang there was a lasting connection with his family firm at Johnstone. Through W.H.L.Orcutt, an American who was a leading expert in the field, Weirs placed considerable orders, in the early 1900s, with Ludwig Loewe & Co. of Berlin, who designed a ball-rod lathe for them. Loewes, through the owning family, had widespread connections in the armaments industry of Great Britain and Germany, which no doubt gave them up-to-date and expert knowledge over the whole range of engineering machinery, since the armaments firms were in the forefront of development. Apart from the products of Harveys, Langs and Loewes, there were machines in the Cathcart works in 1901 supplied by a dozen or more firms in Great Britain, Germany and the United States. Power came from Crossley gas engines, fuelled from the town supply, and from electricity. There was also one of James Weir's boilers in the works, supplying steam for the test shop.

To run the works, which covered five acres 'under roof', Weirs employed 950 men. 'Before the conclusion of the famous engineer strike in 1898,' says *Engineering*, 'Messrs Weir decided that some system of paying their men in proportion to the work done was absolutely necessary.' They decided on 'a modification of the premium system' which seemed to them reasonably easy for the management to apply and for the men to understand. The Weir-Halsey system, as it was called, was based on detailed work study, and the principle was that if a man finished a job in less than the time allowed for it, he was paid at his full rate for half the time he saved.

The system worked reasonably well before 1914, and William Weir, once convinced of the rightness of payment by results in engineering, never changed his mind. He maintained that for the firm it was essential in the face of foreign competition, especially American, and that for the men it yielded more money than time rates. The men, however, always suspected that it concealed some dark plot on the employers' side, and that if they worked too fast they might very easily work themselves out of a job. The parties to the argument were not really speaking the same language, and their fundamental disagreement persisted, now more obtrusive, now less, during the greater part of the period covered by this book.

In 1897 Charles Parsons (1854-1931) formed the Parsons Steam Turbine Company. In 1906 HMS *Dreadnought*, then the world's most powerful fighting ship, was launched, fitted with turbine machinery. (She was built in great secrecy, and estimating for her auxiliary machinery was done by William Weir personally, direct to the Engineer-in-Chief.) Turbines were also fitted in the Cunarder *Mauretania*, which was intended to challenge German supremacy in the North Atlantic passenger trade just as *Dreadnought* was intended to counter the rise of German fighting power in the North Sea. In 1900 the first 1000 kW. turbo-alternators, built by Parsons, were put up at Elberfeld in Germany, and in 1906 the last British electricity-generating plant driven by reciprocating steam engines was built (for the LCC tramways). Both at sea and on land the steam turbine, an invention as important as Watt's separate condenser (1769) had established itself.[27]

At about the same time, coal was being displaced by oil as fuel for steam boilers. The Royal Navy, impelled by Admiral Fisher (who also impelled it towards turbines), experimented with oil between 1902 and 1905. About 1907 the Navy began a decisive changeover: so decisive that in 1912 the Liberal Government, against its political principles, took a half-interest in the Anglo-Persian Oil Company which was intended, in some manner unspecified, to protect supplies of oil for the fleet. Oil fuel came first into destroyers, but in 1912 the battleship *Malaya* was designed for it from the first. Other ships were converted, and by the time war broke out the Royal Navy was predominantly an oil-fired fleet.

Between 1902 and 1904 internal combustion engines, designed by Rudolf Diesel (1858–1913) to run on oil-fuel, were put into a canal boat in France and then into a much larger oil-tanker (*Wandal*) built in Russia for service on the Caspian. The probability emerged, gradually hardening into certainty, that large vessels would eventually be driven by internal combustion engines rather than steam engines of any kind, turbine or otherwise. That, however, was a distant prospect in 1914, though Fisher, as always, was trying to force the pace. 'Oram and the Admiralty are timorous – *of course they are!*' he wrote to Charles Parsons in 1912, 'They were timorous with the water-tube boiler! They were timorous at the Turbine going into the Dreadnought! We've got to push them over the precipice!'[28] Over the precipice, however, the Engineer-in-Chief refused to go, and at the outbreak of war no craft of any consequence in the Royal Navy were propelled by internal combustion engines.

Internal combustion engines in large ships, many years later, were to raise grave problems for Weirs. They do not require feed heating or much in the way of pumping machinery, and they do not provide steam to run pumps for other purposes about the ship, such as Weirs specialized in. Turbines, on the contrary, and the adoption of oil fuel were both entirely favourable to the natural line of development of Weirs' business before 1914.

Turbine-driven ships still needed Weirs' feed-heating apparatus and they could easily spare steam for fire pumps, bilge pumps, and the many other pumps which Weirs made. On top of all this, an additional demand became apparent: independent air pumps (that is, pumps driven independently of the main engines) between the condensers and the boilers. William Weir, in 1912, explained how the demand had arisen:

The most obvious advantage of an independent air pump is its ability to obtain a vacuum in the condenser before the main engines are started, thereby enabling the engines to be manipulated with greater ease and certainty at times when immediate response is of importance. On this account, the first adoption of such pumps was on war vessels, and later for small river steamers while the advent of the marine steam-turbine made the provision of such pumps a practical necessity.[29]

If steam-driven pumps of any kind were required, then Weirs were obvious suppliers, and as soon as turbine engines came in they started making wet and dry air pumps for them. As with all their gear, they took full responsibility for its efficiency after it was in a ship, and would go to great lengths to put it right if it went wrong, with corresponding distress if the breakdown turned out to be their own fault. 'In the early days of turbine propulsion,' said William Weir, 'many forms and combinations of wet and dry air pumps were fitted, but unfortunately these installations, in the majority of cases, were rendered apparently non-effective on account of faulty condenser design.'

Weirs therefore set about designing a condenser of their own. They were not without experience, since James Weir had applied himself to the problem in the nineties. About 1908 they produced a design which would not, they felt, disgrace their pumps. 'The present design of "Uniflux" condenser,' William Weir said in 1912, 'is a direct outcome of the apparent non-success of the independent dry air pump.' The Uniflux condenser, in turn, prompted another look at air pumps. The pressure of naval design, particularly for destroyers and light cruisers, was always towards light, compact machinery, simple, reliable, and economical in steam. Applying these requirements to the design of pumps, Weirs combined wet and dry air pumps in one unit, which they called their 'Dual' air pump.

With the Uniflux condenser and the Dual air pump Weirs were in a position, as they had been with their original feed-heating equipment, to offer a complete package, and they insisted on doing so. 'I quite understand,' wrote William Weir to the firm's French agent in 1909, in response to an enquiry from the French naval authorities, 'that you wish us to quote for Air Pumps of our latest Dual Type. . . . Unfortunately, it is impossible for us to quote for such Air Pumps without at the same time raising the question of the supply of our new Uniflux Condensers . . . as it is impossible for us to give definite vacuum guarantees except [sic] we are controlling the whole of the Condensing Plant.'[30]

The condensers which Weirs had in mind when they complained of faulty design were almost certainly Richardson Westgarth's 'Contraflo' condensers. When Weirs went into the condenser business themselves the quarrel between the two firms became acute, and D.B. Morison of Richardsons chose to carry it on in public, by means of papers read to professional bodies. Weir – secure, no doubt, in the happy knowledge of success – refused for a long time to reply, but in 1912 he was persuaded, or provoked, to do so. The paper which he read before the Institution of Engineers and Shipbuilders in Scotland, on 'Development in Auxiliary Units between Exhaust Pipe and Boiler', was followed by a discussion acrimoniously initiated by Morison, and the printed report of the proceedings runs to well over a hundred pages.

Weirs did not themselves make condensers, partly because they were large and unwieldy and transport costs from Cathcart would have been enormous, and partly, it appears, because they regarded them as a sideline, undertaken to protect their major interests. 'We do not anticipate making a fortune out of it,' Weir wrote to Andrew Laing of Wallsend in 1908. 'If we get a fair recognition we will be satisfied – as our idea in going into the matter was to conserve our Air Pump business as much as possible.'[31]

Accordingly Weirs licensed other firms to build Uniflux condensers on a royalty basis. Laing, whose firm was one of the licensees, must have remembered Weir's remark about not making a fortune. When the agreement came up for renewal in 1914 he got the terms down from £1000 a year for five years to £600. 'If we got the same low rate from all the others,' wrote Weir, 'the job would hardly be worth the trouble.'[32] Other firms haggled also, and Weir used much the same tone, sorrowful rather than angry. 'I honestly think,' he wrote to E.C. Carnt of J.S. White & Co., East Cowes, 'I am justified in asking recognition for our work. . . . At the same time, Mr Carnt, while I am unable to appreciate your point of view, I would infinitely prefer to retain your respect than to charge fees for something which you sincerely consider is not worth paying fees for.' Carnt remained unmoved. The arrangement with Whites was not renewed.[33]

In spite of occasional disgruntlement of this sort, Weirs established themselves quickly and solidly in the condenser business. In 1911 Weir was explaining the terms on which he was prepared to license the German naval authorities to use his condenser designs (they were strong enough to refuse his usual terms, and to make their refusal stick). The letter he wrote to his German associate, Noltenius, illustrates both the wide spread of Weirs' business and the cosmopolitan outlook of the international naval shipbuilding industry before 1914:

It may interest your German naval friends to know that apart from the British Navy, in which [sic] we design all the condensers, we have supplied the designs for the two Argentine battleships building in America, for the *Wyoming* Battleship of the U.S. Navy, for *Courbet* and *Jean Bart* of the French Navy, for the four new Dreadnoughts of the Austrian Navy, for all the Dreadnoughts of the Italian Navy, for all the Dreadnoughts and Battle Cruisers of the Japanese Navy, for the new Battleship for the Brazilian Navy, new Battleship for the Turkish Navy, new Battleships for the Chilean Navy – as a matter of fact, almost all the Warships building except the German Battleships.
With kindest regards and the Compliments of the Season. . . .
P.S. – Also all Russian B'ships.[34]

As early as 1910 Weir had claimed, in a letter to a Dutchman, '98 per cent of the largest marine [condenser] installations throughout the world are now in our hands'[35] and in 1913, writing to Germany again and evidently relying on the same figures, he said 'over 98 per cent of the large turbine-propelled vessels are equipped with our Dual Air Pumps'.[36] To impress customers, usually foreign, with his firm's general dominance of their field he could quote similar evidence relating to other gear. In 1911, for instance, writing to Engineer Commander Y. Makihara of the Imperial Japanese Navy, for the benefit of the home authorities in Tokyo, Weir called a sonorous roll of large British warships with his firm's distilling apparatus: *Invincible*, *Inflexible*, *Indomitable* and *Australia* had 400-ton plant, *Lion* and *Princess Royal* 480-ton plant, *Neptune*, *Colossus*, *Conqueror*, *Ajax* and *King George* 200-ton plant, and he added as an after-thought, 'also eighteen TBD's'.[37] In 1913 he told Noltenius: 'every Dutch Torpedo Boat hitherto has been fitted with our pumps, feed and air',[38] and in the same year, on the title page of a publicity brochure (*The Works and Products of Messrs G. & J. Weir, Ltd*) the company claimed that they were contractors to the British Admiralty and War Office and to the Governments of:

Argentina	France	Portugal
Austria-Hungary	Germany	Russia
Belgium	Greece	Siam
Brazil	Holland	Spain
Chile	Italy	Sweden
China	Japan	Turkey
Denmark	Norway	United States
		etc., etc., etc.

Though who the etceteras were is a little difficult to conceive.

With this imposing list of foreign customers there was a good deal of talk, from time to time, about setting up Weir works abroad, especially in France and USA, two important centres of shipbuilding which Weirs found very resistant to their sales effort. Nothing came of the proposals for directly owned works, either in those two countries or elsewhere. In the years before the Great War, Weirs' foreign trade was carried on by agents in countries where there was enough business to support them, by incessant travel on the part of the directors and others, and by licensing agreements.

Weirs' agent in France was Marius Jullien, a Marseilles ship's chandler who had useful connections in the dockyards. 'I cannot understand,' William Weir observed to Jullien in 1902, 'how France can have a good navy without Weir pumps',[39] and eighteen months later he was urging the agent 'to do your best to obtain an introduction of our Feed Pumps which are now used in every Navy in the world except the French Navy'.[40] Jullien did as he was told and business resulted, but as late as 1909 Weir, confident of success with the Uniflux condenser and its associated air pumps, told Jullien that his methods of the past fifteen years – trying to obtain orders by visiting the contractors – had been 'perfectly useless' and 'we must make a distinct change in our method of obtaining French Naval Work', by which he appears to have meant a direct approach to the Minister of Marine. 'I quite appreciate,' he told Jullien, 'that you will look on this proposal with surprise, but we have waited too long for feed pump orders from the French Navy.'[41] It is not clear that the new method was much more successful than the old. The French dealt with Weirs when it suited them, but that was not often enough to suit William Weir.

Much the same was true of the Americans. Weirs' Directors visited America frequently, and they had close relations with Admiral Chester Bowles of the Fore River shipbuilding company, builders of the largest class of warships. Moreover from time to time, particularly in 1909, enough orders came Weirs' way to be encouraging, but delusively so, so far as any long-term prospects were concerned. The market was protected by a duty of 30 per cent, and Weirs felt the full force of the opposition which established American interests could put up to back any foreign competitor who showed signs of becoming dangerous. William Weir's own opinion of Americans was compounded of admiration and dislike ('Americans are very tricky people'[42]), and he had no doubt that he was being unfairly hampered in his efforts to get into the American market. 'In America,' he wrote in 1913, 'there exists a Pump Trust which possesses very great influence and this concern has hitherto been able to control and influence American shipbuilders to prevent the import of Weir Pumps.'[43]

In Germany, despite hints of anti-British political feeling, Weirs seem to have found none of the half-concealed obstacles which they found so difficult to deal with in France and America. Germany was a very good market for British goods (the best in the world apart from India), and neither German shipbuilders nor the German naval authorities showed any reluctance to buy Weirs' gear if it stood up to competition. In 1905 William Weir and James Latta went in a German destroyer on her sea trials – she was fitted with Weir air pumps – and her captain, who was half English, showed his ship off to them.[44] As soon as Weir came back he put in a report to the Admiralty, and he did much the same in 1913 when he had information about Russian and Romanian warships.[45] The Germans became more sensitive about security in the last few years before 1914, but in the international armaments industry few technical secrets can have been really safe, and governments presumably accepted the risk when they allowed – and encouraged – their own suppliers to tender for foreign orders or accepted tenders from foreign suppliers.

Weir pumps and other gear were manufactured in Germany under an agreement of 1906 with Norddeutsche Maschinen und Armaturen Fabrik, Bremen (otherwise known as Atlas), who also held Weirs' franchise for Russia and Switzerland.[46] The profits went to a small holding company called Deutsche Weir-pumpen Gesellschaft; owned 50-50 by Weirs and Atlas. William Weir described the arrangement as 'peculiar'[47] and in April 1914 he was not pleased with the previous year's net profit – £3000 – which he considered 'very unsatisfactory in consideration of the large turnover which must have been made.'[48] Presumably the German business was not unsatisfactory all the time.

Weirs' arrangements with Norddeutsche Maschinen for working the Russian market provided for a licensing agreement with a Moscow firm, royalties being paid to Deutsche Weir for division between Weirs and their German partners. Weirs had settled these terms 'when ... the Entente between Germany and Russia was very strong, and we considered that the best could be made of Russia by Germans.' Then the political situation began to alter. The Russians employed British designers 'who help us [Weirs] considerably in getting the work.' Progress under the agreement with the Germans was slow, and the Russian Government began to demand improvements to the works of Weirs' Russian associates which would mean capital investment – perhaps as much as £60,000 – by Weirs. Weirs asked the Germans to release them, for a consideration, from the agreement.[49]

The Germans accepted £7000, and Weirs went on to negotiate with the firm of Gustav List, Moscow, for a joint venture. The politics of the matter became very involved, the more so as the Russians were still relying on German advisers for some of their ships. The ships themselves were built in Russia, and the authorities were determined to have as much as possible of their machinery made there as well. The shipbuilders, however, who were being pressed for early delivery, petitioned to be allowed to order foreign-made machinery, and fierce international competition for the order followed.[50]

Through this maze Weir and Latta doggedly pursued their way, frequently visiting St Petersburg to do what Weir called 'a tremendous lot of pushing' with high officials of the Russian Admiralty and General Staff, some holding military rank, some naval, who held the final authority in technical matters. The prize was great. In 1913, according to Weir, the Russian building programme included 4 battle-cruisers, 2 cruisers, 2 light cruisers and 28 destroyers. *Whitaker's Almanac* for 1914 gives even larger figures.

The Austrians and the Italians were building heavily, too. *Whitaker* 1914 shows three battleships building for Austria-Hungary, five for Italy, besides numerous smaller ships. Not many of these vessels, it is safe to say, would have put to sea without Weir gear of some kind. The Austrian Government, like the Russian, was beginning to insist that auxiliary machinery should be built in Austrian territory. Weir resigned himself to the inevitable: 'It is of course an unfortunate development, but I think we have seen it coming.' He opened up licensing negotiations with G.Lindeke of Stabilimento Technico Triestino.[51] The rising pace of naval shipbuilding in 1913 kept Latta almost incessantly on the move. In the summer of that year he made a journey which took him through St Petersburg, Berlin, Vienna, Budapest, Trieste and Naples.

With none of their foreign customers were Weirs' links closer or of longer standing than with the Japanese, who began dealing with Weirs before the turn of the century. They kept representatives permanently in England, and Japanese naval officers, especially Engineer Captain, later Admiral, Fujii, were among William Weir's most frequent correspondents. The Japanese, like other nations, were anxious to build up their own industries, and they came to Weirs to learn as well as to buy. The nature of the relationship is well explained in one of Weir's letters, written in 1912:

... our arrangement with each of the two private firms in Japan is that they pay us a royalty of 15% on the British selling price of all machinery which they build in Japan, and they guarantee to pay us not less than £600 per annum for ten years. Further, each of these firms agrees to give us two-thirds of all the machinery for their present large Cruisers for construction here. In connection with the Japanese Admiralty, they give us an order for two-thirds of the Battleship machinery, together with a sum for the designs of the remainder of the machinery based on 15% of the British selling price, and in addition they pay us £2,500 for the tuition of their men.[52]

The 'two private firms' were Mitsubishi and Kawasaki. The agreements with them and with the Japanese Admiralty had just been made when Weir wrote. They were very quickly put into effect. Within a fortnight of writing the letter quoted above, Weir was writing another letter to say that during the succeeding three months there would be fifteen Japanese officials, workmen and foremen 'pursuing a course of tuition' at Cathcart.[53]

These agreements represent the Japanese determination to make themselves self-sufficient, especially in the manufacture of armaments, and their readiness to buy British experience in order, eventually, to make themselves independent of British suppliers. They are in the same class as an agreement made in 1905 between the Japanese authorities and the Nobel-Dynamite Trust and their German partners who, in association with Armstrongs, undertook to set up the Japanese Explosives Company with a factory in Japan to make smokeless powder for the Japanese forces, especially the Navy, which would be using Armstrong guns. The agreement provided that the factory would eventually pass into Japanese ownership, and the Japanese would then be in control of their own supplies of propellant.[54]

Arrangements for technical aid to the Japanese had their dangers. In 1911, before the agreement with the Japanese Admiralty was signed, the Japanese Navy's London office showed a keen desire to get hold of the working drawings of some pumps supplied by Weirs for cruisers, saying that they were wanted for making spare parts in wartime. There was no offer of payment. Weirs became suspicious and demurred. It then emerged via Admiral Fujii, who evidently did not know or did not approve his subordinates' deviousness, that the real intention was to manufacture pumps in Japan. 'I do not mind saying,' Weir wrote to Fujii, 'that we were very angry about the whole matter as it loooked very like obtaining the drawings under false pretences. It would have been quite a different matter if Commander Shigemura had asked us for a price for the drawings and told us that the pumps were to be made in Japan.' The matter was smoothed over and a price was agreed for the drawings, but the episode is a pointer to the ethics of Japanese officials at the time, and perhaps of some sections of the international armaments industry. In 1914, Fujii was found guilty of taking a bribe from a representative of Vickers, and committed suicide.[55]

Weirs' aim in their negotiations, whether with the Admiralty at home or with prospective buyers abroad, was to get as near as they could to supplying the whole of the auxiliary engine room machinery in a ship or, better still, a class of ships. This machinery Weir defined, in a letter to Jullien in 1909, as:

Main and auxiliary condensers
Main and auxiliary air pumps
Main and auxiliary feed pumps
Forced lubrication pumps
Oil fuel pumps
Fire and bilge pumps
Evaporators and distilling machinery[56]

The prices they might charge are suggested by a quotation made in 1911 for complete pumping gear for the new battle-cruiser *Queen Mary*. The quotation covered, that is to say, all the items on the list above except condensers, evaporators and distilling machinery, as well as spare gear. It came to £24,240.

In 1913, as we have seen (p. 29 above), work for warships of various nationalities accounted for rather more than 60 per cent of the value of Weirs' orders, and merchant ships' business brought in about 24 per cent. Weirs, that is to say, still relied overwhelmingly on shipbuilding for their livelihood. In 1911, indeed, they were so busy with marine work that William Weir positively discouraged the idea of expansion on land. Nevertheless by 1913 orders for land gear, though a slightly smaller proportion of the total than five years earlier, were in absolute figures worth much more (£53,000 for generating plant: £51,000 for other land plant).

Much the largest increase in demand came from the electricity generating industry, but there was also a rising demand for pumping gear for oil pipe-lines, which were being built over long distances to get crude oil from the oilfields to the sea. Weirs equipped two pumping stations, to deal with 6,500,000 gallons of oil a month, on a 270-mile line built for the Burmah Oil Company in Burma, and when that work was seen to be successful they got a contract for pumps on a line built for the Anglo-Persian Oil Company over 150 miles from Maidan-I-Naftun to Abadan on the Persian Gulf. Weirs did their best to get into the Russian oil business, but without success.

Between 1911 and 1914 Weirs tried hard to sell feed heating to the railways, at home and abroad, on the ground that feed heating on railway locomotives would pay for itself in fuel saved. It had been tried before, but it had always failed, in William Weir's words, 'through the difficulty of feeding the boiler'.[57] He claimed that his firm's designers had got over that difficulty, but he found railway engineers difficult men to convince. 'They are quite different,' Weir wrote, 'to any other class of engineer we have come across yet.'[58] Terribly conservative, he thought.

Nevertheless, one eminent railway engineer – Dugald Drummond of the London and South Western Railway – developed his own system of feed heating. Weir poured scorn – 'as regards the Drummond Feed Heaters, ... no intelligent engineer could fail to appreciate their obvious inefficiency, excessive weight and cost.'[59] He showed uncharitable glee when Drummond's heaters gave trouble.

Weirs' own apparatus seems never to have been more than moderately successful, though it was widely sold about the world and at the end of 1913 Weir said the works had 'over 200 sets in hand for different companies'.[60] It seems to have been difficult, however, to show in practice the fuel saving which ought to have been possible in theory, and it was correspondingly hard to persuade locomotive superintendents, accustomed as they were to knowing their own minds and having their own way, that the saving was great enough to justify the extra cost and complications on their engines. The business never seems to have become self-generating, in the manner of business in other Weir specialities.

If the railway engineers were conservative so too, in their way, were Weirs. They were fully conscious of it, and in a speech celebrating the firm's twentieth anniversary William Weir made a virtue of it:

> Gentlemen, to deal with new markets and continually varying requirements, in other words, to be Engineers as well as Manufacturers, means continuous research and experiment for new designs, and while often tempted to adventure, we have progressed along safe and consecutive [sic, but probably he said 'conservative'] lines, feeling that our best guide in this department has been the principles and example set us by my father – the most revolutionary conservative I know.[61]

This conservative temperament showed itself towards 1910, when Weirs had to make up their minds what to do about a rising demand for centrifugal pumps in competition with the direct-acting pump on which their reputation was founded. Centrifugal pumps saved weight and space, and it was claimed for them that they saved steam also, but Weirs were sceptical. Nevertheless they had to take account of the demands of the market, and they 'engaged the services of the best designer in Europe' – Joseph Pietermüller, a German* – 'of small steam

---

* Pietermüller was too late to get away to Germany at the start of the war. Late in August he was staying in Glasgow with a friend, but he was not allowed at Cathcart. Weir, who was evidently sympathetic towards him, heard that he was bored and sent him his drawing tools and notes, so that he could get on with a fan

turbines and rotary pumps'.[62] By the beginning of 1912 they were able to tell Harland & Wolff: 'If you desire Rotary Feed Pumps we are in a position to put them forward [but] . . . for the majority of installations we do not recommend them because we have not the fullest marine experience with them.' A week or two later William Weir told Latta that rotary pumps 'will have a very great effect on our future policy, and I wish to be as cautious as possible'.[63]

Caution was natural and proper, since the rotary pump represented a sharp departure from Weirs' experience of pump design. Moreover it required either an electric motor or a turbine to drive it and these, too, were outside Weirs' normal practice. Experiments therefore continued and were the subject of much correspondence with the Admiralty and others. It is difficult to avoid the suspicion that Weirs' heart was not really in the rotary pump business, and William Weir probably expressed his firm's attitude as well as his own when he wrote to Admiral Fujii in August 1912: 'Generally speaking, you will not obtain any great savings or advantages with Rotary Auxiliaries, but Engineers generally seem to think the Rotary movement should be encouraged, and, in fact, it is more a question of fashion than anything else.'[64]

Somewhat set in their ways, then, Weirs by 1914 certainly were, and indeed for some years had been. But within their own field – restricted, as it was, by their own deliberate choice – they were world leaders. Their trade was expanding, their technical reputation stood high. Indeed at the Engineer-in-Chief's branch they had for years held more or less the status of consultants, being asked from time to time even to pass judgement on competitors' products. The basis of their policy had been explained by William Weir as long ago as 1907:

Truism though it may seem, I think we are none the worse of putting the answer straight that those concerns will best weather the storm [he was contemplating the onset of the 1908 depression]

which he had been designing. He was interned during the war, rejoined Weirs for a short time afterwards, then returned to Germany, where he died (LB XII, 461, 489).

which do not carry too much sail, concerns whose capital is not a burden to them, and whose affairs are managed with rational ideas of proportion between the means and the end. Great fields for enterprise even in new industries may exist, but unless conducted with prudence and sanity, such enterprises cannot be successful.[65]

William Weir, nevertheless, was sorely tempted away from his singlemindedness by one 'great field of enterprise' in a new industry – the motor industry. To that episode in Weirs' history, in the next chapter, we must turn.

3
Weirs and the Motor Industry
1902–12

Motoring became practical in the United Kingdom on 14 November 1896, when the Locomotives on Roads Act came into force, permitting mechanically-propelled vehicles to travel on the highway without a man walking in front with a red flag. Cars, especially in France, had already gone beyond the purely experimental stage, and by the end of the century several classes of users were beginning to appear.

For rich men at leisure, large, powerful cars, each one built to order, provided a new form of sport, with plenty of excitement, mechanical interest, and some danger. The chassis alone might cost over £1000 before the body was built. Tyres did fairly well, in the early days, if they lasted 1000 miles, and several sets of covers in a year could quickly run to a bill in three figures. This was motoring as the Guinness family, for instance, understood it.

But at a less glamorous level, by 1901 it was possible to buy, for £100–£200, a reasonably reliable low-powered car, capable of 20 m.p.h., which would relieve a doctor of the necessity of doing his visits on foot, on a bicycle, or on public transport, without going to the very heavy expense of private horse-drawn transport, which was beyond the reach of any but the most prosperous of the middle class. A writer in *The Autocar* of 1904 calculated the running costs of a two-cylinder 6½ h.p. car, which might cost £175 to buy new or £125 second-hand, at about 4d. a mile for 6000 miles a year, including £1 a week for an unskilled man to look after it. Against that, a horse-and-trap in the country – the cheapest form of private horse-drawn transport – was reckoned to cost something like 6d. a mile.[1]

Again at a utilitarian level, some businessmen quite early began to look at the possibilities of motor vans and lorries. W.H.Lever, the founder of Lever Brothers, was one. As a private individual he once said he was 'in love with petrol'. As a businessman he had 'handsome motor cars belonging to the firm' (as the *Daily Mail* described them) running in London immediately after midnight on 13–14 November 1896. That was no doubt a stunt, but before the end of the century Sunlight Soap was being delivered by motor van.[2]

Developments in the embryonic motor industry caught the eye of many enterprising men. These men were chiefly of two kinds. On the one hand there were those whose existing business and technical training were of a kind fairly easily adaptable (or so they thought) to making motor cars. Some came from the bicycle trade in the Midlands (William Morris, rather later, is the most famous of these) and others from general engineering in many parts of England and Scotland (two of the best-known, Henry Royce and W.O.Bentley, were brought up in loco-motive workshops). Then on the other hand there were those whose contribution was not chiefly in technology but in matters requiring financial acumen and/or salesmanship. Two who entered into the history of Weirs were S.F.Edge (1868–1940), an Australian racing cyclist who formed a partnership with the engineer Montague Napier (1870–1931), and C.S.Rolls (1877–1910) who, following Edge's example, formed a partnership with Henry Royce (1863–1933).[3] Edge had no formal technical education at all. Rolls had read engineering at Cambridge, but it is fair to say that his main contribution to the motor industry, like Edge's, lay in finding a brilliant engineer and supporting his talents with general commercial ability, especially in marketing. Another rather similar figure, an entrepreneur rather than an engineer, of whom we shall have much to say, was Alexandre Darracq.[4]

William Weir was early attracted to cars. He bought a $3\frac{1}{2}$ h.p. Benz about 1898 and after that a steady succession of other cars, not of the very expensive makes. His interest, as might be expected of a young man in his twenties and thirties, was partly sporting, but that did not lead him to cars of great power or to racing cars. His cars were of moderate power, up to about 20 h.p., and he entered them for hill-climbs and reliability trials organized by the Scottish (later Royal Scottish) Automobile Club, of which he was a founder. The speed limit of the day – 20 m.p.h. – brought him more than one brisk brush with the magistrates. Of one such encounter, in 1904, he wrote to Lord Ailsa: 'My case at Norman Cross [on the Great North Road] was dismissed yesterday, this being the first motor case which has been dismissed at the Norman Cross Court for the last three years. They have been uniformly successful until they happened to strike my car. We had a very tough fight, in fact the scene in the court house was more like a pantomime than anything else.'[5]

Cars were no doubt exciting mechanical toys for well-to-do young men. Weir, as an engineer and a businessman, saw them as much more than that. He enjoyed what he called 'the automobile movement', but he also took it seriously. 'There can be no doubt whatever,' he remarked in 1903, 'that in the very near future it will be one of our most important industries if our manufacturers and capitalists would only work better together.'[6]

To find capital to back technical ability is usually one of the biggest problems in developing a new industry. Weir evidently considered that there were plenty of people capable of making motor cars in the United Kingdom and plenty of people capable of financing them, if only the two sides could be brought together in harmony. He evidently saw the motor industry as a logical and profitable extension of the existing engineering industry, requiring only vision and sound commercial management to make it go. If that were so, why should not G. & J. Weir join in?

Several engineering firms already had done so. Early in 1902 Weir bought a 10 h.p. car (£390) from one of them – the Wolseley Tool and Motor Co. Although he liked the car he formed no very high opinion of Wolseleys' commercial efficiency, as his correspondence shows, and by the end of 1902, perhaps as a result of this experience, he seems to have decided to see what Weirs could do in this line of business. His approach was cautious and indirect. He made no attempt, at this stage, to divert Weirs, as a firm, from marine engineering, which might have upset his formidable father. Instead, William Weir interested himself personally in an existing French car business which already had strong English connections. This was the business which Alexandre Darracq had founded.

Darracq, born in 1855 at Bordeaux, had been trained as a draftsman in an arsenal at Tarbes near the central Pyrenees. He came to Paris to work for a firm making sewing machines, Hurtu et Hautin, and in 1891 was attracted into the cycle industry, from which it was a short step to cars. He had, therefore, a technical background. Nevertheless his own account, according to the historians of his car business, was that he approached cars not as an engineer but as a businessman.

He was among the first to realize that there would be a large market for a cheap, reliable car, and he set out to find one. He had dealings with several well-known French makers, and by the end of 1900 he had found the design he wanted. It was by Louis Renault, whose family (with whom the Weir family had friendly relations for many years) was moving from drapery into motor engineering. The car Darracq chose had a single-cylinder engine of 6½ h.p., and the English selling price was £250. 'Every feature of the new design had been chosen with an eye to . . . quantity production, and a far more serious bid was made for standardization than had ever been attempted by any motor manufacturer before.'[7] Darracq decided on a remarkable output for 1901: 1200 cars.

Darracq had considerable success in racing, which by 1902 showed that his basic technical ideas, particularly in the transmission system, could be applied to more powerful cars than his 6½ h.p. model. He became anxious, therefore, to put on a wider range, although he remained determined to keep his prices down, whatever type of car he might produce. He had no intention of competing at the top of the market. The top of the market, in England, was represented by the cars which Montague Napier made and S.F.Edge sold. In 1900 an 8–9 h.p. Napier sold for about £500, against the £250 charged for the 6½ h.p. Darracq. In later years prices for comparable cars were always higher, often much higher, in Napiers' range than in Darracqs', and at the bottom of their list, with cars selling well under £200, Darracqs touched levels which Napiers did not descend to.[8]

To expand his range Darracq needed capital for his works at Suresnes, near Paris. To get it he came to London, in 1902, and a company was floated by J.S.Smith-Winby. It was A.Darracq & Co. Ltd, which came into existence in 1903, with Smith-Winby as Chairman. The capital – £375,000 – was subscribed, the company's historians say, by only eight shareholders. One of them was William Weir. His original interest was small – 750 £1 shares @ 95 – but within a few weeks he agreed to take up 2500 shares @ 25s.[9] The company was English, but its Managing Director was Alexandre Darracq and its sole factory remained the one at Suresnes. It was an arrangement which demanded excellent communications and very tactful Anglo-French (or Franco-Scottish) relations.

William Weir had been sufficiently interested in Darracqs by December 1902 to visit the works at Suresnes. Soon after he came back he ordered a 20 h.p. car, one of Darracq's new models, but later he changed his mind and ordered a car of 24 h.p., which was delivered in April 1903. Weir said it ran 'exceptionally well'. Meanwhile he had joined with his father in buying, for £380, a Darracq 'brougham', probably one of the smaller models fitted with a special body. The new range, launched at the Paris Motor Show in December 1902, ran from a single-cylinder car of 8 h.p. through two-cylinder cars of 9 and 12 h.p. to the 4-cylinder 20 and 24 h.p. cars at the top.[10]

Weir gave a clear indication of his reasons for backing Darracq in a paper on 'Possible Development in Automobilism and Automobiles' which he read to the Western Section of the

Scottish Automobile Club on 9 March 1903. He discussed the British preference for foreign cars, especially French, saying that about 2500 cars a year were being built in Great Britain and about 3500 were being imported. He said that in Great Britain there were about thirty-eight firms building motor-cars 'or alleged to be doing so', that 'only seven . . . merit the slightest consideration', and that 'with very few exceptions, none . . . have up to the present made any considerable profit on the sale of their cars.' His paper was directed chiefly to saying why he thought the British makers were doing so badly.

In his diagnosis he was as positive as usual: 'The chief reason for this state of affairs is, I venture to say, want of specialization and want of enterprise.' He attacked what seems to be a perennial error in the motor industry – marketing too many models – and in what looks like a hit at Napier and Edge ('our premier firm') he said: 'There can be little credit from the commercial point of view due to a firm who only make 100 cars per annum in perhaps four different sizes, at prices which only attract the man of great means. I therefore maintain,' he concluded, 'that the first principle in making automobiles should be to adhere rigidly to one size of car, until it is produced in sufficient numbers to pay well.'

Although, by the time Weir spoke, Darracq had considerably extended his range, he had nevertheless founded his business on exactly Weir's 'first principle in making automobiles', and it must have been Darracq Weir had in mind when he said: 'last year a well-known French company – not the very largest – built 1050 cars of two models only: the result was a very large profit.' Darracq's methods did not amount to mass production, but he made the greatest possible use of standardization and thereby kept prices well down towards the utilitarian end of the market where Weir – rightly – judged that the big business would eventually lie. The general direction of his thoughts shows plainly in a calculation he produced which put the cost of running a motor cab at 3·825d. per mile against 5·936d. for a horse cab – figures remarkably close to those quoted, above, for a doctor's running expenses. It was in this frame of mind, without doubt, that he decided to put his money behind Darracq.

He kept his lines open, however, to the merchants of luxury. In March 1903, writing to S.F.Edge, Weir said he thought Glasgow ought to be 'more active' in the commercial development of the motor industry, because in London (where Napier made the cars that Edge sold) 'you will ultimately be hampered with the wage question, also your ground must be expensive and your building restrictions somewhat annoying.' Then he made what looks like a veiled invitation to some form of partnership: 'without being in any way egotistical, I think a visit [to Cathcart] would be of value to either Mr Napier, yourself, or your foreman, particularly if you are considering extensions . . .'.[11]

There seems, indeed, to be no doubt that at this time William Weir intended to use the Darracq connection as a springboard to launch the family firm into the motor industry. In the same letter to Edge he went on:

I think there is quite room in this country for two or three concerns of the Darracq nature. I cannot see that improvements in design will be of such a revolutionary nature as to affect the laying down of a considerable sized manufacturing plant. . . . Modifications . . . appear . . . to affect the jigs and other fixtures rather than the actual machine tools.

He set about building an experimental car at Cathcart, and when an enquiry came in for production models he did not conceal that production was in fact in his mind: 'I return herewith your order for motor cars, as the car we are at present building is in every way an experiment, and in any case we would not undertake to supply these cars for about two years from this date.'[12]

Weir also developed an interest in motor racing. It was an interest with a keen practical edge to it. 'The great success in the Continental makers', he remarked to a correspondent of July 1903, 'is undoubtedly due to their racing experience, and had there been no racing we would still have been running clumsy, heavy automobiles using twice as much petrol spirit as we do at present.'[13] When he wrote those words, he had just come back from Ireland, where he had been watching the 1903 race for the Gordon Bennett Cup.

The Cup was an elaborate trophy featuring a winged female (the Goddess of Victory) standing on the seat of a motor car driven at speed with one hand by a nonchalant nude of indeterminate sex (the Genius of Progress), sitting on the bonnet and bearing a flaming torch. It was presented in 1899 by James Gordon Bennett (1841–1918), the owner of the *New York Herald*. His intention was to establish an international contest and also, perhaps, to break the prevailing French monopoly of long-distance road races.[14]

Races for the trophy were at first combined with other, more important, events. They were held in 1900 (Paris-Lyons) and 1901 (Paris-Bordeaux). They were won, more or less as a matter of routine, by French cars and drivers, and no one took much interest, although William Weir thought it worthwhile seeing the start of the 1900 Race. Then in 1902 the Gordon Bennett race (Paris-Innsbruck) was won by S.F.Edge, driving a Napier. None of the other three entrants, all French, finished. The excitement was enormous. The prestige of British cars increased dramatically, and the French felt correspondingly threatened.

The 1903 race, by the rules of the contest, had to be held in British territory, and a course was laid out in Ireland. The entry, much larger than ever before, included teams from Germany and the USA, as well as England and France. This was the race which Weir went over to see, after a great deal of correspondence to make sure that cars were properly handled on the railway and on the ships to Ireland. The winner was a German and Edge came in last of those who finished (seven out of twelve did not).

The Gordon Bennett race was now firmly established in the public imagination, and it became clear that the 1904 race in Germany, under Imperial patronage, would be an affair of great splendour.

In this race, for sound commercial reasons, Alexandre Darracq and his associates greatly desired to be represented. So did many other car owners, dealers and manufacturers – so many, in fact, that in several countries eliminating trials were run to settle the composition of national teams. For the French trials Darracq built cars at Suresnes. For the German and British trials cars were built to Darracq designs in Germany and Great Britain.

No other maker was thus triply represented in the eliminating trials for the Gordon Bennett race of 1904. It has generally been assumed – and Lord Montagu of Beaulieu, in his book on the Gordon Bennett races, takes it for granted – that this multiple representation was the outcome of a gamesmanlike plot by Darracq personally to get round the rule which required all cars entered in the Gordon Bennett race to be built entirely in the country under whose name they raced. Darracq was no doubt very pleased to have three chances in the eliminating trials, but it seems unlikely that he craftily engineered the situation. The German car was built by Fritz von Opel who – as Lord Montagu of Beaulieu points out – had a licence to build Darracq-type touring cars. Presumably, therefore, he had faith in them and needed no encouragement to build a racing car to Darracq designs. In Great Britain Alfred Rawlinson, the Darracq company's London manager, decided to enter for the eliminating trials, no doubt to gain publicity for his firm's products. It would have been strange, therefore, if he had gone in for the race with cars designed by anyone but Darracq, so that again there need be no suspicion of sharp practice. In any case, everybody at the time knew perfectly well where all the cars were built and there was no attempt to conceal Darracq's connection with any of them.[15]

When Weir heard that Rawlinson was going in for the trials, he decided that the time had come to launch his firm into serious car building. 'I am presuming,' he wrote to Rawlinson in January 1904, 'you are working to Darracq designs in your Racer which you are building here. Now, I consider, speaking quite frankly, that no one can do this class of work for you better than we can. . . . The Suresnes Works are good, but I can show you something better here, and I think you should take the earliest chance of getting down to see us. . . .'[16] A few days later he wrote: 'Regarding the Gordon Bennett cars, I am glad to note that your arrangements are so far forward, as I think it would be really excellent if a British-built Darracq should beat the French one . . . any assistance we can give you, we shall be delighted to.'[17]

It looks as if competitive fever had got into William Weir, overriding his native caution. He presumably knew, when he made his offer to Rawlinson, that any car or cars he might build would have to be presented to the organizers of the trials, in London, by 16 April, giving him a little over three months to do the whole job, from drawing board to finished car. He had never built a car before, except the experimental one of 1903, and it seems likely that he never got beyond the engine of that.[18] He was always self-confident, but this headlong rush into motor-racing – in which he carried his father and his colleagues along with him – is quite out of character, both for William Weir and his firm. Why didn't they wait for a later race, perhaps the Gordon Bennett race of 1905? They would have lost nothing and they might have gained a great deal.

Anyway off they went on the race to get three cars (not just one) ready for Rawlinson by 16 April. Patterns had to be made and pattern makers worked at night to do it. Materials and components had to be gathered into Cathcart from Sunderland and Wolverhampton. Radiators were built by 'Swiss people' in England. Technical advice was sought in Paris and from T.C. Pullinger of John Marston Ltd, to whom Weir admitted: 'I would like your next visit to be as soon as possible, as you must understand it is very difficult for us without any knowledge of car building to go much further with the assembling.'[19] 'We are being hustled so much with these Racing Cars,' he told Lord Ailsa in February, 'that life is hardly worth living at present, although it is certainly most interesting and instructive.'[20] Weir evidently found the 'hustle' exhilarating, and in the middle of March he reported triumphantly to his father, who was abroad, that the cars would be ready in time 'and when they are done it will be the biggest engineering feat which has been done for many years'.[21]

Weir's confidence was justified. He got enthusiastic cooperation from his men, and on 16 April 1904, a few minutes before the latest time allowed, the cars were delivered (on horse-drawn wagons) for weighing-in by the Automobile Club of Great Britain and Ireland in London, having travelled from Glasgow during the night by special train. On 18 April Weir told Rawlinson: 'This place [Cathcart] is as dull as a graveyard now.'[22]

While these stirring deeds were going forward other measures, less spectacular but more businesslike, were in hand. Weir himself had taken enthusiastically to selling cars to his acquaintances, and during 1903 he was continually badgering Rawlinson (whose ability as a manager he had no great opinion of) to find someone to set up an agency in Scotland. Rawlinson's first choice did not please Weir – he was 'not in a position to tackle the right sort of people' – but Weir had his own nominee ready. Robert Kennedy, whom Weir described as 'one of my assistants,' took over the Darracq sole agency for Scotland on 18 January 1904 and he was set up in a showroom and workshop on the factory site at Cathcart, where Weir could and did keep a sharp eye on him.[23]

Darracqs' normal business, all this time, was going very well, and in February 1904 Smith-Winby proposed a reconstruction of the company to raise more capital. He invited Weir to join the Board. Weir replied that he was 'not without a slight qualification for the position', and if he approved the details of the flotation he would be pleased to accept. The new company eventually came into existence in 1905. Holders of the Ordinary capital of the old company received shares, one-for-one, in the new, and a public issue of £150,000 5% Debentures and £375,000 Preferred Ordinary raised money to pay back the Preference capital of the old company and provided £425,000 new money for the new one. Of the new company [A.Darracq & Co. (1905) Ltd] Weir duly became a director, although he warned Smith-Winby that he was not prepared to make a larger investment than he had previously held.[24]

Weir's entry into the motor industry early in 1904 attracted the attention of the Hon. C.S.Rolls, who had just gone into business as a car dealer with his own firm, C.S.Rolls & Co., Fulham. Rolls had been closely associated with S.F.Edge for four or five years,[25] and he was looking for an engineer with whom he might form the same sort of partnership which Edge had with Napier. He wanted, that is to say, an engineer who would make cars which he, and he alone, would sell. On 26 March 1904 he wrote to William Weir. Rolls's letter is lost, but Weir's reply, dated 1 April, survives:

> Regarding the manufacture of Motor Cars, our facilities for this work are more extensive than perhaps most of the Motor Builders themselves of this country, but up till now we have never done anything in this way. As you are aware we are now completing the manufacture of the three large Darracq Racers for the Gordon Bennett Trials. Before deciding on any definite measure, I think it would be much better if you personally could take a run down here, see our works and the class of work we have carried out on the Racing Cars, and at the same time we could have a discussion for a future policy.[26]

It is clear from this letter that Rolls had made a proposal to Weir which Weir was disposed to accept. Whether Rolls ever visited Cathcart we do not know, nor do we know the precise terms of the proposition or what caused it to fall through. About a month after the date of Weir's letter, Rolls was induced to meet Royce for the first time. Royce had a car ready for the market, and that may have been decisive. The agreement which brought Rolls-Royce into existence, instead of Rolls-Weir, was signed on 23 December 1904.[27]

Rolls, in any case, must have been put off any idea of persevering with Weirs by the performance of the Weir Darracqs when they came to the Gordon Bennett trials, in the Isle of Man, in the second week of May, a week or so after Rolls had met Royce. Accounts vary as to exactly what happened to the three cars, but the main facts are clear from Weir's own correspondence. The propeller shaft broke in the car driven by Rawlinson and in the two others, driven by Frenchmen, the brakes failed. This all happened very close to the start, so that the cars never became serious competitors at all.

The cars had been sent to France after the weighing-in, allegedly for final preparation. Weir, bitterly disappointed and humiliated by the disaster that followed, blamed the French:

Rawlinson's car [he wrote to Lord Ailsa] was ruined by the Frenchmen in France; they took out the cardan shaft* and hardened it glass hard, so that at the first real shock it snapped clean away, their reason for this I cannot tell. The experience they had in their own cars showed them that the brake attachments were defective, they altered Rawlinson's and left the other two unaltered, and under the stress of racing naturally enough they gave way. The Frenchmen were frightened off the course, and had no spirit or courage whatever. In addition Rawlinson's mechanic deliberately put water in the petrol to begin with [why? – Weir does not explain], and it took poor Rawlinson 1½ hours to clean it out before the start. When it did start the mechanic jumped out of the car and refused to go with him, and he had to take a man from the crowd. Add to this that they had no management whatever, no arrangements for anything, and the cars in a filthy dirty condition covered with mud and grease so that they exceeded the weight limit, and you have a slight idea of my feelings. Further, there was no manner of doubt but that the cars were a long way the fastest, and had they not gone to France but been tuned up here by Kennedy and driven by English drivers, I think we would have made an excellent showing. It is no use having any sympathy for the Darracq people as they deliberately threw away all their chances, in fact were it not for the money they have spent I should have said that the whole thing was done intentionally, and perhaps there may be some mysterious reason behind it all, and on that account I have decided to have nothing to do with the new Darracq Company whatever ... except of course as regards the representation of Darracq by Kennedy.[28]

Weir's suspicions about French sabotage, repeated and elaborated in a letter to Rawlinson a day or so later, were probably baseless. The cars had been over-hastily built by a

* An auxiliary shaft between clutch and gearbox.

firm without experience, and the French might reasonably have protested that the alleged sabotage was simply the result of their having had too little time to get the cars ready and test them properly. The idea of sabotage seems inherently absurd, and the mere fact that Weir, usually so cool in his judgement, could entertain it suggests how greatly distressed he was. One of the Weir cars, bought and rebuilt at leisure by Algernon Lee Guinness, later raced with some success, which again suggests that the main thing wrong with the cars which broke down in the Isle of Man was lack of time in which to get them running properly.

This whole episode of the Gordon Bennett cars – which may well have ruined Weirs' chances of a partnership with Rolls – is quite out of character with the rest of the firm's development, and quite inexplicable. We shall never know, presumably, what fit of March madness convinced sober Scottish engineers that in about three months, without having built a car of any sort before, they could turn out three cars fit to enter the most hotly contested international race in the world.

There is little doubt that the fiasco killed any idea that Weirs, as a firm, may have had of becoming motor car manufacturers. William Weir's surviving correspondence contains several categorical denials that the firm had any such intention, and probably they may be taken at their face value. It is difficult to believe that he would have been able to persuade his father and his colleagues to any more adventures in internal combustion, especially during the years when the marine business, as we saw in the last chapter, was growing most lustily.

Weir himself, however, changed his mind about cutting his connection with Darracq. As a director of the new company he concerned himself actively and often testily with its affairs. His correspondence contains frequent caustic comments on Darracq cars – particularly their finish in which he detected a deplorable tendency to sacrifice quality to profit – and on the methods and ability of Rawlinson. More than once he threatened to resign.

His main interest was no longer in petrol-driven cars but

in vehicles driven by steam, especially buses. This was perhaps natural in a steam engineer, especially since it was by no means certain, yet, that the petrol engine would run all competitors off the road. Steam vehicles used paraffin as fuel – cheaper than petrol – had no need for a gearbox, and ran smoothly. They had disadvantages, including the difficulty of carrying water for a reasonable operating range, but disadvantages could no doubt be overcome. Nor were steam vehicles necessarily heavy and slow. Steam cars, like petrol cars, were entered in the long-distance races to show what they could do.

Darracq, with the support of William Weir and his father, began to take buses seriously during 1905. Their experiments with petrol-driven buses were not very satisfactory, but in 1905 Darracq himself was greatly impressed by two steam buses in service at Nice. They were driven by engines designed by Léon Serpollet. He had been building steam vehicles since the eighties, and in 1904 he entered a racing car for the French Gordon Bennett trials which got a good deal nearer the French team than Darracq's cars did.[29]

Darracq's interest must have been very welcome to Serpollet. He was short of capital, whereas Darracq's business was flourishing and was known to have influential backing in the City of London. James Weir was asked to report technically. 'I feel certain,' wrote his son, 'that if his report is satisfactory we can go on with this affair as hard as ever possible with every prospect of success.'[30] James Weir came back from Paris 'quite decided in favour of steam'. Moreover he agreed 'that the name Serpollet would carry distinct weight', although he thought Serpollet had 'claimed a great deal more in the patents than what can be supported'.[31] Even with this reservation, James Weir's recommendation seems to have been decisive. Matters went forward very fast, and in May 1906 the Darracq-Serpollet Omnibus Company Limited was formed, with William Weir on the Board.

The Company's capital was £500,000. £300,000, in Ordinary shares, was issued equally to Darracq and to Serpollet, in exchange for patents and other assets. James Weir had said that he did not think Serpollet's buildings and plant were worth much, and we have seen what he thought of Serpollet's patents. Evidently, then, the promoters of the new Company valued Serpollet's technical skill very highly, and he became a managing director. Cash was raised by issuing £200,000 Preferred Ordinary at 1s. premium, and the company went straight into business.

To Weirs, steam buses were not Serpollet's only attraction. 'There is another side of this Serpollet development,' Weir told Smith-Winby before the company was formed, '... and that is the use of these small engines for Voidette Boats and Pinnaces in the British Navy.'[32] He took the matter up with Oram at the Admiralty and his reception was sufficiently encouraging for him to arrange for J.S.White, of Cowes, to build an experimental boat.[33] The intention evidently was to use Weirs' facilities for development work, but not for full-scale manufacture, and to share the costs with the new company. 'My father,' Weir told Smith-Winby, 'points out that the development of this boat business is ... very costly ... and will occupy not only a good deal of my own time, but we have to put our most expert technical staff on this work. He is of the opinion that we do not wish to carry the business on and develop it quite so far as the regular manufacturing stage. ... On these grounds he is strongly of the opinion that the 50 per cent basis would be the only fair and equitable arrangement.'[34]

In July 1906 a Serpollet bus was brought over from France, and in August it made a demonstration tour in Scotland, James Weir announcing his intention of joining it at Beattock station on its way north from Carlisle. The Caledonian Railway became very interested, especially after the Serpollet bus, on a test run, had shown itself much faster than a petrol-driven Wolseley or a steam bus made by Morton of Wishaw. 'I am beginning to get a little enthusiastic,' Weir told Lord Ailsa on 28 August, '... and now feel quite certain that the problem of heavy traction is solved in a satisfactory manner.'[35]

During the latter part of 1906 the Serpollet enterprise in both aspects – at sea and on land – was pushed energetically along. The Caledonian Railway and the Glasgow & South Western both bought buses, though surviving correspondence suggests that their subsequent management of them was unintelligent.[36] But Weirs, not content with supplying buses for country routes in Scotland, which they looked on rather as a useful test market, had far more ambitious plans. On 30 January 1907 William Weir sent off 'my firm's cheque' to cover the deposit on shares in a newly established business: the Metropolitan Steam Omnibus Co.[37]

This move represents a firm intention to carry G. & J. Weir a long way beyond marine engineering. After the Gordon Bennett affair William Weir consistently indicated that the connection with Darracq cars was his private affair – nothing to do with the firm – but the bus enterprise was different, since he specifically mentioned '*my firm's* cheque'. G. & J. Weir was still essentially a private business, and the owners, with no outside shareholders to consider, did not always trouble to separate their own affairs very clearly from those of the company. Both at this time and later, they were prepared to finance development work privately, with the idea that the company might take over the results if they were successful. In the case of the Metropolitan Steam Omnibus Co. there is no such confusion. Weirs, as a firm, were sufficiently confident of the Serpollet 'system' to back it in the fiercely competitive world of London transport.[38]

The Metropolitan Steam Omnibus Co. was not founded to build buses, nor to sell them, but to run them, and to run them in London. It was an audacious venture for a firm of Scottish engineers, especially since their London associates do not seem to have included anyone who knew much about transport. Smith-Winby was there, but he was a financier. Sir John Durston took shares and placed a son with the company as an apprentice, but Durston was a naval engineer of great eminence, not a bus operator. Moreover the new company was saddled from the start with a prior commitment not only to one form of traction – steam – but to one make of vehicle – Serpollet's. Throughout its career it was looked on as a captive customer for the Darracq-Serpollet Omnibus Co., and no other maker's vehicle was tried. In an undertaking that had to make its living from transport, was this wise?

The company was launched on a flood of optimism about the bus trade generally. In September 1906 Weir told Lord Ailsa: '. . . my only wish at present is that we had 1000 buses ready for sale.'[39] In October the Metropolitan Steam Omnibus's service began, and by November, according to William Weir, there were six buses 'securing good earnings and running most satisfactorily, pleasing the police and the householders on the route'. He hoped that within six weeks there would be twenty buses running.[40]

On 11 February 1907 Léon Serpollet died. This was a major disaster, because there was no one to replace him. Darracq was not a steam engineer and in any case he was fully committed. No one was forthcoming from Weirs, presumably because all the available technical talent was required for pumps and auxiliary machinery. And there is no doubt that the Serpollet engine, on which such high hopes had been set, required a good deal of development. In March 1908 – well over a year after Serpollet's death – a report was sent to Weir on a trial run to Brighton from London and back, undertaken by one of three buses intended for export to India:

We went to Brighton leaving London at 8.25 a.m. We reached Brighton at 2.00 p.m. On the road we had to fill with water once, adjust the pump . . . twice, clean the burner once, clean the exhaust blowing rupples* once. The bus ran well on level or down grades and reached 20 miles an hour often. Uphill however she was painfully slow. On the return journey we had a blinding snow storm, leaving Brighton at 3.00 we reached London next morning at 4 a.m. The car ran poorly and climbed very bad for first 26 miles when we had to refill with water the back condenser and the feed water heater both leaking badly, time taken for this distance was 3 hrs. 45 mins. About the 27th mile we ran into a ditch in the

* The exhaust valves.

dark and spent 5 wretched hours in the snow getting out again. The journey home was made in a series of races downhill at 25 mi. an hour and painful ascents at about 2 mi. with many pauses to seek for water to fill up. It was great sport but did not tend to make one more enthusiastic about Darracq Serpollets.[41]

All this was not on a prototype, but a production model already sold.

The first casualty was not Serpollet's bus, but his boat. When he died an engine was building in France. It was brought to Cathcart, but by November 1907 Weir had to tell Sir John Durston: '... although we spent considerable time and expense on this, the results have not been satisfactory and at present we have so many other things in course of experiment that we have not been able to give it much consideration.' This confession in itself shows how short of available technical talent the Serpollet enterprise was. Early in 1908 Weir wrote mournfully to the builders of the experimental hull: 'We have conducted a number of trials with the boiler and engine, and they have been only moderately successful, the economy being not nearly so good as we had anticipated. ... We have therefore put the Serpollet machinery on one side ... I will be glad to hear if you can help in any way regarding the disposal of the boat under any fairly decent terms.'[42]

The land side of the Serpollet business was killed by the slump which hit the motor industry – the first of many in its history – in 1907–8. Weir was already complaining that the industrial vehicle business was 'in a state of suspended animation' in October 1907,[43] and in the spring of 1909 he told Sir John Durston that there had been no demand whatever for the previous twelve months.[44] The search, at one time intensive, for a firm to manufacture Serpollet buses in England, instead of France, gradually wilted and died. The Darracq-Serpollet Omnibus Company was moribund by the end of 1910, and in July 1912 Weir wrote: '... the Darracq-Serpollet Works have now been sold and we will be able to liquidate the company under fairly satisfactory conditions.'[45]

The Metropolitan Steam Omnibus Company sank at about

the same rate. Weir tried to save it, but if it was saveable at all – which may be doubted – it certainly needed more than part-time attention which was all he could afford. He was taken by surprise by fare-cutting by the London General Omnibus Company, and it would appear that this formidable opponent, as well as the underground railways, was more than the MSOB could stand. In July 1912 'the Underground Railways Co.' (the Metropolitan?) offered £15,000 for the company, subject to certain arrangements for the settlement of debts. No doubt they wished to be rid of a competitor whose very weakness might be a source of danger to themselves, in so far as it might lead to reckless fare competition. Weir was no doubt glad to accept, and put an end to the constant calls for loan capital. His own opinion of the ordinary shares, by that time, was that they were 'really worth nothing'.[46]

In 1912, also, the question of reconstructing the Darracq company was once again raised but not, this time, on account of prosperity.[47] Weir had already shown numerous signs of disenchantment, and as early as 1906 he had been relieved to get rid of Kennedy's agency business from Cathcart. 'I cannot,' he told Ailsa, 'be worried with a business of that class alongside my own office, as it occupies too much time and gives too much trouble.'[48] He disagreed with Darracq technically and over general commercial policy, and at the end of the 1912 financial year he left the Board.[49]

Thus ended William Weir's personal connection with the motor industry and his firm's first essay in diversification outside marine engineering. It was an experiment they did not repeat for many years, and perhaps enough has been said to indicate why. William Weir wrote an epitaph on the episode when, referring to the motor industry, he said in 1911: 'It requires a great deal of capital, a great deal of patience, and a very expert staff.'[50] In other words, it was not for even the best Glasgow engineers to deal with on a part-time basis. Weir's correspondent, who was a shipbuilder, decided to keep to shipbuilding. Perhaps he was wise.

4

The Great War 1914–18

The war that broke out in August 1914 may be said with some truth to have been foreseen by all, but prepared for by none. All the governments of the Great Powers had been intriguing and arming amongst and against each other for many years, and in Great Britain the likelihood of war with Germany had been a growing influence on policy since the turn of the century, when the 'naval race' began. But this war that everyone expected and prepared for was to have been a short, sharp, dashing affair, lost or won in a matter of months. What nobody expected, or prepared for, was the monstrous four years' siege operation which began after the Germans narrowly failed to crush the French within a few weeks of going to war.

In this murderous deadlock the fighting qualities of the opposed armies were about equal. Neither side, that is, collapsed simply under the pressure of the appalling conditions of trench warfare. Therefore each side's chance of winning came to depend on piling up superiority in weapons and equipment. In consequence the war became a contest in industrial strength between two of the greatest industrial powers of the day – Great Britain and Germany – with a third, potentially the greatest – the USA – involved indirectly from the start and directly, with decisive effect, from April 1917 onward.

To meet the unexpected demand industrial effort, both in Great Britain and Germany, had to be improvised, and improvised on the largest scale, reaching eventually into every nook and cranny of the national life in a manner unprecedented in any previous war. The shock to the system, in Great Britain, was profound. At once an alarming degree of dependence on German industry – for dyestuffs, for optical goods, for drugs, for magnetos – revealed itself. Then, as the scale and intensity of the effort required began to penetrate the ministerial mind – especially Lloyd George's – the Government began to take charge of industry; an invasion of the territory of private enterprise almost as shocking to British nineteenth-century ways of thinking as the German invasion of Belgium. Thirdly, the ferocious demand for output, especially in engineering, presented organized labour, on the one hand, with a formidable threat to the privileged position of the skilled craftsman, built up through many years of industrial warfare, and, on the other hand, with unparalleled opportunities for squeezing better pay and conditions out of reluctant employers.

In August 1914, then, most people did not expect the war to last long or to interfere very much with their accustomed way of life, unless they were young men of an age to volunteer for what most of them imagined would be a few months' exhilarating blood sport. In no other war before or since, it may be remarked in passing, has it been so easy – at the outset – for the Government to find soldiers. The war, to start with, was overwhelmingly popular.

Businessmen, unless directly concerned with armaments, did not expect to be very closely involved in the war effort, and indeed there was a general fear that trade would turn dull and many men would be thrown out of work. Then as the soaring demand for weapons, ammunition and all kinds of supplies began to make itself felt, the whole situation was turned inside out. Businessmen found themselves asked – compelled – to undertake all sorts of unexpected and unfamiliar work, some of which turned out to be very profitable, and trade was brisk. At the same time the men in the factories, emboldened by the obvious shortage of labour – something they had never experienced on such a scale before – became militant and intractable, so that tempers rose on both sides, among employers and employed.

The bedrock of G. & J. Weirs' business was admiralty work,

British and foreign. Weirs, therefore, were among the firms immediately and directly caught up with war work. The British Admiralty had been preparing for war, with increasing momentum, for a dozen years or more. There was no call for sudden, unforeseen expansion (in this the Navy differed sharply from the Army), and such extra strain as there was, Weirs were ready to take up. On the day war broke out William Weir saw the Third Sea Lord* and offered to despatch repair squads, obviously detailed in advance from the firm's men, to the naval dockyards.[1] The next day, 5 August, he wrote to the Engineer-in-Chief at the Admiralty:† 'Generally speaking I think you can depend on having an ample supply of Weir gear.'[2]

The Royal Navy, no doubt, was well enough off for pumps, but it soon became obvious that both the British and French armies needed far more shells than the professional armaments industry could supply. Other engineering firms would have to be called in. By the middle of October 1914 – scarcely more than two months after the start of the war – Weirs had had 'a very large enquiry for 75 mm. shell from the French government', which they had turned away because they had already taken on 'considerable shell contracts for Sheffield friends'.[3]

These 'Sheffield friends' were Thomas Firth & Sons Ltd, who were among the principal makers of war material in Great Britain. They ranked with Armstrong Whitworth, Vickers, Hadfields and the Projectile Company, and with their cry for help, evidently, William Weir's eyes began to open to the possibility that the conflict in France might be more than a passing breach of the peace. 'I have been thinking a good deal about this shell matter,' he wrote to Percy Fawcett of Firths, on 13 October 1914, 'and would like to know if the demand is likely to continue, and if the question is very serious, because assuming the war to last 18 months, a certain expenditure of

---

* Admiral Sir Archibald Moore, KCB (1914) etc. (1862–1934).

† Eng. Rear-Admiral (later Vice-Admiral) (Sir) George Goodwin, KCB (1918) etc. (1862–1945). E.-in-C. Admiralty 1907–17. Succeeded Sir Henry Oram as E.-in-C. of the Fleet, 1917–22.

actual capital would be justifiable if only from a patriotic point of view. . . . Would you like us to put down some extra plant, and is there any system whereby we might get some compensation for the exceptional capital expenditure?'[4]

Weir and his colleagues, evidently convinced that the demand was likely to continue and that the question was 'very serious', soon moved beyond this tentative approach. By the spring of 1915, when the shell shortage in France was becoming a public scandal, they had decided to put up two new buildings on the Cathcart site – Albert Factory and Flanders Factory – which were intended specifically for making shell.

Weirs' Board decided to forego normal profit on these operations. They agreed that from 1 June 1915 until the end of the war

all profits arising from the manufacture of Shell under present contracts, after deduction of necessary allowances for establishment charges and capital expenditure, shall be handed over to certain of the various organisations carrying out relief work or Red Cross work which the war has necessitated, and which are supported by voluntary subscription. When the contracts in question are completed, the different shell plants will be available to produce shell for the Government at net cost, and if required, all such future production shall be carried on in conjunction with the proposed Glasgow National Shell Factory.[5]

This resolution is important. It shows the frame of mind in which Weirs' directors launched into shell-making – a frame of mind radically different from that of their men – and it helps to explain why the two sides, soon in head-on collision, found it impossible to understand each other's point of view. The directors, considering themselves to be performing a public service at a time of national peril, rejected the idea of making money, and felt all the better for it, as they sometimes pointed out. The men, on the other hand, though no doubt patriotic enough by their own way of thinking, saw no reason to deny themselves any advantage that might be gained out of a situation in which they very swiftly saw the strength of their bargaining position. Moreover, bred up always to suspect their employers' motives, they were disposed to look behind the curtain of good intentions for signs of a conspiracy to cheat them of their rights, and what they sought they very quickly found, in the shape of plans to bring women into the factories to make good the lack of men, especially skilled men.

Before, however, this threat of 'dilution' arose – before, even, Weirs' Board decided to forego their profits, and well before Albert and Flanders could come into production – management and men at Weirs and throughout Clydeside generally had come into conflict. The men's general grievance arose from what they considered to be their employers' undue delay in settling a claim, put in in June 1914, for an extra twopence an hour. Weirs' particular case was aggravated by a scheme, devised by William Weir, for bringing workmen over from America. The scheme had small beginnings. On 22 December 1914 Weir wrote to a relation (Allen Coats) in America saying that it was practically impossible to find skilled tradesmen in Scotland and asking if Coats could find 'about a dozen good Turners, who might be willing to come over for . . . say, six months.' Weir said he could not offer 'more than the highest local district rate, but of course they will work on the Bonus System, and it helps them to increase their wages considerably. Further, if we find them good workmen, it is in the foreman's discretion to pay them more.'[6]

Weir did not expect any very great response. 'I feel,' he concluded, 'that the terms are not very attractive to a workman accustomed to American wages, but it may attract some old Glasgow men who have gone to the States.' He was unduly pessimistic. Trade was dull in America, and on 23 February 1915 he was able to tell J.R.Richmond that 34 men had already sailed and 30 more were about to come.[7] The fact that he was offering to pay half the cost of a steerage passage may have helped.

The scheme was carefully explained, before any Americans arrived, to union officials, who were shown copies of the agreements made with the Americans. Nevertheless, and it is a lamentable commentary on the lack of trust between the two sides to the dispute, the general belief was that the Americans were all to have a special bonus of six shillings a week. Nothing Weirs' management said, apparently, would convince their own men, or some of them, that the management were speaking the truth when they said 'that no preference of any financial nature was given to the American workmen over our own workmen'.[8]

To this irritant Weir added a tactless pamphlet, written by himself and issued in January 1915, which, under the title *Responsibility and Duty*, called on workmen to give up restrictive practices because 'every hour lost by a workman which COULD HAVE been worked, HAS been worked by a German workman, who in that time has produced, say, an additional shell ... to kill the British workman's brother-in-arms, or perhaps a bomb to be dropped on his wife and children.' Weir, at the time, was justifiably disturbed at the figures of absence from Cathcart after the New Year celebrations (he had told an Admiralty official that 99 per cent had been absent on Monday morning, 4 January, and between 50 and 75 per cent the next day),[9] but he would have been well advised not to show his resentment in the way he did. He admitted, many years later, that the pamphlet itself had nearly caused a strike, and there can be no doubt that it must have been well in the minds of Weirs' men, along with the matter of the American workmen, when they were called upon to strike, in support of the general Clydeside pay claim, on 16 February 1915.[10]

On that day about 2000 engineers and machinists came out at Weirs, and soon 8000 men, all over the district, were on strike. There was great anger in the rest of the country, but without much effect on the 'Red Clyde.' The men stayed out for about three weeks and then accepted a settlement negotiated by David Kirkwood – who was blamed by other strike leaders for 'breaking up the front' – of an extra penny an hour. By 4 March all the men were back at work.

Even before the strike, William Weir had considered his skilled workmen's attitude to war work lazy and self-centred – as, for instance, when so many stayed away after the New Year, 1915 – and in March *The Times* caused his irritation to boil over. An article appeared in which, among a good many other things, the claim was made that men in the factories had been working 'practically incessantly.' 'The actual facts,' Weir wrote to Northcliffe, *The Times*' owner, 'were perfectly capable of verification by your correspondent, but evidently no attempt was made to do so . . . my irritation was increased from the consciousness of my Firm having very early appreciated the needs of the country and our efforts having been directed to meeting these needs in an efficient manner, and then finding that our men were unable to appreciate the spirit in which we were working.' As for the men working 'practically incessantly', Weir pointed out that since the outbreak of war they had earned less than formerly from the premium bonus system (which depended on the amount of work done) and that for four weeks before the strike they had refused overtime.[11]

Northcliffe was not very responsive, so Weir brought the whole matter into the open with a letter to the Lord Provost of Glasgow, published in the *Glasgow Herald* on 22 May 1915.

The skilled workmen [he said] have clearly demonstrated their inability to resist the temptations offered to them . . . by the shortage of men. The proof of this is shown by excessive wage claims, by the enforcement of restriction on production and on conditions of working, by bad timekeeping, and by drink. Engineering workmen are not alone in their lack of appreciation of the position. . . . Every possible opportunity is seized to put forward claims for higher wages, advantage is taken of every innovation . . . to make it a basis for further demands, until . . . an employer has really to consider whether he should or should not take on Government work of a new nature, such for example as shell, in case he involves himself in labour difficulties which will affect his entire normal business, which may also be the furnishing of Government supplies of a different nature.[12]

The publication of this letter coincided fairly closely with the resolution of Weirs' Board to hand their shell-making profits to charity and with the opening of Albert and Flanders factories. These factories came into production, therefore, at a time when Weirs' management, very conscious of their public-spirited behaviour, were permanently at odds with their men – 'every day, endless trouble,' said William Weir – whose behaviour they regarded as downright unpatriotic. It was not a promising atmosphere in which to have to face the most serious labour problem of the whole war: 'dilution'.

Skilled men, as Weir had said, were scarce, and the scarcity had been made worse by unrestricted Army recruiting in the first weeks of the war, for among these workmen, whom their employers found so lacking in patriotism, there were plenty who would volunteer to go and be killed on a private soldier's pay. But the scarcity was to quite a large extent artificial, being fostered and protected by restrictive practices established in engineering, over two or three generations, by determined collective bargaining and strict union discipline. Besides such matters as limitation of output, 'demarcation' of trades and refusal to allow a man to superintend more than one machine, these practices were particularly severely applied to the protection of skilled men's jobs by forbidding the employment of semi-skilled or unskilled labour, and especially the employment of women.[13]

These practices, as Weir had told the Lord Provost, made innovation in Clydeside engineering extremely difficult, because innovation, well before 1914, already meant automatic or semi-automatic machines and a tendency towards mass-production, with a diminishing demand for men skilled in traditional crafts. In peacetime, therefore, there had not been much innovation along the Clyde – not, at any rate, as much as there could have been if American and German machine tools had been more widely adopted – with consequences which cast a long shadow forward into the twenties and thirties, if not further, and to which we shall return. In war, however, innovation there had to be, if the forces were to get arms and ammunition in anything like the quantities they needed.[14]

In the spring of 1915, with the passing of the Munitions of War Act, the setting up of the Ministry of Munitions and the appointment of Lloyd George as Minister of Munitions, the Government set out to force both management and men in the engineering industry into unfamiliar methods, and to compel them to accept the idea of training unskilled workers, mainly women, to do jobs which every trade union instinct sought to reserve for skilled craftsmen.

Broadly speaking, the unions were offered a bargain. If they would accept 'dilution', the Government would take control of industry and see to it that no undue profits were made from war contracts or, if made, that they were clawed back again by 'Excess Profits Duty'. By this means it was hoped to remove any basis there might be for the men's conviction that 'dilution' was simply a device for the employers to make more money by cheap labour.

So deeply held a conviction was not so easily removed. The official union leaders, who accepted the bargain, found themselves widely distrusted by their own men, and their influence was usurped, especially on the Clyde, by shop stewards whose militancy was unsoiled by any compromise with the employers. Organized in the Clyde Workers' Committee, the shop stewards stood resolute to repel the advancing hordes of women.

William Weir, equally determined on the other side, took care to make his views known in the highest quarters. In May 1915 he told an officer at the Admiralty that in his opinion 'nothing other than martial law in munitions districts will solve our troubles and difficulties'.[15] Twice in June he saw Lloyd George ('surrounding himself with . . . pure politicians . . . [who] really know nothing whatever about industrial organization'[16]), and on 24 July he resigned as Managing Director of G. & J.Weir to become a full-time Ministry of Munitions official, with particular responsibility for munitions production in the West of Scotland.

The most important part of this task was the enforcement of dilution on the Clyde. The struggle went on through the autumn of 1915 and the spring of 1916, and the story of it has been told elsewhere.[17] It reached its climax with a strike at Beardmores' works, organized by the Clyde Workers' Committee, which lasted from 17 March to 4 April 1916. The strike, which was illegal, was broken sharply, efficiently, and with complete success by following the general lines of plans drawn up, in January, by William Weir.

The end of the strike at Beardmores saw the end of serious trouble about dilution on Clydeside. The ravaging of tradition could go ahead unhindered. Weirs, before the war, had employed about 3000 men, and the idea of women in the works would have been profoundly shocking; as much to the management, no doubt, as to the men. By 1918 Weirs' total labour force had doubled, and it included about 2000 women. They were employed, moreover, not only on emergency work such as shell, but also on the pumps which lay at the heart of Weirs' being.

Women's work on shell included unskilled labouring and every process after the rough forging: 'Rough turning, rough finish boring and mill threading on the body of the shell; cutting, tapering, boring and facing on the nose, and finishing, turning and forming the outside of the complete shell, cutting the base for weight, recessing for base-plate, and turning the copper band.'[18] Even for the comparatively skilled processes, the women did not need a great deal of training. 'The introduction of automatic and semi-automatic machinery,' say Scott and Cunnison, the historians of the Clyde Valley wartime industries, '. . . converted work which had formerly demanded the judgement and dexterity of the skilled man into a series of more or less repetitive operations; and to learn to tend these machines was the work of a few weeks.' The women's productivity was very high. As Scott and Cunnison put it, 'they were unrestrained by Trade Union habit and usage,' and they quote an official estimate that women produced shell about three times as fast as it had been produced, with skilled labour, in 1913.

Such a female invasion was profoundly disturbing in itself for the threat which it presented to the security of the men's jobs, and to their general conception of masculine superiority. But besides that, it could not have come about without wholesale, and hated, technological innovation. The men, as we shall see, had no mind to tolerate the perpetuation of any of these outrages after the war.

Weirs' two shell factories, Flanders and Albert, came into production about 1 June 1915. On that date their first manager, H.A.Dudgeon, was appointed. He was to have £800 a year, which may be compared with the remuneration of the Board at the same time. Latta had £500 a year (no doubt he had commission on sales as well); J.G.Weir had £700; Richmond, £1200; Lang, £2200; William Weir, £4200.[19] Before the end of the war, production of 8-inch shell at Albert reached 3500 a week; of 6-inch shell at Flanders, 6000 a week. 53,000 4·5-inch shells, 19,350 3-inch shells, and 90,000 1½-inch anti-aircraft shells (for the Admiralty) were also made.[20]

When William Weir went into government service in July 1915 he remained Chairman of G. & J.Weir, but he gave his official duties precedence over the affairs of his business. His brother, J.G.Weir, departed in September 1914 for unorthodox adventures with the Royal Flying Corps. J.G.Latta remained a full-time director until the summer of 1918. Then 'serious differences', the nature of which is now undiscoverable, arose between him and his colleagues, and he resigned.[21] William Weir was succeeded as Managing Director by J.R.Richmond and C.R.Lang, acting jointly, and they had the detailed direction of Weirs' business during the greater part of the war. The work, much heavier, more varied and more harassing than in peacetime, was thus handled by a seriously depleted Board. Perhaps that helps to explain the sudden quarrel, after more than twenty years, with J.G.Latta.

During 1917 shell-making at Albert Factory was given up and the plant was dispersed, probably to the National Projectile Factory newly established at Cardonald, mainly at the instance of William Weir. Into Albert Factory, in place of shell, came aeroplanes.[22]

Before 1914 the military possibilities of aircraft were only dimly apparent to the Imperial General Staff, who regarded them chiefly as a kind of flying cavalry, very useful for reconnaissance and as observation posts for the gunners. The naval staff, who were perhaps rather more adventurous in their thinking, were developing along totally separate lines, in competition rather than in cooperation. Very little money was being spent, and in 1916 the Chief Engineer of Daimlers said: 'The aviation vote in the Army Estimates for the year preceding the war was not more than sufficient to keep a decent-size firm for a year.'[23]

Nothing had been done to prepare for quantity production of aircraft, for no one foresaw that great numbers would be needed – how could they be, in a war that was to be over in a matter of months? The specialist aircraft firms in the country, about a dozen of them, were stronger in enthusiasm than in anything else, and they still built machines individually, without detailed drawings, so that two machines supposed to be of the same design might differ substantially.[24] Between 1910 and 1914, however, there were two heavy-weight recruits to this happy band – Vickers Limited, who started building heavier-than-air machines (after rather disheartening experience with airships) in 1910, and Armstrong-Whitworth, who formed an aircraft department in 1913. In 1913 Vickers produced a two-seater pusher biplane (the FB1) with a Vickers gun in the nose which, in an improved version (FB2), has been claimed 'the world's first real fighting aeroplane'.[25]

To this infant industry the Government made one outstanding contribution: the Royal Aircraft Factory (later the Royal Aircraft Establishment) at Farnborough, Kent, which first came into existence, as a balloon factory, in 1894. In spite of its name, it was not a production unit, like the Royal Ordnance Factories, but an experimental and design establishment, with responsibilities also in setting standards of workmanship, in assisting the private aircraft industry and in watching prices on behalf of the Government. From the RAF's drawing boards came most of the British-designed engines and aircraft which saw action up to 1917, and a considerable proportion thereafter, but at the Factory itself only prototypes were built. Quantity production was contracted out.[26]

At the outbreak of war the Royal Aircraft Factory had a

series of aircraft far enough advanced in design to make factory production possible. They were known as BE (Blériot Experimental) 2a, 2b and 2c. On the advice of the Superintendent of the Factory, the decision was taken to standardize the BE 2c. It has been described as 'an extremely stable, single-engined two-seat biplane – a good platform for reconnaissance, but a sitting duck for the enemy fighting scouts.'[27] Against airships, in home defence, it was more successful. Five were destroyed from BE 2cs.

By insisting on rigid inspection at every stage, and by organizing training courses for managers and foremen, the Royal Aircraft Factory contrived the manufacture of airframes by many unlikely firms – makers of agricultural implements, pianos and furniture among them – and had them delivered to Farnborough. Then they were turned into complete aircraft at the Royal Aircraft Factory itself.[28] More obvious makers of aircraft in emergency, however, were established engineering firms, especially on Clydeside, where in 1913 William Beardmore & Co. (in which both Vickers and Armstrongs were interested) had already taken a licence to build aero-engines. Weirs, at that time fully occupied with admiralty business, had shown no interest in air work, but if firms were required to build aircraft during the war, they were an obvious choice. They were, in fact, the first Clydeside firm to receive a contract for building the BE 2c.

At least nine other Clydeside engineering firms, including Beardmores and the shipbuilders William Denny and Barclay Curle, received contracts as well as Weirs, but Weirs became much the most prolific aircraft constructors. During the Great War they took orders for 300 BE 2c, 386 FE 2b, and 450 DH 9, whereas no other firm took orders for more than 450 aircraft altogether.[29] But whereas Beardmores launched into aircraft and aero-engines as independent designers, and carried out research and development which kept down their production of completed aircraft, Weirs made no attempt to branch out similarly. They built complete aircraft, not just airframes, and they built them by methods of quantity production, but they kept to the specifications set out in their contracts, and there was never a Weir aircraft or aero-engine designed in the firm's own drawing-offices. If any temptation to diversify into this new and very risky industry presented itself, they successfully resisted it.

For the greater part of the war, British aircraft production was bedevilled by the problem of developing good engines. When war broke out there was no British aero-engine in production that would do for military purposes, and for six months British aircraft had to rely entirely on French designs. Moreover British manufacture of engines, to designs by the French or anyone else, was held up very badly for about two years by the lack of British magnetos. Before the war nearly every magneto used in Great Britain had come from Germany.[30]

At the end of 1916 the output of engines in Great Britain was running at about 600 a month. Early in 1917 the Germans were expected to make a strong effort for air superiority, and far more engines were needed. At this point William Weir went to the Ministry of Munitions in London as Controller of Aeronautical Supplies, and almost at once a programme to produce 2000 engines a month was laid down.

To get anything like this rate of production quickly required a gamble on engines that were not properly out of the development stage, especially the Sunbeam *Arab*, the Hispano-Suiza, and a 200 h.p. six-cylinder water-cooled engine known as the BHP, which is the one that concerns us. The gamble as a whole was a disaster, but it must be borne in mind that in April 1917, soon after it was taken, the average flying life of each RFC officer killed or missing on the Western Front was 92 hours, against 295 in August 1916 and a monthly average of about 190 during the whole war.[31] Under that sort of pressure, technical prudence and even common sense gave way to desperation.

The BHP engine was developed by Beardmores to designs by Frank Halford and T.C.Pullinger. A contract for 2000 engines went to the Siddeley-Deasy Motor Car Co. before the great expansion programme was decided on, and on 30 October 1916 they ordered 2000 cylinder blocks from G. & J.Weir, an order reduced to 1000 on 7 July 1917 and then increased again to 2000 on 17 November. In December 1917 Siddeley-Deasy ordered 12,300 cylinder liners for BHP engines.[32]

The BHP cylinder blocks were cast in aluminium, which gave great trouble. In July 1917 Siddeley-Deasy discovered that 90 per cent of the castings were defective, which undoubtedly accounts for the reduction of their order to Weirs. By the end of the year matters had been put right – hence, presumably, the reinstatement of the order for cylinder blocks and the large orders for liners. Then the exhaust valves began to give trouble. The engine finally came into quantity production in the spring of 1918, but by then it was out of date. 'The engine,' in the words of the official historian, 'had become obsolete before the mass production stage had been reached.'[33]

Besides the major lines of war material discussed in this chapter, which included 610 complete aero-engines as well as components, Weirs made 150 gun carriages, 400 trench howitzers, mines, pistols for spherical mines, percussion gear, recuperators for guns, four sets of diesel engines for submarines, and a good deal else besides. During the war their labour force doubled, they greatly enlarged their premises, and they put manufacturing processes into operation, on a large scale, which would have been unthinkable in Clydeside engineering in 1914. Thus transformed – along with other Clydeside firms – Weirs suddenly found themselves confronted, on 11 November 1918, with the problems of peace.

5

Weirs in the Post-War World

In the first eighteen months or so of peace, a wild optimism surged through British business. Lord Leverhulme, about Christmas 1919, contracted for Lever Brothers to buy the entire share capital of the Niger Company for £8,000,000, without having the least idea where the money was to come from. Sir Harry McGowan and the Board of Nobel Industries Ltd, a little later, committed £3,500,000 to an investment in General Motors. On a less spectacular scale, businessmen throughout the country raised capital for all kinds of enterprises to take advantage of the boom which was driving prices up more steeply, between 1918 and 1920, than ever during the war.[1]

It all seemed sensible enough. A great many people wanted a great many things which they had not been able to get during the war. A great many people were better off than they had been before the war, and wanted to spend their money. A great deal of damage had been done during the war, and would have to be put right. A great many people in Europe needed food. Here, surely, were all the makings of good trade.

Glasgow shipbuilders, in particular, had no need, so far as they could see, for gloom. Naval shipbuilding, no doubt, would cease, or slow down very greatly, but 2479 British merchant ships, or 7,759,090 gross tons, had been lost, as well as 675 fishing vessels of 71,765 tons; and 1885 vessels of over 8,000,000 tons had been damaged. There seemed to be no likelihood of a shortage of orders for the Clyde, and indeed in 1919 646,154 tons of shipping were built there, and in 1920, 672,438 – the two best years the Clyde has ever had, except only for 1913 (756,976 tons).[2]

If, as Stanley Baldwin is said to have observed, there were a good many hard-faced men in the House of Commons, in 1919, who looked as if they had done well out of the war, there were also, Professor Medlicott remarks, 'some hard-faced men on the Labour benches who meant to do well out of the peace.'[3] The boom might be an opportunity for the capitalist, but it was scarcely less so for the unions, who could exert a powerful bargaining influence when demand for labour was so brisk. And nowhere were the unions more militant than on the Clyde.

Part of the bargain with the unions over 'dilution' was that after the war everything should be put back as it had been before. The bargain was kept. The Restoration of Pre-War Practices Act, 1919, required firms to restore pre-war practices by 15 October 1919, and if they did not, an aggrieved union might bring a prosecution before the Local Munitions Tribunal, with an appeal, in Scotland, to a judge of the Court of Session appointed by the Lord President. In the Clyde district there were records of 6000 departures from pre-war practice (out of 10,000 for Scotland as a whole), but very few seem to have been brought into court.

This is not surprising, for the employers generally showed little reluctance to go back to the old ways. A good deal of the new plant they had put in during the war was worn out by the end of it, and they were reluctant to replace it, according to Scott & Cunnison, because 'the uncertainty of the industrial future prevented a development on mass production lines'. What this probably means is that 'development on mass production lines' would certainly provoke furious industrial strife, and the employers had no intention of fighting all over again, on a promising peacetime market, the wartime battles to get new methods accepted. Hardly less conservative than their men, many Clydeside employers seem to have been very happy to get back to things as they used to be, heavily dependent on skilled labour, for they had laid preparations in advance. 'Pre-war practices were restored, dilution ceased, and women and unskilled men returned to their pre-war occupations.'[4] There was thus, in the West of Scotland, if not elsewhere, a kind of controlled Ludditism in engineering: surely a unique example of a whole industry deliberately putting itself at a disadvantage against less conservatively-minded foreign competitors.

Weirs came out of the war with large undistributed profits in reserve. In the autumn of 1919 the company's capital was increased from £90,000 to £1,200,000, and new money was found by distributing £940,000 in shares to the existing shareholders.[5] They thus reinvested in the business funds which might otherwise have come to them in cash. But in what direction was the new investment to lie? The answer, as we shall see, was not given in quite the same conservative terms as appealed to other Clydeside Boards in 1919–20.

Decisions on post-war policy fell to be made by a Board strengthened by the return from war service of William Weir (Lord Weir since 26 June 1918) and his brother James. Lord Weir had been Secretary of State for Air from 27 April 1918 until the end of the year, but as soon as the war ended he had made known his determination to get back to Cathcart, and he had left ministerial office early in 1919. Brigadier-General J.G.Weir CMG, CBE, Director of the Technical Department of the newly founded RAF, also came back to the business as soon as he could, and was evidently giving his full attention to it by the late summer of 1919, if not earlier.

The reconstituted Board had to face the sudden end of naval contracts. Naval work, British and foreign, had formerly accounted for about 50 per cent of Weirs' output, but those days, in Lord Weir's view, were unlikely to return. 'I consider,' he said in December 1919, 'that in future we will get practically no orders for this class of work because ... I do not suppose there will be any warship work undertaken for many years to come.'[6] What, then, was to be done to keep the firm's enlarged plant busy and its increased labour force employed? The directors, moreover, with their fair share of post-war optimism, looked for expansion rather than simple continuity.

It was open to them to diversify. During the war they had been the largest aircraft constructors in Scotland, and although wartime contracts had been abruptly cancelled, they could, no doubt, have taken a chance in the peacetime aircraft industry, but William Weir decided against it because he felt sure that service demands would not support a large industry and civil flying would be a slow starter. Some business men, after the war, were attracted by the possibilities of the motor industry, which in America was booming. Sir Harry McGowan, whom Lord Weir knew well, had great confidence in it, and some idea of investing in it certainly passed through the minds of Lord Weir and J.R.Richmond, but they put that, also, aside.[7]

The conclusion the Board reached was that they should stay in the business they knew. 'We do not believe our brains are good enough,' said Lord Weir, rather engagingly, 'to deal efficiently with more than one industry – that industry is to be Auxiliary Machinery and Pumps. It is better than frittering away our efforts on other lines.'[8] Weirs had a number of important technical contributions to make against the days when shipbuilding would revive, especially the development of the regenerative condenser linked to a closed feed system, which would help them to keep their grip on the supply of feed system auxiliaries to shipbuilders.

During the war the Admiralty, much concerned with boiler corrosion, especially in destroyers, looked to Weirs for an answer to the problem. It was provided by J.G.Weir and James Sim, Weirs' chief draftsman, who designed a closed feed system based on modifying the design of the condenser so as to make it a highly efficient de-aerator and then ensuring, through sufficient feed tank capacity and the introduction of overflow and make-up valves, that nothing but completely de-aerated water entered the boilers. The system was later modified and improved through combining the two valves into one, which was servo-operated. It was a major invention, and it re-asserted Weirs' technical leadership in their own field.* Indeed, when shipbuilding revived it became one of the most profitable of the Weir Product lines and so continued until well after the Second World War.

There were markets, they felt, which they had not yet tapped. Some were at home, but others were abroad, particularly in India,

* See Appendix Five.

Australia, South Africa and South America. In all these markets, Weirs would run into powerful American competition: competition based on the productivity of automatic and semi-automatic methods of manufacture – the methods which so many firms and unions on Clydeside were in 1919 getting rid of.[9]

Weirs' decision to challenge the Americans meant heavy investment in new plant, which was no doubt what they needed the £940,000 of undistributed profits for. They had to re-equip both the general engineering side of the factory and the foundry, and the Board were determined that the men who worked the new machinery should be paid on a piece-work system based on work study and cost accountancy. In the engineering shops, where the men and their union – the Amalgamated Society of Engineers – had long experience of payment by results, the re-equipment of the works does not seem to have caused grave trouble, for on 28 October 1919 Lord Weir said: 'Since the Armistice we have made definite progress in our engineering shops – in particular, in the machine shops – and our new systems and methods of production are beginning to make definite progress.'[10] In the foundry, matters were otherwise.

The men in the foundry belonged to the Associated Ironmoulders of Scotland, not to the ASE. They seem to have had a grudge against Weirs, and there is evidence that the interests of the foundry may have been neglected – at any rate, in one meeting with the ironmoulders, Lord Weir said that an enquiry into costs had convinced him 'that we have paid too much attention to the engineering side and that we must now pay more attention to the foundry side'. At the same meeting one of the ironmoulders' representatives said: 'The general opinion of Cathcart is a poor one. I am one of the men who suffered from tyranny in your works. After 15 years' experience I was thrown out on the streets simply because I was not turning out as much work as another fellow workman.' This blunt accusation did not meet with the energetic refutation that might have been expected if there had been nothing in it. On the contrary, Lord Weir replied, evidently rather uneasily, '. . . the instance that my friend on the other side has given us that there have been certain abuses is an indication to us that the conditions in the foundry from the top side have got to be changed.'[11]

It is clear, then, from this exchange and others, that Weirs' Board were not very proud of their own managerial record in the foundry, and that they knew very well what some, at least, of the men thought of them. In this atmosphere, they went very cautiously about making changes. First, in the early part of 1919, they decided what was necessary. Then, in the summer, they explained their proposals to the shop stewards and later, in October, to their whole body of ironmoulders.

Weirs' review of their foundry practice disclosed to them, as they explained to their men and to the union, 'a situation which we believe to be more or less representative of that of British foundry practice in general, yet . . . we find waste of effort, low intensity of effort, a degree of slackness in management, and the existence of certain old-fashioned methods in the foundries, in particular, we find a strong feeling of prejudice against reform in any direction.'[12] To make quite clear what was meant by 'old-fashioned methods', Lord Weir pointed out to the men that they still wheeled sand to the moulding machine. 'That is inefficiency. Sand should either go to the moulding machines by a mechanical conveyor or it should be lifted in a big grab bucket by the crane and instead of six wheelbarrows, one bucket should drop a ton of sand beside the moulding machine.'[13]

In the same speech, Weir touched an even more sensitive spot. 'In our foundries,' he said, 'there is work being done by men who have served seven years' apprenticeship, which can be equally well done by an unskilled man or a girl after a week's training. That is waste of skilled effort.' No doubt it was, but it was also job protection. If the unskilled man or the girl came in, where would the skilled man be? Out, very probably, or so he thought, and that lay at the root of 'prejudice against reform in any direction' which Weir complained of.

Weir made it quite clear why, nevertheless, he was insisting on drastic changes. He showed his men figures which demonstrated that a casting which cost 34s. 1d. a cwt to produce in

Glasgow could be produced for 17s. 3d. in Philadelphia, in spite of the fact that in Philadelphia the man who made the casting would be paid £9 12s. 6d. a week: in Glasgow, £4 2s. 6d. On the reasons for the difference in costs, Weir was outspoken: 'First, the American methods and facilities and appliances are better, and consequently – and we tell you quite frankly – the men in America work harder and steadier. Perhaps the most essential difference is that the men in America are paid only for what they do and not for being in the shop so many hours per day.'

He asked his men to accept the principle of payment by results, based on work study and production planning; to get rid of union restrictions on output; to stop insisting that skilled men should not give up doing unskilled work. Specifically, he wanted to get unskilled men – disabled soldiers, for choice – on to the repetitional manufacture of cores. 'I conceive it,' he said, 'one of the gravest wastes in British industry that your Union compels men who have served a poorly paid apprenticeship of seven years, to spend the rest of their lives shovelling sand and pulling a lever on a moulding machine. The manufacture of small cores in large numbers is a ridiculous thing to ask full-grown men to employ their time at. If these stupid things exist, why do we not face them and clean up the situation?' Lord Weir, Richmond, James Weir and Lang met the Executive Council of the Associated Ironmoulders on 5 December 1919 to discuss their proposals for the foundry, which had already been explained to the Council in a letter. There was a good deal of rather sterile question-and-answer, but the two sides were never really in communication with each other, and there was not the remotest approach to bargaining. Weirs' directors suggested another conference, and left the union to make up its mind. On 11 February 1920, rather more than two months after the meeting, the union's General Secretary, James Fulton, wrote a brief official letter to Weirs. He quoted a recent vote of his members 'against the acceptance of any system of Payment by Results', and said 'the Executive Council does not see that any useful purpose would be served by a further Conference.'[14]

At the end of 1920 a postscript to this episode was provided by

John Whyte, the Organizing Secretary of the National Union of Foundry Workers. It reveals very clearly the profound feeling of insecurity which lay at the root of the Associated Ironmoulders' rigidity:

> Increased production [Whyte wrote to Lord Weir] appears to be the dominant mainspring of all your thoughts and activities, and you never miss an opportunity of showing your bitterest antipathy to that Trade Union which has most relentlessly failed to agree to your proposals.
>
> Moulders know, for instance, that it is inherent under a Capitalist regime of production to have boom periods of employment (with accompanying excess of overtime) and periods of unemployment and short time. This latter is dreaded by all workers, and payment by results encouraging intensified production would bring a period of unemployment much quicker . . . for after all the removal to the Poorhouse, for ever threatening us within its portals, is the main terror.[15]

It may be granted that there was much in the harsh experience of the working class to justify suspicion of their employers' motives. It is tragic, nevertheless, that this kind of suspicion blinded so many of the workmen in British engineering to the danger from efficient foreign competitors, who, as events were soon to show, could bring them within the Poorhouse with speed and finality.

The ironmoulders' intransigence left great bitterness in the minds of Lord Weir and his Board, not least because it ruined the firm's reputation for reliability:

> I can only admit [Weir wrote to Archibald Gilchrist, Managing Director of Barclay Curle, on 5 April 1921] that your complaints in regard to delays in deliveries are thoroughly justified . . . we have had to face a very grave situation at Cathcart . . . I can remember up till the war commenced when people could depend on our deliveries for even the most elaborate contracts to within 24 hours. Recently they have been unable to depend, I might nearly say, to within 24 weeks. . . . For over 18 months we have steadily fallen behind . . . due, in the first case, to lack of moulders and next to obstruction by moulders on the introduction of new processes and

of unskilled labour. To meet these difficulties we attempted lengthened negotiations to obtain co-operation which was finally refused. . . . The result of this has been to throw our production programme entirely out of gear.[16]

To meet the immediate needs of the post-war boom, Weirs had to buy castings 'with the most deplorable results' – according to Lord Weir – 'first in regard to delivery and next in regard to rejections.' Their permanent solution to the problem, however, was to put up a new foundry, away from Cathcart, for repetition work, which was particularly important for the cheaper class of pumps on which they hoped to found their new foreign trade, and for doing this work they would put in plant which needed no skilled labour at all. Payment would be by results, and they intended to give priority to ex-service men, as well as employing women. A subsidiary – Argus Foundry Limited – was set up, a $3\frac{1}{2}$ acre site was bought at Thornliebank, plant was ordered from America, and by the time Weir wrote to Gilchrist, in April 1921, he hoped to have the new foundry in production within a few weeks.[17]

While the quarrel with the ironmoulders was going on, Weirs were preparing to expand their business in turbine-driven centrifugal pumps. They had gone into it sceptically before the Great War (page 44) and they had confined themselves to boiler feed pumps. By the end of the war they had decided that it would be unwise to go on neglecting circulating water pumps, the more so since they could develop a unit to work from very much the same design of steam turbine as they were developing for boiler feed pumps. Within a matter of weeks of the armistice they began negotiating to buy control of Drysdales of Yoker, who already had an established business in centrifugal pumps. Drysdale & Co. had been established (as Drysdale & Pirie, the names of the original partners) in 1868. Like Weirs, they had prospered on pre-war and wartime shipbuilding, although on a very much smaller scale. In 1919 one of the founding partners was still in the business, being then about seventy, and so was George Reid, who had succeeded, more or less, to Pirie's position (Pirie left in 1883). The main direction of the business was by this time in the hands of Drysdale's two sons, who were not on very good terms with each other, perhaps because the younger was the abler of the two and held the position of managing director. The initiative for the sale of shares to Weirs came from Drysdales' side, because the prospect of competition from Weirs filled them with apprehension. Weirs could give up the idea of making centrifugal pumps themselves, and instead make the turbines to drive pumps made by Drysdales.

The matter seems to have been fairly quickly settled early in 1919, the basis being a sale to Weirs of a controlling interest, leaving the two Drysdales, still substantial shareholders, to run the business. Richmond evidently had his doubts about the transaction. When a figure of £45,000 was mentioned, to yield only about 3·4 per cent, he observed: 'From this point of view our offer is much too good, and probably we could spend the £45,000 odd to better advantage in developing our own centrifugal pump here, say in the Albert Factory.'[18] He appears to have been overborne, and in March 1920 Lord Weir wrote to Sir Thomas Bell of John Brown:

After the Armistice my firm acquired the financial control of Messrs Drysdale & Co. Ltd to enable us to deal with the large number of enquiries for Centrifugal Pumps which we could not and would not handle at Cathcart, our policy being only to make turbine-driven Rotary Machinery in our works. The scheme has been very successful, and we have been able to influence the technical character of Drysdale's products in a favourable way.[19]

By the summer of 1920 the post-war boom was running down. The first flood of post-war demand was spent, and in any case the response to it had been exaggerated. Government spending was being cut, credit was drying up, prices were falling. In foreign markets there was a great deal of political instability and the monetary system, stable and smooth-acting before 1914, was in chaos. The collapse, in Great Britain, from prosperity into depression was frighteningly swift and complete. During 1920 the average figure of unemployment stood at about 400,000.

In 1921 it rose well over 2,000,000. After that, in the twenties and thirties, it never again fell so low as 1,000,000, a figure which gradually came to be accepted, more or less explicitly, as the irreducible minimum. The figures for Scotland, as a proportion of the total working population, were regularly higher than the figures for the United Kingdom as a whole.[20]

The slump of 1921 was general, and no industry altogether escaped. In the recovery which followed, however, and which went much further in some other countries, notably the United States and Germany, than in Great Britain, some industries did very much better than others. These, in Great Britain, were chiefly the newer industries, dealing in consumer goods, including motor cars, or in the newer industrial goods, such as chemicals.

The deflated state of the economy, with falling prices, made for a higher standard of living among the employed population, who even at the worst of times were the vast majority. There was a lively market for goods as diverse as toilet soap, canned food, artificial silk stockings, and mass-produced cars. This was the period, in fact, when the car began to become a normal part of middle-class life, and when speculative builders, accordingly, began to include garages in their plans for suburban housing. Recovery, on the foundation of the newer industries, built up into a mild boom. It reached its peak about 1927, when unemployment fell to its lowest figure between the two wars: just under 1,200,000.

In this recovery the late-Victorian 'basic industries', by which Great Britain had long been accustomed to earn a very good living in foreign trade, scarcely shared. Coal, steel, cotton, engineering and shipbuilding all remained thoroughly depressed until the recovery of the later thirties, stimulated by rearmament, began to get under way. The reasons for depression were various, and some had been emerging before the war. Far Eastern competition against Lancashire cotton, for instance, had been building up for many years, and it became very much worse when the Japanese were able to take over markets neglected, perforce, during the Great War. There was severe competition against coal from other sources of energy, especially oil. Economic nationalism – the search for self-sufficiency – led foreign governments to discriminate against British goods, especially ships, in favour of their own manufactures. And something, in all these industries, must no doubt be put down to the generally conservative temperament of both management and men. The whole situation was made very much worse by the ruin of the world's monetary system in 1931, but to that we shall return.

Shipbuilding, on which Weirs so heavily depended, was probably the most severely depressed industry of all. Between 1923 and 1939, on average, about 36 per cent of insured workers in shipbuilding and ship-repairing in the United Kingdom were unemployed.[21] Even in the years of high prosperity before 1914, shipbuilding had periodically gone through bad times (hence the extreme nervousness of the men employed in it), as, for instance, in 1908. The immediate cause of the drop in new tonnage after 1920 seems to have been simply that the immediate post-war demand for new merchant ships had been made good, and it might have been expected that after a slack year or two, as in times past, orders would start to come in again. There was, indeed, some recovery in the late twenties, and in 1928 and 1929 the figures reached the level of a good year – say, 1902 – early in the century.

The demand for merchant ships for British owners, however, was bound to be closely linked with the state of British export trade, which was not flourishing. Demand from abroad, where some countries had built up fleets of merchant ships during the war, might have been expected to be healthy, but governments seeking industrial self-sufficiency were disinclined to see orders for ships placed abroad, and British shipbuilders and ship-owners complained continually of subsidized competition, while they themselves had to make their way unassisted by their own government.

This decline in building merchant ships would no doubt have been supportable if it had not been accompanied by the stop on naval building so accurately foreseen at Weirs. Before 1914, whatever the owners of merchant ships might be doing, it had for many years been possible to rely on a high and rising demand for warships, especially from the British Admiralty. Just before the Great War, according to *Whitaker's Almanack* for 1914, there were fourteen capital ships and seventy other vessels building in British yards for the Royal Navy, besides capital ships and other craft building for foreign powers. After the war, no capital ships at all were laid down in British yards between 1922 and 1937, and there was a very small demand for other vessels. In the early twenties, for example, the Admiralty ordered two destroyers – *Amazon* and *Ambuscade* – as prototypes, and after that they built, for some years, one flotilla a year: that is, an annual programme of about eight ships.

Many of the problems of British shipbuilding were outside the power of the industry itself to solve. It can scarcely be doubted, however, that they were made worse by the reluctance of management and men to face drastic rationalization of productive capacity and shipbuilding methods. That rationalization of this sort was possible was demonstrated in the explosives industry, where the same problem – post-war failure of demand – was foreseen and was met by the Explosives Trades (later Nobel Industries) merger of 1918, which was followed by an extremely ruthless programme of concentrating productive capacity and diversifying the group's interests. A somewhat similar policy was followed in Imperial Chemical Industries after 1926. The methods were harsh, but they worked, ultimately to the benefit of everyone connected with British chemical industry. Rationalization in shipbuilding, on the other hand, started later, did not go nearly so far, and demonstrated only its negative aspect: the shutting-down of uneconomic yards.

The whole situation was made very much worse by the world catastrophe of 1931–2, with its accompanying economic nationalism. In 1933 the tonnage built in British shipyards for British citizens and companies fell to 83,600. There had been no lower figure since 1843, and to find figures significantly and consistently lower it is necessary to go back to the end of the eighteenth century. In 1934 and 1935 the figures recovered roughly to the level of the early 1860s, but right up to 1938 they remained well below the general level of the years just before 1914.[22]

The effect on Weirs of the economic turmoil of war, post-war boom, industrial dispute, slump and recovery is demonstrated in their figures of invoiced sales. In the last full year of peace they were running about £750,000. Wartime demand sent the figure up to £3,000,000 (1918) but the cancellation of war contracts brought it down to £1,700,000 in 1919. It dropped again, to about £1,000,000, in 1920, when the dispute with the foundry-men was having its worst effect. Then in a year that was generally depressed – 1921 – Weirs' sales rose to £1,400,000, probably because the new foundry was by then in production, but in 1922–3 they fell almost to their lowest inter-war point, rather over £500,000, before recovering to about £1,100,000 in the mild boom of 1927.

Weirs' response to bad trade was to reduce rapidly the men and capital employed in the business. In September 1920 Lord Weir told a correspondent (Engineer Captain E. W. Liversidge) that the position at Cathcart was 'determined entirely by industrial difficulties and obstructions' – no doubt he meant the tactics of the moulders – and that the business was carrying 'a wholly abnormal staff quite out of proportion to turnover'.[23] By the beginning of 1922 there were only 1400 employed at Cathcart, against 3000 before the war. Every week more men were being sacked, and only a fortnight later Weir said they were employing 1200. By June, the figure was down to 1000, including the Argus foundry.[24]

A little later the capital of the business was reduced. The new money taken up in 1919 cannot have been fully invested, for at the end of 1923 an Extraordinary General Meeting resolved to cancel all the Preference capital – 60,000 6% CP Shares of £10 each – and to repay the holders in full. The scheme was approved by the Court of Session and took effect from 28 February 1924. Some five years later, in June 1929, it was resolved to repay £4 per Ordinary share from the undivided profits of the Company earned earlier than 31 December 1926, so that by the time the depression of the thirties set in the capital employed in the company had been very much reduced.[25]

For 1925 no dividend was paid, and in the later twenties dividends for two years (1927 and 1928) were paid, in part at least, not in cash but in debentures of Monel-Weir Limited.* After that, for several years, fairly substantial distributions were made, but reluctantly. The reluctance arose from the fact that Section 21 of the Finance Act 1922, as modified by the Finance Act 1927, dealing with surtax, required a 'reasonable distribution', and what appeared 'reasonable' to the Special Commissioners of Inland Revenue was more than the directors really wished to pay, having regard, they said in 1930, to 'the present serious depression in the shipbuilding and other industries with which the business of the Company is so closely associated.'[26]

This all reads like the record of a business conducted with extreme caution during difficult times, which the 1920s were bound to be for any business so heavily dependent on shipbuilding as Weirs. They could no longer rely on rapidly rising naval demand, from all over the world, to underpin the demand for merchant ships, and the demand for land work does not seem to have been great enough to make good the lack of orders from the shipbuilders. The driving force behind Weirs' pre-war expansion was broken, and the exuberance which bubbles through William Weir's early letter-books had gone flat.

Within the narrow limits set by post-war adversity, Weirs' Board did their best to push the business ahead. Soon after the Great War they took over Murray Workman, Cardonald, making air compressors. In 1921 they took a licence from Sulzer Frères of Winterthur, Switzerland, to build diesel engines for driving auxiliary plant at sea or on land. In 1928 they took over the Contraflo Engineering Co. Ltd, London, which owned the patent rights granted to Weirs' old rival D.B.Morison. Abroad, they continued to license foreign firms

* For Monel-Weir, see p. 103 below.

to build Weir gear, and they made determined assaults on the two markets which, above others, had resisted them: France and USA. In the early twenties, with as much tact as possible, they removed their French agency from the ageing hands of Marius Jullien and reorganized their whole conduct of the business, issuing licences in 1926 to the Societé des Ateliers, Chantiers de France and to S. A. des Ateliers et Chantiers de la Loire. In America, in 1920, they licensed the Bethlehem Shipbuilding Corporation, but when depression came in 1921 it was made clear that in the Bethlehem group shipbuilding was subordinate to steelmaking, and Weirs' business was never pushed hard enough to satisfy them. By 1929 Weirs and Bethlehem had agreed to part. In Japan the licence agreement with Mitsubishi Shoji Kaisha ran out in 1922. It was renewed, during a visit to Japan, by J.G.Weir.[27]

We have no day-to-day commentary on the firm's affairs in the twenties such as is provided for the period before 1914 by William Weir's letters. Weir himself, deep in public policy in London, as a rule only attended at Cathcart at weekends, and very little correspondence from other sources has survived. It appears that the main object of the directors was to keep the business alive and reasonably healthy at a low level of activity, holding together as much as they could of skilled staff and labour for expansion in better times – and to do all this, as always, on the minimum of invested capital. They were greatly helped in pursuing this policy by the constitution of the business as a private company with very few shareholders, which made it fairly easy to take decisions and act quickly on them, however unorthodox or disagreeable they might be.

The business was in the hands of two families, the Weirs and the Langs, but there is no evidence that it suffered from the complacency or undue conservatism which is sometimes said to have been a fault of British family businesses, particularly at this period. Indeed, during the twenties two considerable enterprises were in hand well outside the limits of Weirs' normal peacetime business. These were Weir houses and Monel metal, and to them we must now turn.

97

6

Diversions in the Twenties: Housing and Monel Metal

By the time the Great War ended very few private houses – virtually none – had been built since 1914, and not a great many of the cheaper sort since 1910, when the late Victorian boom in that kind of housing came to a sudden end.[1] At the same time great hopes had been aroused about 'a fit country for heroes to live in'[2] and almost completely democratic suffrage, including votes for some women, had been established. The result was that the problem of housing shortage, particularly for the working classes, was pushed to the forefront of politics.

The building of houses by traditional methods provided examples of unrationalized hand craftsmanship as fine as any to be found in engineering or shipbuilding, and quite as strongly protected by restrictive practices. Moreover there was no threat from abroad, as there was to the 'basic industries'. Building, in the phraseology of the day, was 'sheltered'. Both sides of the industry – management and men – were thus very well placed to take advantage of the post-war demand for houses, and if any challenge from new-fangled methods should arise, they would both be found on the same side to oppose them.

The builders' position had one weakness. Houses need not necessarily be built on site by skilled craftsmen – bricklayers, plumbers, painters, plasterers, carpenters – using their traditional materials and observing the customs of their trades, including rigid demarcation. Houses could be looked upon as a task for engineering firms, with the parts, chiefly of steel or wood – no bricks – made in a factory and assembled on the site by unskilled labour. Looked at in this way, the making of houses had a great deal in common with the making of aircraft during the Great War, and any firm which could do that job could certainly do the other. Ideas of this nature, to the scandal of the building trades, began to be talked about in the early twenties, in particular by William Weir.

Weir seized upon the fact that the traditional building industry was not keeping up with demand, even though its resources, particularly skilled labour, were fully taken up. So however nervous the building trades might be of an engineer invading their territory, they could hardly complain with any conviction that factory methods, in the short run at any rate, were likely to take work away from them. 'The existing trade,' Weir explained to Sir John Chancellor, 'cannot meet the country's need, therefore I can call my scheme supplementary, and, if necessary, temporary.'[3]

'His scheme' was to make the components of houses in an engineering works, according to engineering practice, and then to get them erected by unemployed men of any trade or none, paid, if craftsmen, at engineering craftsmen's rates; if labourers, at engineering labourers' rates, but in either case observing the general conditions of employment of engineering rather than of building, since he contended that the traditions of the building industry had no bearing on the case. He was particularly concerned about unemployment in engineering and the steel industry. He could, and did, claim with perfect truth that a scheme on the lines he proposed would make a dent in two major social problems – housing shortage and unemployment. He also calculated that each house built would save the Unemployment Insurance Fund about £75.

Weir's phraseology – 'I can *call* my scheme supplementary...' suggests a hidden motive, and indeed there was one, which Weir revealed to Chancellor but to few others. He was hoping to strike a blow at the restrictive practices of the craft unions in 'sheltered' industries. 'If one is able,' he wrote to Chancellor, 'to offer an alternative technique involving no craft skill or even introducing a new kind of craft, then given enough unemployment in other directions, you have a most effective line of attack.'

On these grounds, during 1923, Weir decided to carry his family firm into the production of factory-made houses. For a firm which had generally refused to diversify, even into activities much more closely related to conventional engineering, this may seem a remarkable departure. It can certainly not be explained purely, or even mainly, by ordinary commercial motives. No doubt Weir and his Board expected to see profits – even, in the end, handsome profits – but a great deal would have to be spent on development and there was certain to be political trouble. They could have found quieter ways of making money if that had been the chief consideration.

It was not, and the decision to commit Weirs to unorthodox housing shows quite clearly that the owners of the business were prepared to use it, on occasion, for purposes of social policy and labour relations. Only a fairly small firm, the owners of which were answerable to none but themselves, could have contemplated such a course of action. It would scarcely have been open to a large public company. There is very little doubt that the decision owed a good deal to resentment at the upshot of the dispute with the ironmoulders, and in some ways it belongs rather to the biography of William Weir than to the history of Weirs. But the decision, taken early in the 1920s, had consequences which only became fully apparent after the Second World War, and for that reason, if for no other, it demands attention at this point in the narrative.

During 1923 and 1924 Weir, firmly established among the nation's rulers, cultivated ministerial opinion, both Conservative and (briefly) Labour. At the same time Weirs, as a firm, went ahead with preparations, and they established at Cardonald a factory, intended as a prototype, which was planned to produce 2500 houses in 1925. By the time the Conservatives were firmly in power again, towards the end of 1924, Weirs were ready to go ahead, having by that time laid out about £75,000 in capital expenditure, salaries, wages and material.

Weir had already announced his intentions publicly, and a Committee set up by the Labour Government of 1924, under Sir Ernest Moir,* had gone into the whole question of unconventional house-building and reported favourably, if cautiously, on Weir's proposals.

The Weir House [says the first catalogue issued] is a composite structure of steel sheets or plates for the outer wall, and a high grade composition sheet for the inner lining, both attached to a strong wooden framing with a double cellular air space between. The interior partitions consist of wooden framing covered with best quality composition lining, or in living room and hall with three-ply wood suitably treated and stained. The flooring is of the usual white pine tongued and grooved. The roof is of wooden sarking† covered with slates of asbestos cement of best quality or clay tiles. The foundations are of concrete with bitumen damp course. These are the main elements of construction. . . .

The catalogue lists four types of house. The largest, built in semi-detached pairs, had three bedrooms and two storeys. The others were variants on a single-storey, two-bedroom plan, but one version provided for two-storey blocks of four houses, two up, two down. On costs and prices the catalogue is non-committal, saying 'the cost of a standardized product cannot be definitely established until production on a fair scale has been reached and until full experience has been gained in methods and processes'. Weir himself, however, in correspondence, quoted £380 at a production figure of 20 houses a week (it is not clear which type of house he was referring to) and £360 at 80 a week, and to Churchill, as Chancellor of the Exchequer, he promised 10,000 houses, over two years, at £340 each.[4]

But would any local authority be allowed to put up the houses Weirs could provide, under the conditions of employment which Weirs insisted on? Not, evidently, if the National Federation of Building Trades Operatives had its way. The first clash came

---

* Sir E.Moir Bart (1916) (1862–1933), Scottish engineer. Partner of Lord Cowdray in S.Pearson & Son Ltd.

† Rough-cut timber.

in Glasgow, where working class housing conditions were among the worst in the United Kingdom. In the autumn of 1924 Glasgow Corporation ordered twenty Weir houses as an experiment. Weirs engaged unemployed men to make them and put them up; offering pay and conditions equivalent to those in engineering. The National Federation promptly made it very clear to Glasgow Corporation that there would be trouble if Weirs, on the sites, did not observe the building trade's rates of pay and conditions of employment. Weirs refused, the Corporation took fright, and the scheme was dead.

Much the same tactics were repeated elsewhere, with much the same results. Local authorities were not prepared to have their entire housing programmes interrupted for the sake of experiments with the Weir house, and a few sharp words from the Building Trades Operatives were usually enough to check any dealings an authority might have begun with Weirs.

The matter therefore fell back into the hands of the Government, who appointed a Court of Enquiry under Lord Bradbury, late of the Treasury. The building employers joined their men in opposing Weirs' schemes. The Court, however, found against them and rejected their claim that the conditions of the building trade should be applied to these radically new methods of producing housing. This decision was of no practical effect. The Government flinched from the certainty of a major dispute in the building industry and refused either to coerce local authorities – which, given local authorities' almost infinite capacity for delay, would have been very difficult – or to push through any scheme of their own, although there were plans for a government-sponsored housing company in Scotland.

In spite of everything, some 3000 Weir houses were put up, chiefly in Scotland, and it appears that most of the tenants liked them. They were well planned, well equipped, and well insulated, which was a great deal more than could be said for many conventionally-built houses. Nevertheless without the support of local authorities or the Government the scheme was bound to fail, and by the end of 1927 it was all over. 'It is an extraordinary thing,' wrote Weir early in that year, 'that,

A direct contact feed water heater of the late nineteenth century

An evaporator for distilling sea water

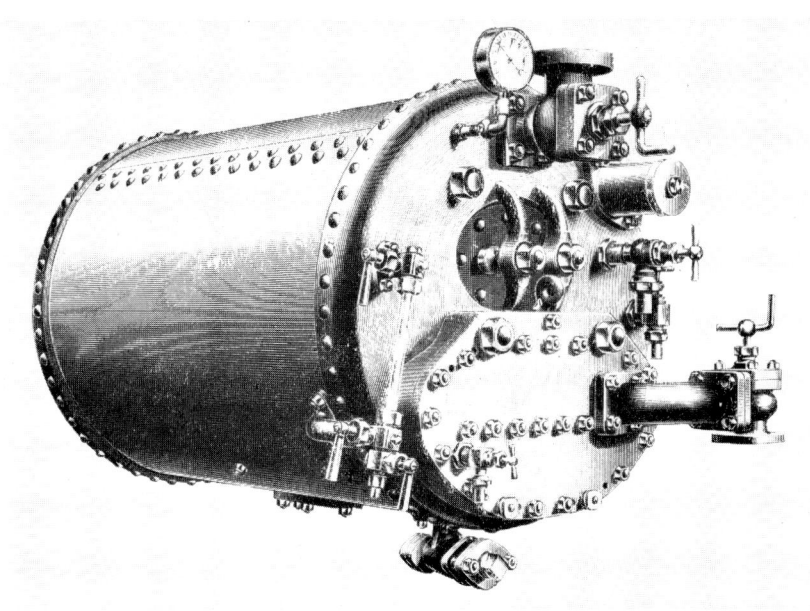

The twin boiler feed pumps which were installed in RMS *Campania*, built by the Fairfield Company, 1893

The founders – George and James Weir

Above, the Works in 1904

Left, an early twentieth-century Uniflux Condenser

Below, the pumps installed for the Anglo-Persian Oil Company before 1914

A locomotive feed pump fitted to a L & NW Railway engine, before 1914

Three Darracq racing cars manufactured at Cathcart, 1904

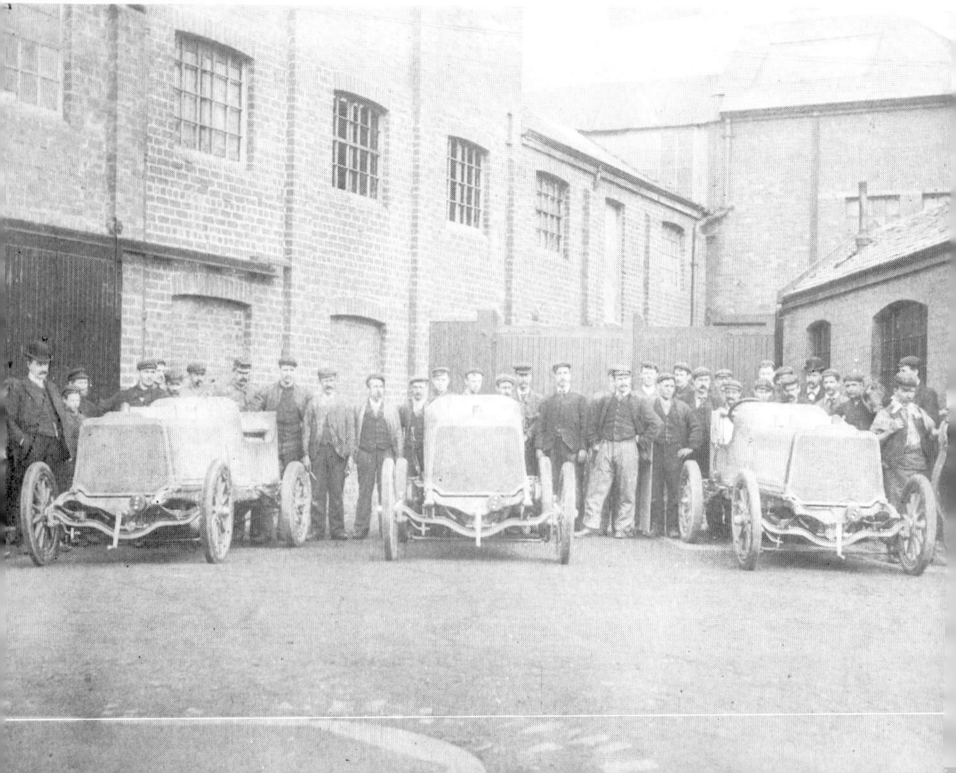

A Darracq Serpollet engined bus, *c.* 1906

Aircraft assembly in 1918

The first Lord Weir
as Controller of
Aeronautical Supplies
at the Ministry of
Munitions in 1915

James Drysdale

An early Weir house at Cardonald, Glasgow, c. 1926

Autogiro W-2, c. 1934

The Autogiro W-3 of 1936

Turbo-feed pump installed in RMS *Queen Mary*

An early Zwicky aircraft refueller

Above, Mr C.R. Lang, CBE, Mr J.G. Weir, CMG, CBE
Below, Mr J. Spittal, Mr M.L. Jamieson

Above, The Right Honourable Lord Weir of Eastwood, PC, GCB, LLD, DL
Below, Mr J. R. Richmond, CBE, Mr J. Craig, Mr H. Hillier

The turbine-driven feed pump designed and built for steam gunboats of the Second World War

Painting depicting the turbine shop at Cathcart during the Second World War

Petrol driven salvage pumps were used extensively on damaged vessels during the war

The finishing touch to the assembly of a 25-pounder field gun carriage

The 25-pounder in action

The 'Hybrid'. This was a 17-pounder mounted on to a 25-pounder carriage

Mr N.M.Niven

The Air Horse, developed by the Cierva Company, 1945–50

The Skeeter, taken over with the Cierva Company by Saunders-Roe and developed during the 1950s

An early 'Quality' house, of the type built of steel between 1945 and 1948

Land-based sea-water distillation plant of the 1950s

The Guernsey sea-water distillation plant

The sea-water distillation plant at Aden

The *Fairtry* fish factory vessel, built by Simons-Lobnitz while a member of the Weir Group

The board of directors,
1961/62

The second Viscount Weir

A Weir Pacific stainless steel Class 150 gate valve, designed to operate at temperatures down to −160 °C, installed in the methane tanker *Methane Progress*

A seven-roomed house completed by Weir Housing Corporation Limited in five weeks and two days at a cost of less than £6,500 using the advanced Multicom system of construction pioneered by the company

Above, the Ashford Common pumping station of the London Metropolitan Water Board is equipped with twelve pump sets, capacities ranging from ten million to thirty million gallons per day. Both pumps and drive motors were manufactured at the Alloa plant of Weir Pumps Ltd

Right, a large pump casting produced in one of the Group's steel foundries at Sheffield

A galley designed and manufactured by C. F. Taylor (Metal Workers) Limited for the Boeing 747 'jumbo-jet'

Three one hundred thousand gallon per minute de-watering pumps ordered from Weir-Warmtekracht N.V. for the Wilton-Fijenoord dry dock at Schiedam, Holland. The pumps were manufactured by the dock owners under licence from Weir Pumps Limited

A boiler feed pump, one of the many designed and manufactured by
Weir Pumps Limited for major power stations at home and overseas

Large cooling tower circulating water pumps designed and built at the
Yoker factory of Weir Pumps Limited and installed in a major British
power station of the Central Electricity Generating Board

The board (and Secretary) of The Weir Group Limited, March 1971.
Left to right, back row: Mr J.J.B.Young, Mr J.A.Lumsden, DL, MBE,
The Hon W.K.J.Weir, Mr J.Russell Lang, CBE, Viscount Weir, CBE,LLD,
Mr F.R.Frame (Secretary), Mr E.D.Bremner and Mr J.W.Atwell, CBE.
Left to right, front row: Mr W.D.Coats, Mr A.C.Smith, Mr John H.Lord,
Sir Charles Connell, DL, Mr S.L.Finch and Mr C.F.Taylor, OBE, DL

although we have demonstrated that the steel house is thoroughly good, that the tenants thoroughly appreciate it, and that it can be built rapidly and with certainty, yet not one single Local Authority in Scotland has the courage to place a contract [presumably he meant a large contract] with us.'[5] What had also been demonstrated, for the second time in Weirs' post-war history, was the immense defensive strength of a trade union fighting, however ill-advisedly, for the preservation of the traditional way of doing things. The Weir House, however, was not quite so dead as in 1927 it seemed to be. When there was a shortage of housing at the end of the Second World War it came to life again in circumstances and with results which we shall examine in their place.

Weirs' other diversionary interest of the twenties, Monel metal, had origins running back to 1910. In that year, in North America, William Weir had been attracted by a nickel-copper alloy, made direct from the ore, developed by the International Nickel Company of Canada from ore produced at their property at Copper Cliff. It had unique properties of high tensile strength under temperature and it was extremely resistant to corrosion. This was Monel metal. Weir saw possibilities in it, especially for steam turbine blading, and the firm took a licence to sell it in Europe and the British Empire.

Before the war there seems to have been practically no development, presumably because Weirs' resources were fully stretched on their ordinary work. By the time war broke out, whatever enthusiasm they may have had for the metal seems to have drained away, for in the autumn of 1914 Weirs' Board, preoccupied with war work, decided to get rid of the rights to Panizzi Preston, a dealer in special metals. 'In the ten days since I have seen you,' Weir wrote to Preston on 13 November 1914, '. . . . I have been quite unable to do more with the Monel Metal question than to discuss it with my other Directors and to come to the decision to hand over to you, on reasonable terms, all the rights we possess as regards the Metal for Aeroplane work, Automobiles, Propellers, Railway work, and Marine Engineering, with the exception of perhaps a very few firms. In other words, practically the whole affair other than our own personal requirements.'[6]

When Preston looked more closely at Weirs' agreement with International Nickel, which he would have to take over, he did not like it, because it seemed to him to give International Nickel altogether too free a hand after the term of agreement – it was for five years – ran out, by which time he might have spent a lot of money getting Monel on to the market without having had time to get much back.* Weir said that his firm had 'found it very difficult to get INC to consider a proposition at all', and admitted that the agreement was 'a bit weak, but it is the best we could get and we took the risk'. Preston was not so bold, and the negotiations lapsed.[7]

At the end of the war Weirs were still in possession of the Monel rights, presumably by then secured by an agreement extended or made permanent. By 1920, probably as part of their campaign to make good the loss of naval orders for auxiliary machinery, they were working up uses for Monel metal, particularly in condenser tubes, since they had come to the conclusion 'that the only permanent and definite cure for condenser tube troubles rested with the provision of . . . non-corrodible material.'[8] 'We are busy,' wrote Lord Weir in 1920, 'developing the use of Monel Metal for all classes of engineering work, and tubes constitute one of the most important spheres of activity.' He did not, however, at that time intend to go in for full-scale manufacture himself. 'At the moment,' he went on, 'we have two firms in England working on the problem [of tubes], and under practically no conditions would we contemplate starting the making of tubes ourselves.'[9]

This kind of semi-detached development did not run smoothly. In May 1922 Sir Charles Parsons' firm at Newcastle

* Weirs' agreement was with the Bayonne Castings Co. which 'is practically a subsidiary of the International Nickel Co., New York, which controls the supply of material . . . the Agreement . . . has the approval and sanction of the INC who were prevented from entering into an agreement with us [because] . . . they do not consider it desirable that it should be made public that the two businesses are interlocked [no doubt for fear of anti-trust proceedings].' LB XIII, File 61, 216. It is not clear when the term of the agreement was due to run out.

complained of the quality of Monel metal supplied by Weirs for turbine blading and cancelled their orders. Weir, writing to Sir Charles, said the difficulties had arisen 'through looseness and reticence on your part in ordering the material', but he was much disturbed by such a complaint from so distinguished a customer. 'Monel,' he said, 'is undoubtedly becoming the standard blading for all difficult turbine propositions ... I think it would be a pity for your firm to fall out from the Monel circle in view of the developments taking place and the increasingly valuable results which are being obtained generally.'[10]

Then in the making of condenser tubes Monel metal turned out much more difficult to work than steel, and Weirs found it 'impossible to get any enthusiasm awakened in the ranks of British tube makers on the subject of Monel metal'. In the autumn of 1927 Lord Weir went to America to see 'an entirely new process of making brass condenser tubes in the hope that it could be applied to Monel metal', and what he saw impressed him 'very much', though it also made him wonder whether 'thoroughly good brass tube at a very slight extra cost' might displace Monel metal altogether. By this time Weirs were already making tubes on a small scale – probably not more than pilot plant – and they had reached the point where they had to consider whether to commit themselves to 'very large' capital expenditure – £50,000 or so.[11] By May 1924 they had evidently made their decision. 'In view of our outside difficulties,' Weir told a correspondent, 'we are now having a shot at making tubes ourselves.'[12]

Weirs put up plant, both for turbine blading and for condenser tubes, at Zenith Works alongside Argus Foundry, Thornliebank, but at least until 1928 they continued to employ an outside contractor, Talbot-Stead of Walsall, who put in a new shop for cold-drawing Monel metal tubes.[13] What Lord Weir described as 'our new process of manufacturing Monel metal tubes'[14] came into operation during 1925, and at the beginning of 1927 Richmond told Weir: 'Monel is doing quite well, and we have an order for 2580 tubes from Werkspoor for the Dutch Destroyers. The total output invoiced since 1 January from the Department is £9,803, and more still to price.'[15]

This letter is an indication of the important continental market for Monel metal. It had developed in Germany in the early twenties, and by the beginning of 1926 Weirs were ready to set up a German selling company – Monel Gesellschaft – with offices in Frankfurt. It appears to have been started by A.Foianesi, Weirs' French agent, who was installed at Frankfurt in February 1926.[16] At about the same time Weirs decided not to form a French Monel Metal Co. 'until ... financial conditions in France become more stabilized',[17] and the business was conducted through G. & J.Weir SARL, Weirs' French company, which also handled sales in Belgium and Switzerland. By the beginning of 1928 Monel Gesellschaft, with sales for the previous year of £22,000, was doing much better than the French. 'I do not think,' Weir wrote to Richmond after seeing the balance sheets, 'any of us have appreciated how poorly Paris has done. I think you should have a cold-blooded talk with Foianesi.' It was being suggested that Weirs should have a Monel agent in Switzerland and another in Brussels, 'and make Foianesi concentrate on exploiting France in much greater detail.'[18]

During 1928 a company called Monel-Weir Limited was set up at Cathcart. To it, for £196,274 1s. 10½d., G. & J.Weir sold the assets of their business 'of merchanting and manufacturing Monel Metal and Rolled Malleable Nickel carried on ... at Holm Foundry, Cathcart, and elsewhere.' They also contracted to 'use our influence' to have Monel-Weir appointed by International Nickel sole concessionnaires for the purchase and sale of Monel Metal and Rolled Malleable Nickel 'in Great Britain, Europe and elsewhere' as nearly as possible on the terms that Weirs themselves had had.

The concession was duly granted. £186,000 6% Mortgage Debenture Stock of Monel Weir Ltd was taken up by G. & J. Weir, and some at least of this stock was used in paying Weirs' dividends for 1927 and 1928 – an arrangement agreed upon before the stock was issued.[19] This device was intended to conserve the cash resources of G. & J. Weir in difficult times, and it would appear, therefore, that the motive for setting up Monel-Weir was partly to provide defence works for Weirs' main business.

Monel-Weir was very successful, depression notwithstanding. By 1932, when shipbuilding was at its lowest point, Weirs' directors found themselves obliged to decide whether the main business of their firm should henceforth be engineering, as it always had been, or the merchandizing of metals, which was the backbone of Monel-Weir's operations. The directors decided on engineering. They sold Monel-Weir's business, including the Zenith Works, to International Nickel, keeping only selling rights in France, to be exercised through G. & J. Weir SARL.

What made Weirs sell this flourishing asset? Broadly, a shrewd forecast, eventually justified, that the development of stainless steel would sooner or later deprive Monel metal of most of its market, because stainless steel, containing perhaps 3–4 per cent of nickel, is much cheaper than Monel containing 70 per cent. When the offer came from International Nickel, Weirs' Board considered that it gave them a good opportunity to get out of Monel at the top.

International Nickel, for their part, by acquiring Mond Nickel had acquired Mond Metal, a competitor to Monel. They had also taken over Mond Nickel's mining property in Canada, their refinery at Clydach in South Wales, and Henry Wiggin, a Birmingham subsidiary which specialized in the manufacturing and sale of nickel products. By buying Monel-Weir International Nickel rounded off a very tidy transaction.

The story of housing and Monel metal outlined in this chapter, taken with the account of Weirs' main business set out in the last, shows contradictory and co-existent inclinations towards caution and adventure, almost amounting to a split mind, which was characteristic of Weirs' second-generation management. William Weir, before the war, had on occasion made a virtue of conservatism, but on other occasions he had carried his colleagues into flirtation with motor cars and steam buses. After the war, similarly, the declared policy of the firm was to stick to the business they understood – pumps and auxiliary machinery – and eschew seductive by-ways, and after the post-war boom collapsed the directors pursued this policy with sufficient single-mindedness and skill to keep the firm in sound financial health against better times. Yet at the same time they permitted themselves to venture twice into new territory. Housing, as we have seen, was chiefly a political excursion and came to a political end. Monel metal, on the other hand, was much the most successful diversification, of a strictly commercial nature, which Weirs had ever made. Then, when it showed signs of overshadowing the pumps, it was resolutely stripped away and Weirs became once more unambiguous steam engineers.

But not for long. As we shall see in the next chapter, the urge towards new things once again broke through. In the thirties, alongside their orthodox activities, Weirs took to the air.

7

Depression, Autogiros and Rearmament 1929–39

In the first third of the twentieth century the British people
suffered, in quick succession, the Great War and the slump of
the early thirties. Loss of life in the war and unemployment in
the slump were neither so great as in some other countries,
but the psychological damage seems to have been greater –
perhaps, in the case of the slump, because self-confidence and
self-respect had been gravely injured by the post-war sickness
of the 'basic industries' long before the disasters of 1931–3.
However that may be, the events and general atmosphere,
real or imaginary, of the period we are about to deal with have
sunk deeply into national folklore, and their shadow lay over
British policies at least into the 'affluence' of the later 1960s,
if not beyond.

The boom of the late twenties, always far more apparent in
the USA than in Great Britain, collapsed at the end of October
1929 in the sudden ruin of prices on the New York Stock
Exchange. Over the next two years the shock spread, shattering
confidence, credit, and eventually the frail post-war payments
system, such as it was. This was the machinery of international
trade, and by the end of 1931 all nations which relied for their
well-being on the state of world markets, whether for primary
produce or manufactures or (like the USA) for both, were
deeply in distress. The average figure of unemployment for
Great Britain in 1932, taken over the whole year, was 2·75 m.,
representing about 22 per cent of insured workers.[1]

Since the central feature of the depression was the collapse
of world trade, it hit industries heavily dependent on exports

much harder than others, and shipbuilding hardest of all. Activity in British yards fell disastrously, and in 1932 the percentage of all insured workers unemployed rose to 62 per cent – much the highest figure recorded for any British industry. On Clydebank 1931 came to a calamitous end when on 11 December all work suddenly stopped – because Cunard could no longer finance it – on what was intended to be the largest ship in the world, put in hand at John Browns' yard a little over a year previously. 1932 opened under the shadow of the immense unfinished bulk of the ship that eventually put to sea as *Queen Mary*.[2]

Weirs' own industry, general engineering, was not hit quite so hard as shipbuilding. The percentage of insured workers unemployed, under 10 in 1929, rose to its highest point, 29·1, in 1932, and then began to fall, slowly at first and then, as rearmament got under way, quite rapidly. The worst figures, by the standards of the day, were scarcely more than moderately high, and by the later thirties, in engineering, there was what passed for full employment – that is, percentage figures of unemployment fairly comfortably below 10 per cent, which no doubt chiefly represented movement from one job to another.

Weirs had been quick to trim their affairs when the steam went out of the post-war boom, and the moderate prosperity of the later twenties had never tempted them into over-expansion. They had reduced their labour force, their plant and their capital, and they evidently persuaded Drysdales to pursue much the same policy, for in 1929 their capital was reduced from £150,000 nominal to £112,500 by returning 5s. a share to the shareholders and reducing the value of shares from £1 to 15s.[3] By the time the depression set in, Weirs can have had little in the way of idle but expensive resources, and they had considerable reserves, invested outside the business, which seem to have held their value reasonably well. 'We feel we have done pretty well,' Weir wrote in January 1931, 'in reducing the effects of depression in the last few years at Cathcart, and only now is the depression hitting us really hard.'[4]

Sales, which had risen after the depression of the early twenties to a peak of slightly over £1,000,000 in 1927, fell rapidly after 1928 to little more than £400,000 in 1933. Overheads rose with falling output and profit margins shrank, at the same time as falling commodity values had to be met from reserves. On top of everything, important customers – shipbuilders, no doubt – were in trouble and there was a risk of bad debts.[5] Even at the worst, however, in 1932 and 1933, profits were made, and the directors came under pressure to make a distribution – not from the shareholders, but once again from the Special Commissioners of Inland Revenue, under the terms of Section 21 of the Finance Act 1922.[6] They complied, but not without misgivings.

Weirs showed the strength of their finances in 1933, when the old-established Colchester firm of A.G.Mumford Limited (incorporating John Kirkaldy Limited) went into voluntary liquidation. Among Mumfords' assets there was one item which interested Weirs. It was a boiler feed regulator of Mumfords' own design. Weirs accordingly offered the liquidator £50,000 in cash – *in cash*, at the bottom of the depression – and when they got Mumford's business they closed the works and transferred all activity to Cathcart.[7] This was scarcely the action of a firm which had been overborne by events, however dire.

But the most convincing demonstration of Weirs' vitality amid depression was their work on rotating-wing aircraft from 1932 onward. Like the housing project, this was a highly idiosyncratic venture far beyond the normal bounds of the firm's activity, in which the profit motive, as it is usually understood, played little part. It was a piece of development work in new technology, showing little, if any, hope of commercial return except in some problematical future. It could only have been undertaken by a firm very sure of its technical and financial strength and also, probably, only by a firm in which ownership and direction, undivorced, lay in very few hands.*

* The alternative might have been a very large firm, committing only a very small proportion of its resources. But it would have required a very imaginative large firm, especially in the thirties.

Aircraft with rotating wings were developed alongside fixed-wing aircraft, but much less rapidly. Their chief advantages – very slow speed through the air, almost to the point of hovering, and their need of very little space for take-off and landing – were less obviously useful, especially for war, than the high speed of the fixed-wing aeroplane, even with its attendant disadvantage of long runs on the ground. But the fact that there were advantages was recognized, and there was always the hope that in some form of rotating-wing aircraft would be found a safe, simple machine, fairly cheap and requiring little space, which could become the private car of the air. Therefore ideas continued to be put forward in many countries – France, Russia, Austria, Germany, Great Britain, USA – and backers could sometimes be found to develop them.[8]

In the early twenties the most successful designer of rotating-wing aircraft was Juan de la Cierva y Cordonia (1895–1936), an aristocratic Spaniard with family money behind him. On 9 January 1923 his fourth experimental design, mounted on the fuselage of a Hanriot scout, flew across a field in Spain, and on 20 October 1925 he flew another machine, built up on the bodywork of an Avro 504K, at the Royal Aircraft Establishment, Farnborough. The Air Ministry's officials were sufficiently impressed to want to experiment with a Cierva machine of their own, and in 1926 they had one, also using Avro 504K bodywork.

Most of the early designers of rotating-wing aircraft built helicopters, in which power-driven rotors both lifted the machine and drove it forward. Cierva's conception was different. His machines were propelled, like fixed-wing aircraft, by engine-driven airscrews, but they were lifted by rotors driven by the airflow created by the aircraft's motion, and for that reason they were called *autogiros*.

If the engine of an autogiro failed, it would probably come down safely, because the speed of its fall would be sufficient to keep the rotors going. If an early helicopter's engine failed, it would crash, because the rotors would stop with the engine. The helicopter, however, could take off much more sharply than the early autogiros, which needed quite a long run to get their rotors going. Both kinds of aircraft could come down into a very small space. But in the twenties the main advantage of the autogiro over all contemporary helicopters was that it worked. It needed development, but by 1925 it was already quite plainly a practical aircraft.

So, at any rate, thought J.G.Weir, who saw the demonstration at Farnborough on 20 October 1925 and was greatly excited by it. 'Yesterday,' wrote William Weir on 21 October, '. . . Jimmy rang me up to say that he had been at Farnborough to see the performance of a new autogiro aeroplane. . . . In Jimmy's opinion, it marks the real beginning of aviation, apart from its war importance. It is the invention of a young Spaniard, and Courteney, who flew the machine, came to see me to report that in his opinion, commercial aviation could now commence.'[9] In the same letter William Weir announced, evidently with relief, 'that Jim has now settled down, having bought Skeldon, Adam Wood's old place, eight miles from Ayr, having two miles of splendid salmon fishing.' But 'settling down', for J.G.Weir, simply meant a heavy investment of time, talent and money in that most hazardous and expensive of industrial operations: the development of an aircraft of revolutionary design.

William Weir was quite as enthusiastic as his brother. 'I realized at once,' he wrote in 1928 to Henry Ford, 'that this machine would solve completely the problem of aviation as a public utility,'[10] and in this optimistic mood he agreed to serve on a committee, set up within ten days of the Farnborough demonstration, to advise Cierva who, it was said, 'evidently feels rather overweighted . . . as he has to devote a good deal of time to the technical side of improving his patent position while at the same time enquiries are reaching him from many quarters which have to be dealt with.'[11] One enquiry was from the Air Ministry, for a licence to build four autogiros, which soon became five.

The members of the committee, apart from William Weir, were J.G.Weir, Frank Courteney the demonstration pilot, and

Sir Robert Kindersley,* and it was preliminary to the setting up of a company to develop Cierva's invention. Early in 1926, after correspondence with Cierva's father, the general form of the company was settled. It was to be an English company 'to exploit the world patents of the Cierva machine including the English patents . . . [it] should not do anything in the nature of building aeroplanes itself, but merely negotiate the selling outright of patents and the granting of licences and royalties.' The capital required, £30,000, was put up by J.G. Weir, Kindersley and others, but William Weir decided 'that it would be undesirable for me to have a financial interest in the concern, as matters might develop where I would be placed in an invidious position.' By this he meant that as an ex-Secretary for Air, and a much respected one, and as a personal friend of the Chief of the Air Staff (Trenchard), he was frequently called upon for advice, and sometimes felt obliged to offer it on his own initiative, and his financial disinterestedness must be beyond question.[12]

With the founding of the Cierva Autogiro Co., Great Britain became Juan de la Cierva's main base. He developed his aircraft technically and promoted them energetically by demonstration throughout Europe. He aroused a great deal of interest in autogiros all over the world, and during ten years or so some five hundred rotor planes were built, not all under Cierva's patents. Cierva, nevertheless, was the leading designer in his field.

Technical progress was not matched by demand, at any rate on the scale or with the speed that the Weir brothers and their associates seem to have expected in the autumn of 1925. In 1928 Lord Weir tried to interest Henry Ford, obviously with the idea of mass production. 'I am now glad to inform you', he wrote, 'that . . . machines can be built with the same degree of safety as, and with no more manipulative skill than, that required for a motor car.' Edsel Ford, Henry's son, very politely turned Weir down.[13] On the military side the Air Ministry, after the

* Lord (1941) Kindersley (1871–1954), prominent financier, Director of the Bank of England 1914–46.

first, uncharacteristic, rush of enthusiasm, went very cautiously, spending only about £16,000 over several years, probably because several incidents in the test-flying of rotorplanes (not all Cierva Autogiros) received a good deal of publicity, perhaps more than they deserved. There was some hostile lobbying, too, from the makers of conventional aircraft.

'During this seven year period,' wrote Lord Weir in 1933, with a hint of bitterness, 'the development quite naturally met with lukewarm and half-hearted support and encouragement from all Authority and even from the scientific world. Such is the normal history of all great inventions. No reflection whatever is made on the Air Ministry policy during practically the whole period. They did spend some money. They did give some encouragement, and it is true to say that at no stage were they ever pressed to help in any great degree.'[14]

For the first six years of the Cierva company's life there is no evidence that Weirs as a company, distinct from J.G.Weir as an individual, were in any way financially committed to the autogiro project. By the summer of 1932, however, Cierva's affairs had reached a crisis, and J.G.Weir turned to his family firm for support. On 6 July 1932, say the minutes of Weirs' Board, 'Consideration was given to a proposal that the Company should enter into arrangements with the Cierva Autogiro Co. Ltd, whereby the Company would acquire the right to develop a type of small Autogiro up to a point when a definite decision could be taken either to go into the business of production or to abandon the project. Mr J.G.Weir presented an estimate showing the approximate outlays on the scheme and it was resolved to authorize the conclusion of an agreement with the Cierva Company and to limit the commitment of this Company as regards expenditure on the scheme to a sum not exceeding £8,000.'[15]

J.G.Weir's appeal came when Weirs' regular business was still being dragged downwards by the slump in shipbuilding, and when no end to the depression in world trade, which had caused the shipbuilders' troubles, was even remotely in sight. In America and Germany, indeed, matters were scarcely yet at their worst. Nevertheless Weirs' directors felt sure enough of themselves and their resources to promise £8000 for a project in the eventual outcome of which, as is evident from the wording of the Minute, some at least of them had precious little confidence. It was a remarkable demonstration either of J.G.Weir's persuasiveness or of the Weir Board's enterprise in hard times – perhaps of both.

Under the terms of the 1932 agreement Weirs immediately undertook development work, including the development of an autogiro engine of their own design. Their first autogiro, C28 or W-1, flew in May 1933 and between that date and the end of 1937, in quick succession, they produced W-2 and, in two versions, W-3 and W-4.[16] These latter two models, unlike earlier autogiros, could take off in a space about as large as a tennis court, because the rotors could be connected to the engine, in a position of 'no-lift', before take-off, to give them speed, and then, at the moment of take-off, they could be disconnected from the engine and made to lift the aircraft off the ground.

This device removed one of the autogiro's most serious disadvantages against the helicopter, and its importance was recognized. But it also converted the autogiro, for purpose of take-off, into a helicopter, thus carrying it away from the original conception of the inventor. Then Cierva himself was killed, in an airliner which crashed at Croydon Airport in December 1936. Weirs had by this time a design team of their own, and they completed the process of standing Cierva's invention on its head. Moving on from an autogiro which could become a temporary helicopter, they proposed a helicopter which, in emergency, could become a temporary autogiro by disconnecting the rotors from the engine, thus enabling it to land safely, something which, up to that time, no disabled helicopter had been able to do.

The men who developed this device were Dr J.A.J.Bennett, C.C.Pullin, K.Watson, G.E.Walker, F.L.Hodgess, R.F. Bowyer, R.A.Pullin, T.Nesbitt, L.Pullin and W.Stein. The Board recognized the importance of their ideas, and on

28 December 1937 resolved 'that the power-driven dual-rotor phase-displacement system of autogiro warrants experimental development and demonstration and that without further review this will be carried on for twelve months. They added, unkindly, 'that the method of carrying this out is to be by scientific experimentation and not by the hit and miss of the past.' In the same resolution, they decided to make a new agreement with the Cierva Company giving Weirs free use of their patents, advice and technical checks. No royalties were to be paid 'until £60,000 of development costs incurred by G. & J. Weir are exhausted'.[17]

Experimental versions of the Weir helicopter were built and flown during 1938 and 1939, and in July 1939 Weirs virtually took over the Cierva Autogiro Company.[18] Autogiros were still built, under licence, by A.V.Roe & Co., and they played some part in the war, but Weirs themselves had turned decisively to helicopters. At Cathcart they produced two, W-5, first flown in June 1938, and W-6, first flown in October 1939. In 1940 Air Vice Marshal Tedder went up in W-6 thereby becoming, it is said, the first helicopter passenger. By that time, however, wartime demands were diverting Weirs' resources away from helicopter development, and on 5 September 1941, after it had been given up altogether for a while, the Board resolved 'that these activities should be resumed, but on a small scale for the present, to take the form ... of little beyond design work'.[19]

Cierva was not the only aeronautical pioneer, between the two wars, who had reason to be grateful to Weirs. Another was (Sir) Frank Whittle. In the late 1930s, as a serving officer in the RAF, he was struggling with the development of a jet engine. The Air Ministry allowed him to engage in his eccentric activities, but they gave him no financial backing, for which he was obliged to look to private enterprise. That, as he makes clear in his autobiography,* was something which his left-wing

---

* Sir Frank Whittle, *Jet, the Story of a Pioneer*, London (Frederick Muller), 1953. See esp. pp. 49-50, 82, 89, and Chapter 49.

political principles and his views on his duties as a public servant made him very chary of doing, but there was no alternative. He was lucky enough to be put in touch with O.T.Falk & Partners, a firm of investment bankers in which two of the members – L.L.Whyte and Sir Maurice Bonham Carter – had sufficient technical insight to be prepared to back him. Under Falks' guidance a company, Power Jets Limited, was formed in March 1936 to develop Whittle's invention in cooperation with British Thomson-Houston.

Power Jets was never rich, and by the end of 1937 it was short of capital. Sir Maurice Bonham Carter approached Lord Weir, and Weirs put up £3000, to which in the spring of 1938 they added £2000. Together with sums contributed by others, the money helped to keep Power Jets going at a moment when Power Jets badly needed help. The investment was made, like others of Weirs' investments, without regard to the possibility of profit but simply as a contribution to technical progress – a point which, to judge from the general tone of Whittle's autobiography, seems to have escaped his brilliant but bigotedly anti-commercial mind.

Power Jets' stormy career ended, in 1944, in nationalization by the war-time Coalition Government, acting through Sir Stafford Cripps. The transaction was exceptionally acrimonious, and when Weirs were offered three times the cost of their shares they protested that profit was not what they were in Power Jets for and they did not want to sell. Cripps made it plain that nationalization would nevertheless be forced upon them, and they therefore accepted his offer. £15,625 was paid to Weirs and they applied £10,625, representing the element of capital appreciation, to a Special Research Account, thus emphasizing the disinterested nature of the original investment.

Through their investment in Power Jets Weirs may claim to have played some part in ensuring that a major invention did not die in infancy of financial malnutrition. The sum contributed, as Whittle observes, was 'small . . . from the point of view of the [firm] concerned', and it was followed by much more massive investment of public money. Nevertheless

Weirs deserve more credit than they have so far received for supporting an enterprise of great value to the State at a time when the State would spend nothing on it, although a few years later it was prepared to use dictatorial powers to take it over.

While Weirs' work on autogiros was going forward, the worst clouds of depression began to lift. 1933 seems to have been a slightly better year than 1932 (or perhaps it would be nearer the mark to call it not quite such a bad one) and 1934 was better again, though unemployment did not fall below 2,000,000 until 1936 and was still about 1,500,000 in 1939. Of these figures, in the later thirties, well over 80 per cent represented people 'temporarily stopped', whereas in the late twenties, before depression set in, the figure was under 70 per cent, meaning that 30 per cent or more of the unemployed were officially regarded as permanently unemployed. The improvement in these figures is one indication, among several, that in the thirties the structure of British industry was at last beginning to alter radically.[20]

In shipbuilding, the figure of tonnage commenced in 1933 – 242,000 – though pitiable in comparison with the experience of the beginning of the century, was a great deal better than the 72,000 tons commenced in 1932. Then in 1934 work started again on *Queen Mary*, largely as a result of Lord Weir's work in promoting a merger between Cunard and White Star, and after that the rise in shipbuilding figures was dramatic. Over a million tons were commenced both in 1936 and 1937, and although the figure dropped by half in 1938, it came back over a million in 1939. These figures in the late thirties were of the same order of magnitude as before the Great War, even though they were much lower than the figures of tonnage launched in 1912 (1,739,000) and 1913 (1,932,000).[21]

From about 1935 onward, a rising proportion of the new tonnage was for the Royal Navy, as the world began to get ready once again for war. The last period of preparation for war, before 1914, had been the period of Weirs' greatest growth and prosperity, and the late thirties, as we shall see,

I

brought prosperity also. But there were great differences between the circumstances of the two periods.

First, before 1914 preparations for war were going on for twenty years or so, whereas serious preparation for the war of 1939 lasted for barely four. Next, before 1914 British preparations for war were heavily concentrated on the Navy, and throughout the world, at the same time, other Powers were enthusiastically ordering warships, for most of which Weirs supplied the auxiliary machinery. In the thirties, British naval construction was inhibited, until 1937, by the Washington Naval Treaty with USA and Japan, reinforced by the decisions of the London naval conference of 1930, and even after 1935 it was influenced by the treaty with Germany made in that year. In any case, the Fleet had never been run down so far as the other two Services, and although many of the ships were old, particularly in comparison with Germany's, naval building was not regarded with such urgency before 1939 as before 1914. In the world at large, in 1939 warships were less fashionable than in 1914, so that there was not so great a foreign demand for auxiliary machinery.

The main emphasis, in British preparations for renewed war with Germany, was on the RAF. As for the Army, the Government doubted whether recruits would come forward for land fighting of the 1914–18 type, which was the type of fighting generally expected, and they proposed to provide only a small expeditionary force for cooperation with the French, as well as anti-aircraft defence at home. The Air Force, on the other hand, was to be provided with a formidable bombing force to hammer Germany. The force had to be created practically from nothing, and it was barely in existence at the outbreak of war. Nevertheless, the figures of expenditure on armaments, and the distribution of expenditure between the Services, show the way things were going from 1935 to 1939:[22]

Gross Public Expenditure (£m.) on:

	Army & Ordnance	Royal Navy	RAF
1935	39·7	56·6	17·6
1936	44·6	64·8	27·5
1937	54·8	81·1	50·1
1938	77·9	102·0	82·3
1939	121·4	127·3	133·8

Weirs' direct interest in equipment for the RAF was comparatively small, arising chiefly from the business of Zwicky Limited of Slough, specializing in small pumps for petrol and other light hydro-carbon liquids and in fine filtration, all of which had applications in aircraft refuelling. Weirs bought control of Zwicky in 1930. Zwicky's finances were not strong, and Weirs guaranteed their subsidiary's bank overdrafts. The guarantees rose from £1000, hopefully for six months only, in 1932 to £3000 in 1936, and then to £10,000 in 1938 and £15,000 in May 1939. The rise represents, no doubt, the gathering pace of air rearmament, and especially the provision of ground equipment for newly-built airfields. [23]

The main impetus behind Weirs' revival in the late thirties came from their traditional lines of business. As early as the Annual General Meeting of 1934, the Chairman spoke of 'the more hopeful outlook for the immediate future', and when he looked back on 1934 he called it 'a successful year'. [24] In these years shipbuilding was reviving, but preparation for the German war had not begun, and a good deal of the improvement probably came from land work, particularly for oil companies and for power stations. In both these fields there was powerful American competition, some of which Lord Weir did not consider over-scrupulous. [25]

Sales began to rise, for the first time in the thirties, during 1934, and after a slight check in 1935 they went rapidly and steeply up from the extreme low point (just over £400,000) of 1933 to £2,100,000 in 1939, without showing the slightest tendency to falter even during the fairly severe recession which affected trade generally in 1938. For this rise, from late 1935 on, naval rearmament was chiefly responsible. Sterry B. Freeman of the Blue Funnel Line, visiting Cathcart in October 1935, found it 'refreshing . . . that the shops which were closed up a few years ago were again fully occupied'.[26] In April 1939, writing to the Prime Minister, Lord Weir said: 'Here at Cathcart we are engaged up to about 80 per cent on naval rearmament.'[27]

For the whole of the twenty years between the two wars the ultimate direction of Weirs' affairs lay with the Chairman, Lord Weir, and with three other representatives of the founding families: J.R.Richmond, J.G.Weir and C.R.Lang. These latter three, with the assistance of John Craig on the sales and commercial side, ran the business from day to day. Lord Weir, heavily engaged for almost the whole inter-war period in public affairs, was not a managing director. His influence on policy, however, as we have had occasion to observe, was strong, unorthodox, and often decisive.

In the thirties new men began to move into higher management, though not yet into control of policy. J.R.Lang and Kenneth Weir, from the founding families, were appointed to the Board in 1930, Lang being then twenty-eight and Weir twenty-five. Lang went into the works under his father, Weir to assist John Craig, whom he succeeded in 1938. Harold Hillier, who had been Chief Engineer with Contraflo, was in charge of design work and joined the Board, at the age of forty-two, in 1933. The Production Manager, M.L.Jamieson, a pupil of C.R.Lang, came on the Board at the same time as Hillier, being then forty-one. John Spittal, fifty in 1936, who had been a cost accountant at Argus Foundry, was at the head of the accounting department.

These men represented the third generation of Weirs' management from the company's foundation. In 1939 they held positions that were highly responsible but not supremely decisive. After the war they, or some of them, would be faced with the task of reorganizing Weirs' affairs in the world of the forties, fifties and sixties, just as their fathers' generation had had to cope with the problems of an earlier post-war world.

Before we pass to this latest phase in Weirs' history, and to the foundation of the Weir Group, we must examine the effects of the Second World War upon the business which was still, at that time, chiefly concentrated at Cathcart.

8

The Second World War
1939–45

At the outbreak of war in 1939 Great Britain was much better prepared, administratively, than in 1914. No one, any more than twenty-five years earlier, had any idea of what the true nature of the war would turn out to be, and such ideas as people had were mostly wrong. There was no immediate air bombardment nor, during the whole course of the war, was the British army engaged in land fighting on the scale of 1914–18, although both possibilities had been looked on as certainties, even in high places. But it was realized from the start, as it had not been realized in 1914, that a major war in the twentieth century would require total mobilization of the nation's industrial strength, and measures had been taken accordingly, well beforehand. They were based on the experience of the previous war, especially at the Ministry of Munitions, and since the interval between the two wars was short many of the men who had run the Ministry of Munitions in the Great War were available to plan and direct the organization of supply in the war against Hitler. Prominent among these men were William Weir and his brother, J.G.Weir.

Much of the planning of war production was based on distinguishing between the 'professional armaments industry', as it was officially known, and other firms, chiefly in engineering, which could be turned on to armaments work if necessary. The main preparations for war, it was assumed, would be carried out by the professionals who included the Vickers group, ICI and the bigger aircraft firms. When war broke out the others would be brought in, having been advised of what would be required of them and given some training during peace. They would operate under professional guidance, both in their own factories and in 'shadow factories' built and equipped by the Government. The conception of 'shadow factories' originated with Lord Weir and a committee of industrial advisers in 1934. They did not intend these factories to come into operation until war actually broke out, but in fact in 1936 the situation was already so menacing, and the need for arms so urgent, that the shadows very quickly acquired substance.

Weirs found themselves both on the 'professional' and the 'shadow' side of the line. Few, if any, British ships, whether warships or merchantmen, put to sea without auxiliary machinery built by Weirs, Drysdales or their licensees, and to that extent Weirs' main work, before and during the war, was cut out for them. They were 'professionals' in armaments as much as if they had been shipbuilders. But to their main task was added, as we shall see, very considerable 'shadow' activity in the building of field artillery, just as, in the Great War, aircraft building had been added to Weirs' normal business in auxiliary machinery.[1]

Rebuilding, renewal and enlargement of the Royal Navy began in 1935-6. The pre-war programme was undertaken in the knowledge that the Navy might have to face three enemies at once – Germany, Italy, Japan – but no real attempt was made to plan a fleet capable of the task, largely because war was expected long before any such fleet could be brought into being.[2] The programme which was put in hand, by pre-1914 standards, was quite modest, though by the standards of the twenties and early thirties it was enormous. It included five *King George V* battleships, six Fleet aircraft carriers, about twenty cruisers, large and small, three fast minelayers, numerous destroyers and a variety of smaller warships and auxiliaries, as well as submarines.

In the early years of the war the main emphasis in naval building was on convoy protection, for the German submarines were just as menacing as during the Great War. Extra capital ships were not needed and the only one laid down – *Vanguard* –

was not completed until after the war. Extra cruisers, however, were built, and from 1942 onward light fleet carriers were developed. Building of smaller craft was heavy, particularly destroyers, corvettes and, latterly, frigates. For coastal work, against German E-boats, steam gunboats were developed, which needed powerful machinery of very light, compact design.

In 1943 the strategy of the Grand Alliance began to turn from defence to attack, both in Europe and in the Pacific. In naval building, during the last years of the war, that meant light fleet carriers, destroyers of the *Battle* class specially designed for Pacific service, and landing craft varying from large ships designed to carry tanks over considerable distances down to assault boats. And all the time there were merchant vessels building – more from 1940 to 1943 than from 1915 to 1918 – and for repair.

Shipbuilders, not only in the United Kingdom but also in Australia and Canada, needed all kinds of Weir and Drysdale auxiliaries, and a list of what was supplied, for various classes of ships, can be found in Appendix Two. As well as the items mentioned there, Weirs' regenerative condensers, built under licence by the main machinery contractors, were put into almost all the high-powered vessels. For gun-moving gear in battleships and for assisted take-off gear in aircraft carriers, Weirs supplied hydraulic pumping sets of a type originally developed for the Imperial Japanese Navy.

The shock of battle brought demands unforeseen in peacetime. To recover sunken or heavily damaged ships Drysdales built large numbers of salvage pumps. The design of ships' pumps and auxiliary machinery had to be altered to take account of underwater explosions caused by mines dropped from aircraft. Air attack, again, made it necessary to fit ships with extra fire-fighting equipment redesigned, in some cases, to be driven by steam turbines instead of electric motors. All the time there was a heavy load of repair work.

Pumps, fire-fighting equipment and other machinery were built for land service. As devastated territory was re-conquered, drinking water was needed both for troops and for the liberated populations, and Weirs built evaporating and distilling plant to provide it, as well as similar plant for ships engaged in the Pacific. Output from Cathcart, in total, rose between 1935 and 1945 by about 350 per cent.[3]

Zwicky Limited, much smaller than either Weirs or Drysdales, was engaged chiefly on refuelling equipment for the RAF. Before the war, Zwickys had developed gear suitable for tanker lorries stationed on airfields, and during the war they built about 5000 tankers of this kind, as well as 862 tankers for lubricating oil, others for water, and a variety of other fuel-handling equipment, as well as components supplied to other firms. Zwickys grew very greatly, and their output from Slough rose $17\frac{1}{2}$ times in ten years (1935-45).

What we have so far examined in this chapter has been the 'professional' side of Weirs' war work – work of the kind which Weirs themselves, Drysdales and Zwickys carried on as their main business in peace as well as war. But even when this kind of work had expanded under the pressure of rearmament, it still did not take up all the factory space at Cathcart, which still had spare space as a legacy from the war before. Here, indeed, was a 'shadow factory'. How could it best be used?

The answer was found to lie in an activity far removed from anything that Weirs or their subsidiaries had previously engaged in: the supply of field artillery. How Weirs came to take up the building of guns illustrates the nature and methods of the administrative machinery prepared in Great Britain, in the late thirties, in preparation for war. It is also a case-history of the kind of problem the 'shadow' system was designed to solve, and the methods used in solving it.

About 1925, the military authorities began to think about a new field gun for the British Army. New weapons, however, were politically very unpopular in the mid-twenties, money was correspondingly tight, and there was in any case no serious danger of war. Matters therefore moved very slowly indeed until serious rearmament began, and even then the army's requirements, except in anti-aircraft guns, had low priority: certainly much lower than the requirements of the RAF.

In 1936, after Hitler occupied the Rhineland, the development of the new gun, along with most other measures of war preparation, accelerated remarkably. The General Staff produced a specification – for a 25-pdr gun with a range of 13,500 yards – pilot models were delivered in 1937, a production design was approved in December 1938, and in February 1940 bulk deliveries began. The period from conception to specification had been about nine years, but from specification to delivery it was barely four, which shows how greatly fright can speed up gestation.[4]

Behind this string of dates lies one of the major achievements of pre-war planning for wartime supply. In the thirties the main difficulty in providing weapons for the army, leaving matters of priority on one side, was to find firms capable of producing them. Ships and aircraft are both needed in peace, and plenty of firms could produce them, though the shipbuilders had run down during the inter-war depression and the aircraft industry needed very great expansion. But even so the Admiralty and the Air Ministry were better placed than the War Office. Army weapons, especially tanks and artillery, are only needed in war or under threat of war, and they need specialized firms to produce them. Before 1914, firms of this kind had been supported by a thriving international trade in arms, but in the twenties that trade had withered away, and British firms that had prospered on it went out of existence or turned to something else, so that outside the Vickers group and the Government's own establishment at Woolwich the capacity to produce heavy armaments almost ceased to exist.[5] To meet this situation the supply system of the War Office, centred on the ancient office of Master-General of the Ordnance, was drastically reorganized from 1936 onward.

Lord Weir was at this time adviser to the Air Minister, Lord Swinton, and at the peak of his influence in war planning generally. He saw how serious the problem of army production was, and his advice was to set up in the War Office a Department of Munitions Production 'with sufficient technical, production, inspectional, commercial and financial experience, coupled with a spirit of "drive", to enter into and settle promptly, effective business negotiations with, for example, 100 selected firms ... [to] create and adapt existing facilities to enable them to supply highly technical products of which they perhaps have no previous experience.' Weir's advice was accepted and the Department was set up. The Director General of Munitions Production, at Weir's suggestion, was Engineer Vice-Admiral Sir Harold Brown, appointed in the summer of 1936.[6] His Department left the War Office in 1939 and became the nucleus of the Ministry of Supply.

In this way it happened that the man chiefly responsible for bringing into existence the department responsible for, amongst much else, the production of field artillery was the Chairman of G. & J.Weir, and that the first head of the department was Sir Harold Brown who, as Engineer-in-Chief of the Fleet in the early thirties, and for many years before that as an officer of the E.-in-C.'s branch at the Admiralty,* had had very close relations, personally and in business, with Weir and with Weirs. Therefore, when Weirs' Board came to consider how the spare space at Cathcart could best be turned to use, the problem of the 25-pdr gun came quickly to their notice.

This was exactly the kind of problem which the 'shadow' armaments industry was designed to solve, by providing production facilities when matters of design had been settled. A gun department was set up at Cathcart which Weirs ran as an 'agency factory' – that is, a factory which they ran as agents for the Ministry of Supply, making no profit but earning a fee, like other wartime contractors in the 'shadow' industry. The War Office, following the usual practice with 'shadow' contractors, placed an 'educational' order first and then, in May 1939, a substantive order for carriages, since the supply of carriages was holding up delivery of complete weapons.[7] The first carriage built was shown to the King and Queen when they visited Cathcart on 27 February 1940.

Weirs became considerably the largest producers of 25-pdr carriages. They built the recoil system themselves, sub-contracted

* Engineer Lieutenant H.A.Brown was at the Admiralty in 1914 (above, p. 24).

other parts, and assembled and delivered complete carriages, with the guns mounted on them. In 1940 the Ministry of Supply decided on their final requirements, and Weirs decided to aim at a monthly output of 240 recuperators, 150 cradles and 150 complete carriages. In July 1940, under the threat of invasion, they built fifty carriages – one-third of the planned maximum only six months after production began. The maximum was reached in October 1941. By the end of 1943 the Ministry had all the guns and all the spares they needed, and Weirs, who were required to meet an expansion in the frigate programme, stopped building 25-pdr carriages. By that time they had built 3625, representing about one-third of the army's total needs, and far more than the number built by anyone else.

In 1941, with the building of field artillery well under way, Weirs became involved in the development of anti-tank artillery, an undertaking far less fortunate, though not through any fault of Weirs. The fault lay with those who, between the wars, had neglected the development of armoured warfare generally. The tank broke the machine-gunner's domination of the battle-field and made it possible, once again, for attackers to carry fortified positions. Combined with aircraft, it made trench warfare, on the 1914–18 pattern, very unlikely: a point which completely eluded most British military planners (though not Lord Weir). It completely altered the nature of land fighting. It was probably the greatest British military invention ever made, but its supreme importance, seized upon by the Germans and others, was never grasped by those in authority at the War Office in the twenties and thirties.

Anti-tank artillery, naturally, was neglected as much as the tank itself. The General Staff seem to have regarded tanks as a kind of mechanized big game – rogue elephants, perhaps – for it was their fixed conviction, from 1927 on, that infantry could defend themselves from tank attack with some kind of small arms, and in 1939 they were sent off to war with the Boys ·55 inch anti-tank rifle, which would no doubt have been very formidable against elephants, since it could penetrate the armour of contemporary German tanks up to a range of 400 yards. So could a ·303-inch machine gun, which had the advantage of automatic fire.[8]

The first gun specifically intended to stop tanks was a 2 pdr, adopted in 1934 when the General Staff realized that all Continental armies were intending to fire at tanks with guns rather than small arms. The 2 pdr was designed primarily to be used in tanks, not against them, and the requirements were not precisely the same. In 1938 the Director of Artillery, looking at the problem the other way round, started designing a 6-pdr gun for use against tanks which might also be mounted in them. For that purpose it turned out to have too long a barrel, and for anti-tank work it did not meet the General Staff's requirement that it should perforate 70 mm. armour at a range 'something over 500 yards'. The point, however, was not pressed, and in March 1940 the 6 pdr was accepted to replace the 2 pdr.[9]

On the later development of the 6-pdr gun Weirs came to exercise a strong influence. To see how they did so it is necessary to look at their influence on administration generally, which was considerable.[10] It arose from dissatisfaction with the system in force at the Ministry of Supply in the early months of the war, which seemed to Weirs over-centralized and very apt to lead to duplication of effort, especially in the placing of subcontracts.

J.R.Lang, Weirs' works director, and M.L.Jamieson, production director, suggested putting a great deal of the planning of production in the hands of the main contractors for major items of equipment. They proposed that each group of main contractors should form a committee which would coordinate the work of sub-contractors, bring the best practice into common use throughout the group, arrange for the distribution of sub-contracted items in short supply and make representations on questions of design which interfered with production. Each committee would have a full-time Chairman and secretary to coordinate its work and to keep in touch with the Ministry on such matters as additional orders and their distribution, the allocation of machine tools and the supply of materials.

The scheme was not received with universal joy. The Royal Ordnance Factories, whose practice Lang and Jamieson wanted to bring closer to the methods of private industry, were reluctant to change their ways. Sir Harold Brown had doubts which he communicated to Kenneth Weir. At the Ministry of Aircraft Production the proposals were welcomed, which probably did nothing at all to increase their popularity at Supply. There, however, they had one influential supporter – Brigadier F.G.Wrisberg,* Director of Gun Carriage Production – and on 21 June 1940 the 25-pdr Gun Carriage Production Committee was formed.

The Ministry naturally expected Weirs to support their brainchild, so Kenneth Weir was put in as Chairman. He served on the Committee until its work was finished. It was set up too late to put into force all the suggestions put forward by Lang and Jamieson, but it distinguished itself by being the first to finish its programme which, as we have seen, was completed in 1943.

The work of the 25 pdr committee was complicated by production difficulties inherent in the design, and the contractors were only able to make one important modification, a welded cradle developed by Harold Hillier, Weirs' Chief Engineer.[11]† When, in 1941, the 6-pdr Tank and Anti-Tank Ordnance Production Committee was set up, also under Kenneth Weir, their work was made smoother because Hillier, who had been appointed Consultant Adviser to the Director of Artillery, was able from the start to modify the design of the gun so as to make it much easier to build, though no less efficient.

This group pooled the best efforts of their production engineers to standardize manufacturing processes and achieve the greatest possible production. In collaboration with the Ministry, they centralized the programming of materials for

* Later Lieut.-Gen. Sir F.G.Wrisberg, KCB, CBE.

† Baker Perkins designed a very effective welded recuperator but too late to be widely adopted in the 25-pdr. programme.

drop stampings, heavy forgings, and other components. 'The 6-pounder production in highly specialized and liberally equipped factories,' says Professor Postan, 'was much more economical than that of any other gun of comparable complexity.'[12]

Production of the 6-pdr gun, desperately needed in 1941-2, was ordered 'at all costs', and about 16,000 guns were built, 1940 of them by Weirs themselves, who also produced 3180 breech rings, 2407 breech blocks, and thousands of other components of breech mechanism. But the 6 pdr, produced so efficiently and in such numbers, was very quickly superseded. It was only assembled at Weirs for fifteen months.

It was superseded after bitter controversy of the kind which bedevilled the whole wartime tank programme – controversy which might not have been necessary but for the pre-war years of neglect. The gun which superseded the 6 pdr was a 17 pdr, needed to deal with the very much heavier armour plate which by 1942 German tanks were known to be mounting (just as, before 1914, progressively heavier naval guns had been needed to deal with the progressively heavier armour plate of warships). In the 17-pdr programme Weirs played no very great part, except in one brief and crucial episode.

The 17 pdr, like earlier guns, was intended to be used both in and against tanks. Designs for an anti-tank gun and carriage were approved in the summer of 1942, but guns became available before carriages. It had been possible to mount the 6 pdr on a carriage originally designed for the 2 pdr, but the 6-pdr carriage could not be adapted to take the 17 pdr, an altogether heavier weapon. Yet delay in getting the gun to the troops was intolerable. A solution occurred simultaneously to Kenneth Weir, to Harold Hillier, and to Douglas Smith, Weirs' Gunshop Manager. Why not mount the 17 pdr, for the time being, on a 25 pdr carriage?

From War Office approval to the successful trial of the first 'hybrid' took ten days. During the autumn of 1942, in great secrecy, 150 were built. They went into action, to the great satisfaction of Winston Churchill, who is said to have referred to the weapon as 'the pheasant', during the later battles in North Africa, in Sicily, and in Italy. They provided formidable opposition to the German Tiger tank, the arrival of which had been foreseen and greatly feared.

Weirs' activities in the Second World War, like the activities of British industry generally, were better planned and directed than their activities in the Great War. And there can be no doubt that Weirs were enabled to play some part in the planning and direction by having friends in high places. Sir Harold Brown, as we have seen, was Director General of Munitions Production in the early years of the war, and Lord Weir himself served at the Ministry of Supply until 1942, by which time some of the worst problems had been solved. Harold Hillier was consultant to the Director of Artillery. J.G.Weir was a member of the Allied Purchasing Commission in Washington from 1940 to 1943, serving temporarily as Chairman when Arthur B.Purvis was killed in 1941. Weir apparently also simultaneously held the post of Director General of Mechanical Equipment (Design and Development) at the Ministry of Supply, which gave him an oversight of tank design.[13] Kenneth Weir was a member of the Industrial Advisory Panel at the Ministry of Production, set up under Oliver Lyttelton in 1942. None of these appointments, except Hillier's, had any direct connection with Weirs' work, but the mere fact that they were held by the individuals named must mean that they opened up channels of communication which would otherwise have remained closed. British administration, in war or peace, has always depended on informal contact at least as much as on official schemes of organization.

Towards the end of 1943 the heaviest pressure of war began to slacken. Gun work came to an end, as we have seen, and the value of orders for auxiliary machinery began to fall, though within the total the value of Admiralty orders rose somewhat in 1943 itself, no doubt because of the expanded frigate programme of that year. For the whole eleven years of rearmament and war Weirs' order books at Cathcart show the following figures:

Year	Total	Marine	%	Land	%	Admiralty	%
	£	£		£		£	
1935	793,104	168,269	21	179,089	23	445,746	56
1936	1,519,910	389,790	26	185,578	12	944,542	62
1937	2,303,009	1,079,545	47	278,820	12	944,644	41
1938	1,115,251	412,569	37	221,496	20	481,186	43
1939	2,804,560	560,100	20	311,260	11	1,933,200	69
1940	2,018,238	320,535	16	271,806	13	1,425,897	71
1941	1,716,931	438,507	25	201,842	12	1,076,582	63
1942	3,238,395	524,443	17	305,372	9	2,408,580	74
1943	3,070,310	367,698	12	121,217	4	2,581,395	84
1944	2,504,164	340,310	14	352,053	14	1,811,801	72
1945	2,203,568	758,156	34	539,815	24	905,597	41

Throughout the period, the fluctuations from one year to another were wide. In 1938, which was a bad year for trade generally, orders, including Admiralty orders, fell in value by over 50 per cent, and there was another large drop in 1941, though in that year, presumably, the gun programme took up the slack.

Weirs were much more economical with labour than in the Great War, presumably because their work was more efficiently organized. In 1918 there had been 4000 men and 2000 women working at Cathcart. At the peak period of the second war, there were 4009 men and 1214 women at all Weirs' establishments – Cathcart, Yoker, Thornliebank and Slough.[14]

The men in this labour force gave their employers far less trouble than their fathers had done, probably because they were committed to the war against Hitler in a way the older generation had never been committed to the war against the Kaiser, even to the extent of accepting without serious opposition very drastic measures of industrial conscription. The worst that seems to have happened at Cathcart, as at a good many other firms' works, was a fairly high rate of absence, which was castigated in several wartime numbers of *The Weir Bulletin*. On 14 July 1942, for instance, 978 men, 28 per cent of Weirs' labour force, failed to turn up for work after an extra day had been granted for the Glasgow Fair Holidays. 'When I think of what our allies, the Russians, have borne for us,' wrote Sir

John Richmond, in the spirit of the times, 'and what they are suffering now, I write this with shame and humiliation . . . and I sincerely hope I may not have to refer to it again.' He did, though.[15]

As the problems of war began to recede, the problems of peace began to appear. During 1944 the Secretary of State for Scotland, alarmed by the growing housing shortage, approached Lord Weir to help the Government by reviving his steel house, or something like it. The Scottish Secretary was Tom Johnston, at one time a figure of the Clydeside Left and a bitter opponent of Weir during the Great War and after. 'Lord Weir, and others of his kidney,' said Johnston in Parliament in 1926, '. . . had spent their time in breaking the rates of wages and the conditions of life of the people.' And how had the wicked Lord and his accomplices gone about their nefarious purposes? By putting up steel houses.[16]

By 1943 Johnston and Weir had long been reconciled – indeed, it is doubtful whether there was ever any personal enmity, in spite of the politician's language – and Weirs put experimental work in hand. The rebirth of Weir housing, with surprising consequences, is part of Weirs' post-war history, but as early as July 1944 they had put up a demonstration single-storey house, the *Paragon*, at Sighthill, Edinburgh. During the next year or two they followed it with a hundred more, built in differerent parts of Scotland as demonstration models for local authorities.

At the outbreak of war, as we saw at the end of Chapter Seven, a new generation was moving into Weirs' higher management. The Board then, however, and for some time afterwards, was a two-tier structure. The minutes refer to 'the Senior Directors' and the 'younger shareholders', and it is clear where the final authority still lay.[17] Lord Weir, in spite of his public commitments, was a very active Chairman. Richmond and C.R.Lang were joint Managing Directors. J.G.Weir, considerably the youngest of the Senior Directors, was detached on government service during most of the war, but his influence, particularly on technical matters, remained powerful well into the peace.

Charles Lang died, aged seventy-eight, in 1940. Richmond was then seventy-one, Lord Weir sixty-three and J.G.Weir fifty-four. In 1944 the balance of power was altered considerably, in favour of the younger men, and the functions of directors were recorded and defined, apparently for the first time, although a division of duties had long been recognized. Lord Weir remained Chairman and two Deputy Chairmen, Sir John Richmond and J.G.Weir, were appointed, clearly with the intention of creating an Upper House, advisory rather than executive. Kenneth Weir, his task with the guns finished, became Managing Director and J.R.Lang, Works Director. Hillier was Engineering and Technical Director, Jamieson Production Director, Spittal Finance and Accountancy Director, and A.H.Laidlaw, a new director but an old servant of the company (forty years) was appointed Sales and Commercial Director. At the same time J.D.Imrie, Secretary since 1912, resigned in favour of John Davidson. The minutes record explicitly that these measures were undertaken with a view to 'strengthening . . . the structure and operation of the Board to enable the Company to enter on the difficult times ahead with a machine appropriate to the work.'[18] Weirs' wartime exertions brought no very fat reward in profits. A great deal of work was carried out on an agency basis, deliberately

Profits for year ended 31 Dec.		Profits before Tax	Tax	Net
	1936	£202,498	£ 29,964	£172,534
	1937	342,799	64,492	278,307
	1938	448,330	112,000	336,330
	1939	618,910	156,000	462,910
	1940	527,795	190,000	337,795
	1941	476,362	340,580	135,782
	1942	428,858	338,298	90,560
	1943	461,262	253,149	203,113
	1944	500,538	281,418	219,120
	1945	335,570	122,469	213,101
	1946	420,770	168,312	252,458

Note: The above profits before tax include dividends from Drysdale, Zwicky and Contraflo.

calculated to return no profit to the company, and as soon as the war was over wartime contracts were cancelled. These cancellations, together with expenditure of £65,477 on housing, caused a very sharp drop in profits in the last year of the war. For the whole period of rearmament, war, and the uncomfortable transition to peace, the accounts of G. & J. Weir Limited show the profit figures on page 137.

Weirs' business was carried further. First, in the autumn of 1945, Weirs bought out the minority shareholding – 49 per cent – in Drysdales, giving 291,076 Weir 5s. Ordinary shares for 72,769 Drysdale 15s. Ordinaries. J.W.W.Drysdale, accompanied by John Young, joined Weirs' Board, but towards the end of the year he withdrew from the management of his family firm in favour of Young, who had N.M.Niven as assistant Managing Director. The purchase made £269,107 cash available to Weirs. They used it for equipping machine and assembly shops.[19]

As soon as the Drysdale takeover was complete, G. & J. Weir Limited was turned into a public company, constituted in 1946. The consolidated balance sheet, taking account of G. & J.Weir, Drysdales, Argus Foundry and Zwicky, showed capital employed of about £2,300,000. J.W.W.Drysdale became a Deputy Chairman of the new company, along with Richmond and J.G.Weir, and Niven joined Drysdale and John Young on Weirs' Board.

Conversion into a public company gave Weirs' much wider access to the capital market for whatever finance might be needed after the war, when it was quite certain that problems of change and development, all likely to be expensive, would arise. At the same time it carried Weirs a long way from the character of a family business, managed by the owners, which it had had since its foundation. After 1946 the ownership of Weirs would be even more widely dispersed, the management increasingly a matter for salaried professionals. In the post-war world they would increasingly be obliged to question the adequacy not only of Weirs' organization, but of the traditional bases of their prosperity.

9

Direction-Finding in the Fifties

In the world after the war, great changes came over the world's shipbuilding industry. First, it grew. In 1946 about 2·3 million tons were launched; in 1950, 3·5; in 1955, 5·3; in 1960, 8·4. Then, in this expanding market British shipbuilders lost the lead which they had so long held. Just after the war there was very little competition, but by the mid-fifties other nations were challenging strongly, and in 1955 a greater tonnage was launched in Germany than in Great Britain. But the most serious threat was from the Japanese, who by 1960 were well ahead – 1·7m. tons launched in Japan against 1·33m. in Great Britain. By 1963 the tonnage launched in Japan was 2·4m., 970,579 in Germany, 927,649 in Great Britain, and 887,738 in Sweden. And later, worse, for out of 15·8m. tons launched in the world in 1967, 7·5m. were launched in Japan. The British figure was 1·3m., beaten by the Swedes (1·31m.) and closely followed by the Germans (1m.).[1] Over this sad tale we shall not moralize, but the point is driven home even more brutally when we recall that in 1913, out of a much smaller tonnage built in the world, 765,976 tons were built on the Clyde alone – a figure never afterwards closely approached, let alone surpassed.[2]

The output of British shipbuilders, nevertheless, was higher during the fifties than for many years, and much higher than in any year between the wars except 1920 – a freak year – and 1927–9. The outbreak of war in Korea (1950) stimulated the demand for general cargo vessels and the Suez incident (1956) encouraged the development of tankers large enough to by-pass the Suez Canal economically. The effect of competitive failure was to some extent masked, and for Weirs, as we shall see, the

139

fifties were prosperous. But the unchecked relative decline of British shipbuilding was bound, eventually, to bring problems to any business heavily dependent upon it, and hence to Weirs, and we shall see that it did.

For Weirs, predominantly steam engineers as they still were during the fifties, the situation was made worse by the change-over throughout the world from steamers to motor vessels. During the fifties the tonnage launched, of steamers as well as motor vessels, rose. Diesel engines, although greatly improved, still required fairly heavy maintenance and on the whole they were less reliable than steam turbines. Many owners, therefore, still preferred steam propulsion, and in tankers, which accounted for a high proportion of tonnage built, steam was needed for heating the oil, for cleaning the tanks, and for driving the cargo oil pumps. For some years, therefore, the swing from steam to motor was checked. It did not become really dramatic until the sixties:[3]

World Launchings (m. gross tons) 1950–67

	Total		Steam		Motor	
1950	3·5		1·4		2·1	
		100%		40%		60%
1955	5·3		2·2		3·1	
		100		41		59
1960	8·4		3·4		5·0	
		100		40		60
1963	8·5		2·6		5·9	
		100		31		69
1967	15·8		2·1		13·7	
		100		13		87

For Weirs, the change from steam to motor propulsion was almost as far-reaching in its effects as the decisive swing from sail to steam in the 1870s. But whereas that earlier change had created conditions in which James Weir could profitably make his inventions and found his firm, this later one threatened the very existence of the steam-driven auxiliary machinery which for ninety years had been the chief foundation of Weirs' prosperity. It became increasingly necessary, as we shall see in this chapter, for Weirs to find other means of livelihood, and that necessity, as well as the growth in the scale of their operations (for growth, during the fifties, was very considerable), raised those difficult problems of business organization which always go with growth, change and diversification.

The immediate transition from war to peace, for Weirs, was fairly smooth. There was at once a sharp drop in the value of Admiralty orders, from £1,811,801 in 1944 to £905,597 in 1945, and to £109,943 – the lowest figure for Admiralty orders so far recorded in Weirs' history – in 1947. This fall was a natural consequence of the onset of peace. The same thing had happened after 1918, and after 1945 Weirs were better prepared for it. The end of the Second World War was long foreseen – as the end of the First was not – and by 1945, as we saw in the last chapter, war construction programmes had for some time been running down. Moreover Weirs' main business in auxiliary machinery had been less dislocated than in the First World War and was more easily brought back on to a peacetime basis. There was some wrangling with the Admiralty over terms for settling contracts, but by the end of 1947 the last remnants of Weirs' wartime activities were well on the way to winding-up.[4]

The cancellation of Admiralty orders was not a grave inconvenience. There was plenty of work in prospect, and both Cathcart and Yoker were reorganized, physically, to cope with it. The plans for Cathcart, approved by the Board in May 1945, contemplated expenditure of about £100,000, provided a way could be found through the luxuriant jungle of post-war restrictions, regulations and priorities. By the autumn of 1945 the work was under way.[5]

In shipbuilding, there was a great deal to be done in making good wartime damage and destruction, and for a few happy years British firms were unharrassed by output from the shattered yards of Germany and Japan. Of the 2,300,000 tons launched in the world in 1948, 1,200,000 (52 per cent) were British, and of the steam tonnage launched (791,860) the British share was 63 per cent (502,045). The long-term promise of this situation, so much in Weirs' favour, was blighted by the fact that the steam tonnage launched was barely more than half as great as the motor tonnage (1,518,000), but it provided a firm base and, for some years, a rising one for Weirs' post-war business.[6]

On land also post-war business in auxiliary machinery was brisk and the long-term prospect was rather better. The main users were power-stations running on coal or oil, and although competition from atomic energy was certain, it was equally certain that atomic energy would not knock out coal or oil for a long time, if ever. Meanwhile the British Electricity Authority (later the Central Electricity Generating Board) was putting in hand an ambitious programme of new power-stations and there were orders from abroad, as well.

The general effect, then, on Weirs' main business, of the change from war to peace was to reduce the importance of Admiralty work very greatly, to confirm the importance of work for merchant ships and to emphasize the importance of land work, chiefly for power-stations. It is well illustrated statistically by analysis of the input order figures for Cathcart:

Weirs' Input Orders 1944–50

	Total £m.	%	Marine %	Land %	Admiralty %
1944	2·5	100	14	14	72
1945	2·2	100	34	24	42
1946	2·6	100	47	44	9
1947	2·8	100	45	51	4
1948	3·0	100	41	52	7
1949	2·5	100	42	39	19
1950	3·1	100	41	46	13

Towards the end of 1943, as the strain of war relaxed a little, Weirs' interest in helicopters – sustained, as always, chiefly by J.G.Weir – began to revive. The circumstances were not particularly propitious, largely because the development of helicopters was one of several lines of technical development relinquished, by agreement, to the Americans during the war, with disastrous competitive results for Great Britain afterwards.

In helicopters, the work of Sikorsky and others put the Americans well ahead. By 1946 only two British prototypes then under construction seemed to have any future, whereas there were sixteen types flying in America and at least two in limited production.[7]

Weirs, nevertheless, optimistically reassembled their dispersed design team, who went to work at Thames Ditton, with slender resources, for the Cierva Autogiro Co., controlled by Weirs. Basing themselves on ideas which they considered sounder than Sikorsky's, they produced a two-seater research machine known as W9 or 'the drainpipe'. It was unfortunate that wartime economy forced them to use rotor hub gears taken from another experimental helicopter, which made W9 unsafe in translational flight of more than ten feet above the ground. W9 had no direct descendants, but it taught its creators, according to one of them (J. Shapiro), 'some very valuable lessons'.

The Cierva company moved to Southampton and about the end of 1945 began a development which other teams seemed to have ignored. A good deal of interest was developing in the use of helicopters to spray crops, and that raised the question of heavier payloads. A helicopter with a very large payload would be attractive both as a transport and as a crane, because in all aircraft the economics of payload improve with size, and applications both peaceful and warlike might be expected. The Weir-Cierva team set about designing a helicopter with a disposable load of about three tons – much more than anyone else had so far contemplated – using a Rolls-Royce Merlin engine.

The project took shape as the Air Horse, a three-rotor machine which was by far the largest helicopter of its day, with rotors of 47 ft each. Development was driven ahead very fast by J. G. Weir, who also carried a good deal of the financial risk. During 1948 he joined Lazards and others in guaranteeing a bank loan of £30,000 to the Cierva company. Towards the end of the year he himself lent £13,000, and it seems probable that he made other commitments as well, including the acquisition of a factory for leasing to the Company. By the beginning of February 1949 he seemed to be in sight of his reward. 'The prospects of the [Cierva] Company,' Weirs' minutes record, 'had improved considerably as a result of recent satisfactory air horse tests.'[8] In September 1949, barely four years after the first stirrings of an idea, an Air Horse flew at the Farnborough Air Show, and about the end of the year it lifted the full all-up weight it had been designed for – 17,500 lb. In the spring of 1950 a pilot from the Ministry of Supply began learning to fly it. On 1 June 1950 No. 1 Air Horse took off with a crew of three, including Alan Marsh, Britain's most experienced helicopter test pilot, and another test pilot, F.J.Cable. Metal fatigue caused a small component to fail in the pitch control mechanism of the front rotor. The Air Horse crashed and all three men on board were killed.[9]

The Air Horse died with its crew. It was only a viable project as long as there was a reasonable prospect of Government support, and the object of J.G.Weir's subventions had been to bridge the gap between reluctance and confidence in the official mind. By the spring of 1950 confidence had been established. The pilot was a Ministry pilot, and the machine was a Ministry machine. The Air Horse's future seemed as secure as anything is likely to be in the plane-maker's world. The disaster changed all that. The Ministry of Supply withdrew, apparently on the ground that development had been too rapid and research ought to be directed to different ends.

There was no prospect of the Cierva company going on alone. Even before the accident, J.G.Weir had told Weirs' Board that 'the prospect of insolvency was not far ahead'. After it, in October, he told the same audience that Cierva 'would be unable to carry on'.[10] All that remained was to find a comparatively painless way out.

The Cierva company had on hand another promising project, for a light, simple machine known as the Skeeter, which represented J.G.Weir's perennial faith in rotorcraft for the private owner. The Ministry of Supply had also shown an interest in this machine, but at the time of the Air Horse accident it was far from fully developed, and there was no likelihood of sufficient Ministry support for the Cierva company to keep it going. Nevertheless it represented a saleable asset, especially after the Ministry, in October 1950, agreed to pay £50,000 for the completion of the development contract then running, as well as taking over the prototype Skeeters then in existence.[11]

In December 1950 Saunders-Roe agreed to take over 'the Cierva premises and selected members of the staff and labour force, together with such contracts as the Ministry of Supply desired to have completed.... The effect would be to hand over all technical information and assets to Messrs Saunders-Roe.'[12] In other words, Saunders-Roe took over all that remained of the Cierva business as a going concern, although the company itself, with its patents and drawings, a prototype Skeeter, a small wind-tunnel, and a model test apparatus remained the property of the shareholders. The equipment was put in a garage near Winchester, and the company was left with an overdraft of £10,000, guaranteed by J.G.Weir.[13] Eventually, in 1958, after a reduction of capital, J.G.Weir bought G. & J.Weirs' interest in the Cierva Autogiro Company for £5000.[14]

The Skeeter was the ancestor of successful military helicopters, but not in Weirs' hands. For practical purposes the interest of Weirs as a company in helicopters, though not of J.G.Weir as an individual, ceased in the autumn of 1950. Commercially speaking that was probably just as well, considering the subsequent history of the aircraft industry. It was a sad end, nevertheless, to a sustained flight of technical imagination, which during a quarter of a century had more than once seemed to come very near to success on a large scale.

Weirs' connection with helicopters, sustained at all times by the private enthusiasm of J.G.Weir, was never an orthodox commercial venture, though if the history of the Air Horse had been more fortunate it might have become one. Another post-war diversification, steel housing, was also carried along, in its beginnings, by an individual – William Weir – whose motives were not entirely commercial. Its outcome, however, was very different.

The practical result of Tom Johnston's approach to Lord Weir (Chapter Eight) was an order in the autumn of 1944 from the Department of Health for Scotland for 5000 steel houses.[15] These were not to be like the houses of the twenties, which had wooden frames clad with steel. The Weir *Quality* houses of the forties, which drew on the contemporary practice of the aircraft industry, were built entirely of steel. To make them, Weirs set up the Weir Housing Corporation, and early in 1945 took a lease of a Ministry of Production factory at Coatbridge.[16]

Weir Housing Corporation, financed partly by borrowing from the Finance Corporation for Industry, worked up production at Coatbridge until by the autumn of 1947 it was running at about thirty-four houses a week. This housing enterprise of the forties, in contrast to the project of the twenties, had no ulterior political motives. Lord Weir accepted all the conditions laid down by trade unions and about 4000 houses were assembled from factory-made parts without obstruction. Trouble arose, however, from the post-war shortage of steel. In March 1948 the Government decided that no more orders would be placed for houses containing more than a ton of steel each and that no more orders for steel-framed houses would be placed at all. Nevertheless they wanted Weirs to submit plans for the 1949 programme of 'non-traditional' houses. These decisions faced Weirs, so far as they could see, with three alternatives. They could close Weir Housing altogether as existing contracts ran out. They could run it down to a skeleton staff until steel became more plentiful. Or, as the Board Minutes put it, they could 'continue in the housing business in an alternative type of fabric construction, with interior parts as supplied at present', and they could accept an order for 1000 houses built from 'no-fines' concrete, with a 'traditional' roof, 'as the most practical means of filling the gap, pending an improvement in the steel situation.'[17]

This was the policy which the Board chose, noting as they

did so that it was 'a mere temporary expedient, to be abandoned in favour of the original type of Weir House whenever an improvement in the steel situation was in sight'. It turned out to be nothing of the sort, especially after corrosion in steel houses already erected led to a prolonged wrangle with the authorities in 1952-3.[18] The steel shortage passed, like other shortages, but Weirs never went back to the steel house.

They stayed, nevertheless, in the building industry, first with a timber factory-made house and later with houses of 'traditional' construction embodying factory-made timber interiors. They became in fact, straightforward building contractors, applying factory methods or 'traditional' methods as they seemed appropriate. Their early work was all for local authority housing, and by 1962 they had provided about 10 per cent of all housing built in Scotland after the war. They moved on, however, in the middle fifties, to house-building for private sale, buying a small building firm (Drumpellier Building Co. Ltd) for the purpose,[19] and they contracted also for the building of schools. Housing became a permanent feature of Weirs' operations and an important contributor to group profits.

In the curious manner thus described, an old-established Glasgow firm of marine engineers slid sideways into the building trade, protesting loudly that they intended nothing of the sort. The ultimate origins of this unintended venture lay in Lord Weir's plan – or plot? – of the twenties to relieve the housing shortage of the day by methods which were intended to deal a shrewd blow at the craft unions. The immediate origins lay in an approach to Lord Weir by one of his political opponents of the twenties. Success came, after the forced abandonment of the all-steel house, by applying engineering principles and factory methods, rather than the principles and methods of the building trades, to the interior, which accounts for about 60 per cent of the completed cost of a house. Altogether, scarcely a development which an economist would have been likely to predict or a management consultant to recommend, because neither could be expected to take account of the personality and motives of the first Lord Weir.

In the early fifties, while helicopters were put aside and the housing venture grew, the central business of Weirs and Drysdales, marine auxiliary machinery, prospered, largely because of the rising demand for tankers, the reason for which is evident from the figures of world production of crude petroleum:[20]

1950	525,000 metric tons	1960	1,051,070 metric tons
1951	770,100 „ „	1965	1,503,335 „ „
1952	978,439 „ „		

Steam-driven tankers represented a particularly good market for Weirs and Drysdales in combination. As well as the standard auxiliary machinery for the engine-room, they needed centrifugal cargo pumps for loading and discharging. Centrifugal pumps were Drysdales' speciality, and Weirs made the turbines to drive them. The turbines needed steam but that, in a steam ship, presented no problem. Towards the end of the fifties, as we saw earlier, a very rapid changeover to diesel engines set in, but of that more later.

The shipbuilders' rising demand, early in the fifties, evidently took one good judge by surprise. In the spring of 1949, at a Board meeting, Lord Weir 'made reference to the apparent unhopeful trend of mercantile shipbuilding orders due to the incidence of high costs, and suggested that both Weir and Drysdale might expect a falling off in this section of their work. He emphasized that the field of land work presented a better prospect, and . . . he felt that the long-term position should be studied and a policy agreed upon to meet any eventuality.'[21]

With this pronouncement we approach the central *malaise* of Weirs' position in the fifties. It arose from the contradiction between the long-term and short-term prospects of British shipbuilding, which made sound forward planning almost impossible, at any rate until towards the end of the decade, when the contradiction began all too plainly to resolve itself. Looking at Weirs' prospects for marine business over a period of twelve or fifteen years, Lord Weir in 1949 was undoubtedly right to point to the menace of high costs in British shipbuilding, which by the early sixties was in a fair way to being over-whelmed by foreign competition. Over any shorter period, however, Weir was wrong, and it is by periods shorter than twelve or fifteen years that policy-making in business must be regulated.

At the moment when Weir gave his warning, British ship-building was already on an upward curve, and from 1948 to 1958, apart from a sharp check in 1952, the figures were fairly buoyant:[22]

Tonnage of Ships commenced in British yards, 1948–59

	'000 gross tons		'000 gross tons
1948	1180	1954	1445
1949	1212	1955	1378
1950	1418	1956	1343
1951	1484	1957	1599
1952	1188	1958	1312
1953	1279	1959	1140

Weirs' order books at Cathcart over the same period, show the following pattern:

	Total		Marine		Land		Admiralty	
1948	£3·0m.		£1·25m.		£1·6m.		£0·2m.	
		100%		41%		52%		7%
1949	2·5		1·0		1·0		0·5	
		100		42		39		19
1950	3·1		1·25		1·4		0·4	
		100		41		46		13
1951	7·5		4·8		1·7		1·0	
		100		64		22		14
1952	6·6		3·6		2·1		0·9	
		100		55		32		13
1953	5·2		2·6		1·3		1·3	
		100		50		25		25
1954	4·2		1·8		1·7		0·7	
		100		43		40		17
1955	4·8		2·6		1·5		0·3	
		100		55		31		14
1956	8·1		3·9		3·0		1·2	
		100		48		37		15

	Total		Marine		Land		Admiralty	
1957	£9·7·		£4·2·		£4·1·		£1·4·	
		100%		44%		42%		14%
1958	5·4		2·1		2·1		1·2	
		100		40		38		22
1959	4·8		1·4		2·7		0·6	
		100		30		57		13

The unforeseen increase in orders in the early fifties, large and sudden, caused acute problems of delivery from 1951 onward. In January 1952 Weirs' Board 'considered a schedule giving delivery promises for the years 1952 to 1957. They viewed with concern the mounting commitments in the years ahead, both at Cathcart and Yoker, and the embarrassment caused in dealing with the requirements of old customers... [the] Board suggested that the Sales Department should endeavour to be as selective as possible in accepting orders, and delivery dates extended to the utmost limit.'[23]

The natural result of this embarrassment was a scramble for extra factory capacity. Drysdales had begun expanding at Yoker, on their shut-in seven-acre site, in 1948, and all through the fifties 'hectic expansion took place as part of a constantly updated three-year plan'. A warehouse which they took over at Anniesland, a couple of miles from Yoker, gave 48,000 square feet, and by one means and another they doubled the value of their production between 1951 and 1964, although the number of people employed only rose from 1200 to 1400.[24]

Weirs themselves, at the prompting of the Managing Director, Kenneth Weir, were considering expansion beyond the limits of Cathcart in the summer of 1950. A factory at Queenslie, outside Glasgow, looked like becoming available in March 1951, and the suggestion was to relieve the pressure on delivery dates by transferring valve work out of Cathcart altogether. At the same time, Weirs would be meeting a desire expressed by the Admiralty that they should disperse their activities as a precaution against bombing. The Queenslie factory was taken, and a new company, Weir Valves Limited, with a capital of £100,000 and 'ample borrowing powers', was set up to deal both with Weirs themselves and with customers on the open market.[25]

In 1952 Weirs' tender for evaporating plant to produce drinking water from the sea for Kuwait was accepted, and other large evaporators, for Aden and Curaçao, were in prospect. These orders threatened or promised (the choice of word, in the circumstances, is rather difficult) to add to the congestion in Weirs' shops. Accordingly, towards the end of the year Weirs bought, for £125,000, iron and steel foundries at Newmains, Lanarkshire, belonging to the Coltness Iron Company. The buildings were old and scattered but 'there was a collection of assets of immediate and considerable value', and Weirs intended to carry the foundries on as a going concern, to provide a tied source of steel castings for their own business.[26]

Coltness was not a fortunate purchase. The foundries attracted very little demand from outside Weirs' business and six months' experience showed heavy losses which neither J.K.Weir nor J.R.Lang saw any prospect of making good without unjustifiable capital expenditure. Towards the end of 1953 the two foundries were closed. The land, the buildings, and some of the assets were sold to John Connell & Co., scrap merchants of Coatbridge, at a small capital gain.[27]

Weirs' Board thus found themselves faced, once again, with the problem of factory floorspace. In May 1954 Lord Weir proposed a solution. Having reviewed 'the growing figures of output at Cathcart', he 'stressed that this...had been attained as a result of the acquisition of additional plant and equipment, substantial help from the factory at Queenslie, from a growth in subcontracting, and by much overtime and double-shift working.' What was needed, he said, was extra space and new plant, especially for heavy work, and 'perhaps the most important factor of all was the need for a large addition to our facilities for...research, experimental and prototype development.' He said there was, in fact, plenty of room at Cathcart – 80,000 sq ft of it – in the iron and non-ferrous foundries, and to set it free he suggested transferring the foundries elsewhere, 'preferably to Argus'.[28]

Why Argus? Probably because for some time it had been the least prosperous of the Weir subsidiaries.[29] The foundry at Thornliebank was intended principally to supply iron and gunmetal castings to Weirs and Drysdales, but cast iron was being driven out of use by steel and the main gunmetal customer – the Admiralty – offered no prospects of growth. Argus was not well equipped for general foundry work on the open market, and attempts to break into it had failed.

All this must have been in the minds of Weirs' directors as they listened to the Chairman's proposal to transfer the Cathcart foundry to Thornliebank. Having broached the matter in May 1954, Lord Weir returned to it in October, emphasizing the advantage of treating Cathcart solely as an engineering unit. 'Having regard,' he said, 'to the domestic earnings and financial position of the Engineering Division at Cathcart, he submitted that never before had circumstances appeared more favourable to enable it to consolidate and maintain its prosperity.'[30] Drysdale was nervous of 'labour troubles . . . because of redundancy', but the Board recorded its opinion 'that the fusion would result in greater efficiency and economy', and 'resolved to proceed at cost estimated to be £190,000'.

The proposal to transfer the Cathcart foundry to Thornliebank was the last important executive act in the business life of the first Lord Weir. In 1954 he was seventy-seven, still alert and masterful. During the year, nevertheless, he decided to retire. He handed over the Chairmanship to his elder son, Kenneth Weir, and on 14 June 1955 became Honorary President of the company.

Sir John Richmond left the Board at the Annual General Meeting of 1954. J.G. Weir retired in 1956. Sir John had joined the Board about 1895, Lord Weir in 1898, J.G. Weir in 1908. They represented the second generation of Weirs' management – the generation which had seen the brave days of the old private company before 1914, when the Royal Navy had sixty-five battleships at sea and more building; when young men could cheerfully undertake to build three racing cars in three months; when more than half the merchant ships at sea went down the ways in British yards, and most of all on Clydeside. They had carried the business through the Great War and nursed it through bleakness afterwards, until the brief and final revival of British naval shipbuilding in the late thirties and the Second World War.

With the retirement of this group in the mid-fifties, the second generation finally handed over to the third. The second generation still represented, very largely, the traditions of private ownership and control. The third was the generation of the public company and professional management. Their influence had been growing, as we have remarked, for many years, but it was not absolute until Lord Weir retired. Then the direction of the company's affairs passed without reservation into younger hands. The founding families were still strongly represented by J.K.Weir and J.R.Lang, as well as by J.W.W.Drysdale, who remained a director until 1965, but they were supported by a growing team of professional managers represented on the Board, in 1955, by Harold Hillier, N.M.Niven and John Young.

Weirs at this time stood at the peak of their post-war prosperity. Shipbuilding in the world generally and in the United Kingdom in particular was very active – at the Annual General Meeting of 1956 Weirs' new Chairman remarked that world shipbuilding capacity was 'fully booked, in some cases until 1963' – and Weirs' profits were correspondingly buoyant. From less than £400,000 in 1948, net profits rose in 1954 and 1955 to more than £1,500,000 – much the highest figures, up to that time, in Weirs' history.

Board and management together faced problems of a different order of size and diversity from those which had confronted their predecessors. By 1955 the capital employed in Weirs' business was nearly £7,000,000, against £2,600,000 in 1948, and it was still growing fast. The activities of the business, though still heavily concentrated round steam-driven auxiliaries, had come to embrace the Weir Housing Corporation as well as Zwicky, Weir Valves and Argus. Moreover water treatment, as we shall see in the next chapter, was showing promise.

A group of this nature needed the best possible planning, and more so as the outlook for British shipbuilding began to darken in the late fifties. As early as 1953 it was recognized that the organization set up after the war, in which G. & J.Weir Ltd was both a manufacturing company on its own account and a holding company for the group, was no longer right. The developments which followed led directly on towards the Weir Group of the late 1960s. To them we must now turn.

10

The Holding Company

Weirs' situation in the middle and late fifties was paradoxical. On the one hand the business had never been larger or more varied. It was no longer devoted overwhelmingly to a fairly narrow field of steam engineering, and it disposed of resources much greater than ever in the past. On the other hand, the future had never been so uncertain. All round Weirs, the foundations of their world were shifting. New opportunities were appearing: old certainties were dissolving. For the business to survive and prosper, heavy risks would have to be run, calling for the nicest possible judgement of prospects in the engineering industry.

Policy henceforward must be made in consideration of the resources and interests of the group as a whole, without undue regard to any individual unit. And what if that unit should chance to be Cathcart, with all the emotional weight, to say nothing of the financial and technical importance, attached to the birthplace of the group, which was still the site of the largest member of it? The direction of the group must be detached from the management of G. & J. Weir Limited.

The matter of reorganizing Weirs' direction and top management was brought formally before the Board, no doubt after lengthy informal discussion, on 29 December 1953. The Chairman – the first Lord Weir – 'submitted . . . a paper in which he reviewed the Group Organization and Management, the continued expansion and turnover of the business, and the consequent heavy strain on Executives. These developments had inevitably disclosed certain weaknesses in management, which he considered it was the Board's duty to repair as soon as possible. He accordingly offered for consideration suggestions and proposals as to General Policy and Action.'[1]

Weir suggested two key reforms:

a that the parent Board should be relieved entirely of its present Executive responsibilities in directing the activities of the Cathcart Organisation, leaving it free to function purely in a parental and statutory manner for the Group.

b that a new Executive Board should be formed to manage the activities at Holm Foundry, this Board to be composed of the younger Cathcart members of the parent Board, together with Cathcart departmental heads.

In parallel, he suggested that he and Sir John Richmond should leave the Boards of all subsidiaries, and that Sir John should leave the main Board also. As the seniors withdrew, their juniors were to advance, for Weir also suggested that Niven should be confirmed as Joint Managing Director of Drysdales, that A.F.Cargill should become Managing Director of Weir Housing, 'and that such of his Assistants [should] be added to that Board as Mr Lang and he considered suitable.'

These proposals were accepted. They came close to setting up a holding company, divorced from manufacturing, and that was always the intention behind them, but it took some years to carry fully into effect. The Articles of Association had first to be altered to allow 'Executive Directors' – heads of Cathcart departments – to serve on the Cathcart management board without being directors of G. & J.Weir. When the new body was set up, in March 1955, it had Kenneth Weir as Chairman and two other Weir directors. Five 'executive directors' represented the professional management of the Cathcart factory. There, for the time being, major organizational reform was allowed to rest, although other preparations for a holding company, particularly in matters of finance and accounting, went ahead.

Thus reconstituted, Weirs' Board and top management had before them what promised to be a development of major importance, particularly attractive since it might reduce their

dependence on shipbuilding. This was the design and construction of large plants for the evaporation and distillation of
sea water, to provide drinking water for considerable communi-
ties. The process, in the mid-fifties, depended on heating sea
water by steam in submerged tubes. The capital costs were
heavy and so were the running charges, particularly since the
heating coils quickly scaled up and became inefficient. It was
therefore only a commercial proposition in places where the
extraction of oil or minerals, or some other local industry, was
sufficiently profitable to carry the costs.

As early as 1930, Weirs supplied evaporating plant for the
islands of Curaçao and Aruba, in the Netherlands Antilles,
where refineries were built to deal with Venezuelan oil. After
the war, the rapidly rising demand for oil, much of it supplied
from the arid coastal states of the Persian Gulf, made it evident
that water treatment would probably become big business.
All Weirs' past experience fitted them to profit by it, and from
1953 onwards, under Hillier's direction, the economics of the
process were improved, partly by chemical treatment to remove
scale and partly by linking the evaporation process with electricity generation so that sales of electrical energy offset the
cost of producing drinking water. In 1955 Weirs contracted to
supply four large evaporating and distilling plants for Aruba.
The contract, at £1,500,000,* was the largest Weirs had ever
made, and it was followed in less than a year by a contract,
worth £1,400,000, for similar plant in Curaçao. The Aruba
plant was to supply 10,000 tons of fresh water a day; the
Curaçao plant, 4000 tons, as well as electricity at the rate of
7·5mw.[2]

On 27 August 1955 Harold Hillier died, aged sixty-four. He
had never been inclined to delegate, and he left no obvious
successor. There was, however, a candidate outside the business
altogether. This was Dr R.S.Silver,† a physicist by education
but an engineer by choice. He had worked for Weirs previously,
having joined them in 1939, from ICI's explosives factory at

---

* This figure is from the 1956 Report. The 1955 Report gives £1,250,000.
† Later James Watt, Professor of Mechanical Engineering at Glasgow University.

Ardeer, to become, at the age of twenty-six, the head of Weirs' research. His relations with Hillier had not been easy, although in business training he admitted a debt to him, and in 1946 Silver left. In 1956 J.G.Weir invited him back. The way was open, and Silver came. He was appointed Chief Development Engineer, and he applied himself chiefly to sea-water evaporation.

Silver's achievement, a very notable one, was to develop flash distillation of sea water. The principle of flash evaporation is not, as with submerged tube evaporators, to boil the sea water immediately by heating it with steam passing through submerged coils but to heat the sea water under sufficient pressure to stop it from boiling and then, by allowing it to flow in series into chambers at successively lower pressures, cause a proportion of it to boil off (or flash) into vapour in each chamber.

While this principle significantly reduced the deposition of scale on the heating surface, its economics were often less favourable than those of the submerged tube plant. Silver showed that this situation could be reversed if the number of stages of flashing were increased so as to be at least twice the plant performance ratio (the ratio of the weight of distilled water produced to the weight of heating steam used). The heat for the process can be supplied from power-station steam, so that in this process as in the other costs are offset by the sale of electricity.

Silver came back to Weirs in 1956. By 1958 Weirs were confident enough of the 'flash' process to enter into a contract with the States of Guernsey Waterworks Department for a plant to produce 500,000 gallons of fresh water a day. It was intended as stand-by plant to rescue the tomato crop if the rain failed. From Weirs' point of view it served very well as a large-scale experiment or pilot plant, and it was also a convenient show-piece for prospective customers.

In 1959, not long after the Guernsey contract, Weirs contracted with the Government of Kuwait for a much larger installation, which when it was completed would be the largest 'flash' type sea-water distillation plant in the world. It was to have four times the capacity of the Guernsey plant – 2,000,000 gallons of fresh water a day – and it was to consist of two units of nineteen stages each, each producing 1,000,000 gallons. This plant and the plant in Guernsey both came into commission during 1960.[3]

While the 'flash' process was developing, other plants, either on the 'flash' principle or of the old style, were contracted for or commissioned elsewhere. Much the largest – indeed, the largest single installation of its kind in the world – was the plant at Aruba, with its five sextuple-effect evaporators yielding 2,000,000 gallons a day. Apart from its value to the oil industry it was intended to help with the task of developing the island's tourist industry, and on 9 May 1959 it was opened by Kenneth Weir with appropriate official pomp, running even to the issue of a commemorative postage stamp.[4]

The size of large evaporating and distilling plant may be judged from the illustrations. Weirs had never built anything so big before, and as the orders came in it quickly became apparent that Cathcart had no room for them. 'The type and size of Heat Exchange units,' the Chairman reported to the Board on 4 July 1956, 'had already outstripped the size of the existing bays, with the result that an increasing amount of heavy work required to be subcontracted. The situation had led him seriously to consider the desirability of acquiring another business with facilities suitable to undertake this work.'[5]

By September 1956 'another business' had been found – Wm Simons & Co. Ltd of Renfrew, engineers and shipbuilders. The firm dated from 1810, and for many years it had specialized in dredgers, having built what was perhaps the first suction dredger ever to go into action. Simons' equipment included heavy machining and boiler shops and they had vacant land, all of which would be useful to Weirs.

Weirs knew Simons well, having often employed them on sub-contracts. In 1956 their business was not in the best of health. Ownership was split between a number of families, none of whom had control, and although the technical management was good there had been no move to professional commercial management, so that the company's financial policy was unsound and the plant and equipment had been allowed to run down.

Weirs offered £17 10s. a share for 25,000 £10 Ordinary shares. For 12,500 £10 5% Preference shares they offered £10 each, making a total outlay of £1,000,000. The deal went through late in 1956, and Simons passed under Weirs' control. Kenneth Weir became Chairman of Simons, with J.R.Lang and J.W.W.Drysdale with him on the Board.

Weirs' outlay brought them more than fixed assets and land. It brought them a going concern which at the moment of takeover had in hand 'a large suction hopper dredger for the Calcutta Port Commissioners, two diesel electric fish factory trawlers and two diesel electric paddle tugs for the Admiralty.' Moreover the Admiralty had just ordered two boom defence vessels.[6] Thus in the course of developing promising business on land, Weirs became shipbuilders: a move without precedent in their previous history. Why did they choose to make it in 1956, when the long-term outlook for British shipbuilding was scarcely reassuring?

The answer lies in the specialized nature of Simons' business. They built chiefly dredgers, for which the market was limited but fairly dependable, and less liable to violent fluctuation than the market for sea-going ships. Besides the dredger trade, Simons had a long-standing connection with the Admiralty, not for warships (apart from boom defence vessels) but for tugs, netlayers and other service craft. And when Weirs bought Simons, they had just developed fish factory vessels of advanced design, in which the catch was taken in over a ramp at the stern and then immediately passed below for processing.

This was a business which Weirs considered they could profitably carry on. But there was more to it than that. As so often in Weirs' moves outside their own branch of engineering, there was an underlying motive that was not wholly commercial. Weirs desired to see this old-established dredger-building business preserved for Clydeside, and they took it over partly with that end in view.

In 1956, when Weirs acquired Simons, shipbuilding figures had been falling for a couple of years, from 1,445,000 tons commenced in 1954 to 1,343,000 in 1956 itself. Then there was a sharp, sudden improvement to the best figure for thirty years – 1,599,000 tons commenced in 1957 – followed immediately by what Weirs' Chairman, in the Annual Report for 1958, called 'recession conditions generally and in the shipbuilding industry particularly'.

In this gloomy year of 1958 an approach was made to Weirs by another old-established firm of dredger builders. They were Lobnitz & Co. Ltd, who had a shipyard and engine works near Simons at Renfrew. They wanted a merger with Simons, 'the main purpose' – as it was reported to Weirs' Board – 'being a desire on the part of Lobnitz to be associated with Weir so as to strengthen the engineering side of the business.'[7] Presumably they could feel shipbuilding giving way under them.

Weirs were not at first attracted. They saw only too clearly the strength of foreign competition. 'Any advantage,' the Board minutes record, 'to be had through the use of the better machine shop facilities at Lobnitz as compared with those available at Simons was largely ruled out by the fact that the prospects of obtaining orders for either of the two shipyards in the years ahead were extremely poor due to competition from and greater efficiency of the Dutch yards.'[8] Moreover it was not easy to come to terms financially, and at the end of the year Weirs decided to go no further.

During 1959, while British shipbuilding slid ever further into recession, Weirs' Board changed their mind. They decided, as the Annual Report put it, 'that considerable advantages would be secured if the two Companies were operated as a single unit. This would not only strengthen and improve our competitive position in the world market for dredgers and associated craft, but would also augment machine shop and welding facilities and benefit the heavy engineering resources of the Group as a whole.' Weirs took over Lobnitz, and at the end of 1959 Simons-Lobnitz Ltd was formed to run the two shipbuilding subsidiaries as one.

In this curious way, between 1956 and 1959, the success of Weirs' business in sea-water distillation led them to a direct and increasingly heavy commitment to shipbuilding, an industry which they had never ventured upon before, in which many of their customers were engaged, and in which the risks were heavy. At the same time they were seeking to reduce their traditional indirect dependence on shipbuilding prosperity, which was increasingly clearly at hazard, by cultivating new markets for the products of Cathcart, Yoker and Queenslie.

They looked principally towards developments in power-plant engineering. Before the war Weirs had supplied boiler feed pumps for power stations at home and abroad and Drysdales had supplied circulating and feed-water extraction pumps. From 1947 on, at Kenneth Weir's insistence, Weirs began to develop a serious interest in feed heating and condenser plant for power stations, and they had it very much in mind in negotiating the Simons purchase, which would provide extra manufacturing capacity.

In the early fifties the rise of the nuclear-powered generating station seemed to offer exciting new possibilities. Nuclear stations had conventional steam-raising plant which needed the usual auxiliaries. They also had special requirements for pumps and valves in the cooling systems of the reactors. As well as the electricity authorities, another old customer appeared in the nuclear field – the Admiralty. In 1956 Weirs received an order for main coolant pumps for the land-based reactor proto-type of the first British nuclear submarine, *Dreadnought*.[9]

When Weirs set up Weir Valves Ltd at Queenslie in 1950 they had nuclear business in mind from the start. In 1951 they took on a Government contract, known in the minutes as Contract X, which was reported at the time to require about a quarter of the existing floor space.[10] In 1952, with Treasury consent, they arranged to raise £200,000 fresh capital, and in March 1953 Weirs' Board had before them a proposal to double the manufacturing space at Queenslie. The Board of Trade raised 'strong objections . . . on the grounds that at the rate of intake of orders, it would be years before this space could be fully occupied'.[11] Weirs, who were supported by the Ministry of Supply, cut their proposal by about half, and in September arrangements were concluded to push the work ahead. By that time, rather ominously, a 'major question' had arisen 'as to how and to what extent this additional capacity should be employed, having regard to the fact that there would be a considerable release in about a year's time of existing space and of machine tools now employed on the Atomic Energy contract.'[12] It was decided not, for the time being, to order new machine tools for the extension.

The development of atomic energy was a great disappointment for British engineering in the later fifties. Weirs, who like other firms at first placed great faith in it, were approached in 1955 to join one of the consortia then active in research, development and manufacture. 'Additional valuable technical knowledge,' they recorded, 'would be likely to accrue from such a connection, and there was reason to anticipate that a new demand for our products would arise through association with a Group.'[13] There was nothing, however, in the early magnox reactor circuits to interest them, and in the end they decided not to join – 'Weirs' wisest non-decision', it has been called.

Products required in nuclear engineering, both on land and at sea, did become a permanent feature of Weirs' business, but hardly on a scale to justify the high hopes once placed in them. The Atomic Energy Authority gave Weir Valves a large order for valves required in the gaseous diffusion plant at Capenhurst, but by 1959 the work was running down, as Weirs had known all along that it would, and Weir Valves were losing money. 'The contracts for the supply of valves to the Atomic Energy Authority,' said Weirs' Annual Report, 'for gaseous diffusion plants have been substantially completed, and unfortunately there seems little prospect of further orders of this type in the near future.'

Alongside these developments, and the developments in

sea-water distillation which we have already examined, Weirs' Board had to deal with the continuing problem of Argus Foundry. In 1954, as we saw in the last chapter, they decided to shift to Thornliebank all foundry operations carried on at Cathcart, allowing about £190,000 for the purpose. The move was completed by the summer of 1957, but it cost about £175,350 more than the estimate. 'The principal causes of the excess,' the Board observed, 'were the lack of proper supervisory staff to control the initial planning, failure to allow a margin for contingencies . . . and the inadequacy of the second-hand buildings and equipment bought from Coltness.'[14] In other words, another strong argument for administrative reorganization, but to that we shall return.

The move, principally intended to gain space at Cathcart, did nothing to cure Argus. Indeed, rather the reverse, for the men at Thornliebank, as J.W.W.Drysdale had foreseen, resented the intrusion from Cathcart, and inter-union disputes followed. Weirs' Board heard recurrent complaints about inadequate management at Thornliebank, but the fundamental trouble lay deeper, in changing demand for the foundry industry's products. The matter came to a head on 4 June 1958, when a special Board meeting was called 'to consider a memorandum from the Managing Director [J.R.Lang] which recalled the decline in production efficiency, the unsatisfactory management of the Argus Foundry Ltd, and the need for immediate steps being taken to reorganize the Company.'[15]

The main argument of Lang's memorandum, published with elaborations in the Annual Report for 1958, was that since 1954 the demand for light iron castings had fallen off, and it had not been made good by demand for heavy iron castings, because since 1956 new engineering developments had emphasized welded construction. The demand for brass castings had also fallen too low to be profitable, although non-ferrous demand generally had kept up. So had the demand, especially within the Weir Group, for low-carbon steel castings.

Weirs could have closed Argus and withdrawn from foundry operations altogether, but then there would probably be delay in getting castings from outside suppliers at times of heavy demand. Weirs preferred, therefore, to have some 'tied' capacity. But what they had was a foundry supplying iron and non-ferrous castings. What they wanted was a foundry which would supply steel castings instead of iron. They also wanted the best possible foundry management.[16]

Weirs therefore looked for partners with experience of steel founding, and their search led them to Catton & Co. of Leeds, 'steel founders of high repute', who 'indicated their interest in establishing an association with Argus which both parties felt might be to their mutual advantage.' The first contact was made in the spring of 1958, a draft agreement had reached an advanced stage by September, and on 28 November the definitive agreement was executed by the Weir Board.[17]

It provided for the foundation of a joint company. Weir-Catton Limited, to hold the shares in Argus, re-named Weir Foundries Limited, and in Catton & Co. Limited of Leeds. Iron-founding at Thornliebank, both heavy and light, ceased forthwith. Weirs' holding in Weir-Catton was at first 50 per cent, but in 1960, pleased with their investment, they bought the other half, and Weir-Catton became a wholly-owned subsidiary.

While the Catton negotiations were in train, in the latter part of 1958, the plans for setting up a holding company reached maturity. On 30 December 1958 G. & J. Weir Holdings Limited was formed to take over the group as a whole, including a newly formed private company, G. & J. Weir Limited, which was to run the business at Cathcart. The Chairman of Weir Holdings was Kenneth Weir, who became Lord Weir when his father died, aged eighty-two, on 4 July 1959. J.W.W.Drysdale was Deputy Chairman, and J.R.Lang and N.M.Niven, directors. There were also four directors from outside the Weir group – Sir Charles Connell, a leading shipbuilder; I.M. Stewart, Chairman of Hall-Thermotank; J.A.Lumsden, the Company's lawyer; and J.H.Lord, a director of Dunlop Rubber and later Chairman of Whessoe.

On formation, Weir Holdings took over nine subsidiaries.

Eight were in the United Kingdom and one, newly acquired, in Canada. This was Peacock Brothers Ltd, selling agents for Weirs and Drysdales for about half a century and manufacturers, under licence, of Nordstrom valves and of Weir and Drysdale auxiliaries. Weirs bought control in 1957, but the Rockwell Group of Pittsburgh, USA, continued to hold 33 per cent of the equity.[18]

Weir Holdings' balance sheet, at the start, showed share capital and reserves of £6,863,000, represented chiefly by investments in subsidiary companies. Much the largest subsidiary was G. & J.Weir, followed by Drysdales, Weir Housing and Peacocks. Capital and reserves of the subsidiaries, at 31 December 1958, were as follows;[19]

Weir	£4,466,000	(Lobnitz*	£250,000)
Drysdale	2,171,000	Weir Valves	525,000
Weir Housing	1,114,000	Zwicky	279,000
Peacock	878,000	W.R.Skinner†	59,000
Simons	867,000		

Profit figures, at the same date, illustrate the prevailing troubles of Weir Valves (above p. 163) and the profitability of repairs and servicing:

Net available profits 1958

Weir	£571,000	(Lobnitz	not yet owned)
Drysdale	377,000	Skinner	£15,000
Weir Housing	104,000	Zwicky	4000
Peacock (60·9%)	61,000	Valves	3000
Simons	58,000		

Total available profits of the Group 1958: £1,123,000, as in published accounts.

These figures catch the Weir Group in the act of changing course, away from overwhelming dependence on the traditional activities of their two largest members, Weirs and Drysdales. The investment in housing, begun nearly fifteen years before, is already massive, and the contribution to profits important.

* Acquired 1959.
† A London company later re-named Weir, Drysdale Service (London) Ltd. Acquired 1952 (part) and 1954 (whole) as a London base for repairs and servicing.

There is a new and heavy commitment, through Peacocks, to the North American market. Weir Valves are showing the fading of the first bright hopes of nuclear energy. The new policy towards the foundries is still concealed in the Cathcart figures, but it will emerge in 1959 under the heading of Weir-Catton. Most important of all, the development of sea-water distillation has led to much the largest of the group's post-war acquisitions, Simons-Lobnitz, through which Weir Holdings are closely tied to the fortunes of British shipbuilding.

As the Holdings Board took charge, with these changes in progress but far from complete, Weirs approached the crisis of their post-war fate – the sharpest crisis, indeed, in their history. For Weirs were still heavily dependent on shipbuilding – through Simons-Lobnitz more directly dependent on it than ever – and from 1958 onward into the sixties British shipbuilding slid downwards under the pressure of foreign competition to the worst figures since the thirties. In 1960, 1962 and 1965, in an expanding market for shipbuilders generally, under a million tons were commenced, each year, in British yards, against nearly 1,600,000 tons in 1957.

Weirs' Board, then, as the centenary year of the foundation of G. &. J. Weir came up, found the necessity of drastic change thrust ever more brutally before them. Their resources, built up chiefly since 1945, were considerable, but times were changing fast, and not to the advantage of their established interests. The redeployment of the Group's resources, during the adversity of the early and mid-sixties, would be a test of nerve and judgement as severe as any that any British firm had to face during the post-war turmoil of industrial change.

11

The Weir Group
by The Viscount Weir

With the entry of Weirs into the 1960s the last decade of this history is reached and the past begins to merge with the present. Moreover, the decade now to be reviewed is probably the most significant in the Group's history. During its course the Group not only expanded to an extent which currently gives it a respectable position amongst the top two hundred British companies but as we shall see, the increased emphasis on diversity meant that by 1969 the companies comprising the Group in England and overseas substantially outnumbered those based in Scotland. The Weir Group, therefore, by the end of the decade differs as much from its predecessor in the fifties as that entity did from the private company days of the late twenties.

In the last chapter the problems which faced the Board were clearly indicated. By 1959 the Group's Consolidated Profit was £3·302m. and after adjustments for depreciation and taxation the Net Profit attributable was £1·256m. By 1962 Consolidated Profit had fallen to £1·18m. and after depreciation, taxation and other adjustments, the Net Profit attributable had fallen to £225,000, the lowest figure ever recorded since G. & J.Weir became a public company. These are a measure of the difficulties the Board had to face.[1]

These disappointing results arose mainly from the heavy losses incurred by Simons-Lobnitz, and the Board saw no possibility of improvement. They therefore decided to sell the business and during 1961 sought a buyer. As a result a provisional agreement was concluded with Alexander Stephen &

Sons Ltd, the well-known Glasgow shipbuilders, under which the entire business was transferred to them.

The agreement was sound industrial logic. By embarking into the dredger business Stephen would acquire a share in a market which would supplement their activities as builders of high-class merchant vessels and warships. Moreover, they had recently invested substantial sums in modernizing their shipyard and possessed a well-equipped engine works, a pre-requisite to successful operation in dredger construction.

The transfer involved the completion by Simons-Lobnitz of a number of outstanding contracts and could only be effected gradually. It did, however, involve the closing down of shipbuilding and engineering operations at Renfrew and this operation was not accomplished without difficulty as the closure could foreseeably have involved unemployment in the town of Renfrew. However, the closure was arranged to be as gradual as possible and indeed the whole operation was not finally completed until 1964. By this time a substantial number of those employed at Renfrew had managed to find work at Linthouse and elsewhere on the Clyde. This brought the Group's unprofitable adventure to a conclusion.

In retrospect, the main reasons for this failure were the losses incurred on the shipbuilding side. These in turn reflected high production costs during a period of low prices and also fundamental changes in dredger design with associated high development charges. On the engineering side operations were always profitable but never to an extent against which the yard losses could be offset. Moreover, the rapid changes in size of power-station equipment and the invention by Dr Silver of the 'flash' distillation process, greatly reduced the potential load in the machine shops which had been originally envisaged.[2]

The removal of a major source of loss, however, did not solve the Board's main problem which can be summed up in the words 'increased diversification'. This process began, as has already been noted, with the Group's entry into steel founding and the development of the Multiflash distillation plants. This policy had therefore been commenced in 1958 but in his statement of 1961[3] the Chairman summarized what the Group had in mind. He announced Group policy to be on the following lines:

1 To build up manufacturing load by new product development.
2 To enter process fields other than power.
3 To acquire interests in allied and associated undertakings, thus increasing the range of the Group's activities, and strengthening existing ones.

This statement is of considerable importance as it laid down guidelines for Group action and this action, as will be seen, was resolutely pursued throughout the decade.

New product development to a large extent involved a closer survey of the pump market. Drysdale, it is true, purported to cover the whole range of centrifugal pump manufacture but for many years their business had involved preponderant specialization in marine applications and only to a limited extent in land work. Weirs were perhaps even more specialized in their traditional preoccupation with boiler feed pumps. Clearly both companies would have to widen their market approach and the most obvious of the pumping fields for them to enter was process pumping, covering the expanding markets in which the principal users were the chemical, petro-chemical and oil refining industries.

Both companies possessed design capability to produce pumps which could meet the exacting requirements of process engineering, but such developments would take time and time was clearly not on their side in view of the declining demands of shipbuilding. Moreover, other firms, notably American, had been long established in the process field and had acquired substantial experience and reputation. Obviously, time could only be bought through an association with one of these companies, preferably taking the form of a licence agreement.

Similarly, Weirs could expand their interests in air and gas compressors. The firm had established a reputation as builders of such compressors for marine applications but had never at any time contemplated entering the land field. Here again time would be required and here also the quickest access to the market would be through licence agreement for manufacture, or acquisition of the business of an established maker. So, in 1959 Weirs entered into an agreement with Clarke Brothers of Olean, NY, to manufacture under licence the complete range of Clarke reciprocating and centrifugal compressors. Clarke was one of the leading American manufacturers and their machines enjoyed a high reputation for efficiency and reliability.[4]

The Clarke range, however, only covered part of the spectrum of air compressor applications and in 1960 Weirs acquired through purchase from Alley & McLellan Ltd, the goodwill and designs of their air compressor interests. With this purchase Weirs' range of manufacture now covered a substantial part of the demand for industrial and process compressors.[5]

The history of Weir Valves at Queenslie, near Glasgow, has already been mentioned and its lack of progress was undoubtedly the result of its product range being too narrow. This was rectified through an arrangement with the Pacific Valve Co. of Long Beach, California, who had developed a new and interesting type of ball valve. Pacific indeed were interested in having a holding in the Company and in return for the licence arrangement they became a minority shareholder, the company's title being changed to that of Weir Pacific Valves Ltd.[6]

In 1961 the Pulsometer Group of Companies came into the market and was acquired jointly by Booker Brothers McConnell Ltd and Weirs. Pulsometer had a pump works at Reading which Bookers were anxious to have. They also had a licence agreement to manufacture Pacific Pumps (not to be confused with Pacific Valves) which Weirs wished to acquire. Pacific Pumps had an established name and reputation in the field of process pumping and through this purchase Weirs achieved the quick access to this market which they desired.[7]

Important as these acquisitions were in bringing the Group

into new product lines, it must not be inferred that their design staffs were not equally active in improving existing products. For G. & J. Weir in particular, boiler feed pumps still took pride of place as one of their most advanced products. Boiler feed pumps for modern power stations represent the most sophisticated of the entire pumping range. Here the designer is called upon to deal with problems associated with pumping large volumes of water at high temperature and high pressure. The pumps have to be designed to meet severe changes in temperature ('thermal shock') apart from the severe regime of their normal working conditions. They must be of the highest efficiency as the cost of pumping water under these conditions is considerable, and above all they must be unfailingly reliable.

Although Weirs continued to enjoy a high reputation in this market during the forties and fifties, competition was intense as represented by such highly reputed manufacturers as Sulzer, Harland and Mather & Platt. There was indeed little to choose in technical merit between the three companies but towards the end of the decade it might be said that Weirs' designs enjoyed a measure of superiority.

Nor did they limit themselves to developments in the power station field. During the late fifties and early sixties they produced a new and revolutionary design of marine boiler feed pump, the TWL, whose design showed inherent simplification resultant from the adoption of a water lubricated bearing between the pump and the turbine.

In the important field of heat exchange equipment too, the firm's development of improved condenser design was of considerable significance and this, together with some new concepts in the design of feed heaters, enabled them to secure valuable contracts for condensing and feed heat plant during the period when the power station programme in the United Kingdom was advancing rapidly.

Another important advance in the design of an old and familiar Weir product was in ships' distillation equipment and by the end of the decade evaporating and distilling plants were being supplied to ships which not merely produced water of the highest degree of purity but operated under a simple system of push button control.

Nor was new product development confined to Cathcart alone. As pioneers in cargo pump systems for ships, Drysdale continued to lead the field and by the adoption of careful and meticulous model studies they advanced their position substantially as suppliers of large circulating water pumps for power stations and the emptying of dry docks.

In housing also, development continued. The Housing Corporation, based on their extensive and unique factory construction techniques at Coatbridge, developed a system known as Multicom which was as far ahead of its competitors as the original Weir house of the mid-twenties had been over conventional building. This system was specifically designed to offset the common criticism of industrialized housing that it relied too much on a limited number of house types. Under the Multicom system, which concentrated on component production, architects and builders could have at their command sets of housing components which could be translated into dwellings of almost an infinite variety and number.

Finally, much thought was being given at Leeds to improving foundry techniques. Shell moulding was increasingly adopted for the more economical production of lighter castings but also during this period the management team were studying a far reaching and more fundamental concept in steel foundries which, when realized, would result in Knowsthorpe becoming the most advanced steel foundry in Europe.

So far, we have endeavoured to trace the action taken under the first and second of the objectives. It remains to trace the developments under the third heading where the Board aimed at acquiring interests in allied and associated undertakings to increase the range of the Group's activities and strengthen their position in existing ones.

Chronologically the first of these was the acquisition in 1959 of a controlling interest in a French company whose full title was Société D'Installations Thermiques et Auxiliares de Machines – ITAM. This company had been a formidable competitor in France. It was in fact the French counterpart of Contraflo Engineering Co. whose competition with Weirs in the twenties had been an embarrassment. Like Contraflo, ITAM was basically a design and contracting company who sub-contracted the manufacture of contracts they had obtained. ITAM indeed occupied, relative to French shipbuilding, a parallel position to Weirs in the United Kingdom and, like Weirs, when the demand for steam installations in ships began to fade, looked elsewhere to fill the gap. Like Weirs also, they soon acquired an excellent connection with the French power authority known as Electricité de France, a similar State owned undertaking to CEGB. This acquisition was to prove of considerable importance and still remains Weirs' largest acquisition in Europe. The company was renamed Weiritam.[8]

During 1960 a minor acquisition, designed to extend their activities in the wider field of water treatment, was that of the County Water Softener Co. Ltd, but of greater significance were the other constituent companies arising from the deal with Pulsometer which we have already noted. The water treatment interests were further strengthened through the acquisition of G.S.Tett & Co. Ltd and the Zwicky interests were broadened through the acquisition of Skyhi Ltd, who had developed a range of aircraft lifting jacks which fitted well into the pattern of the Zwicky products. Finally, the Pulsometer deal resulted in the purchase of BAL Ltd, makers of packings and sealings in rubber and commercial polymers. This at first sight would appear to fall outwith the concept of associated diversification but many of the customers served by BAL were also customers of Catton and, in the event, this acquisition turned out to be probably one of the most profitable of those involved in the Pulsometer deal.[9]

In 1961 the Group bought a substantial interest in C.F.Taylor (Metal Workers) Ltd, of Wokingham. This was subsequently extended until the company became a wholly owned subsidiary. It arose from Taylor's association with Zwicky as a supplier of tanks for their refuellers, but the Board were much impressed by the company's other activities.[10]

C.F.Taylor had established in Wokingham a very successful business in sheet metal working and panel beating and he had important contacts with the British aircraft industry. Moreover, he had diversified into a number of other fields such as plastics, heating and ventilation, wood working, vending and wrapping equipment, and a design organization. The Board could look back on their interest in the aircraft field which had been terminated when they gave up their interest in the Cierva Autogiro Company. To have some stake again in the industry appealed to them. In addition, there was the proximity to Zwicky, somewhat out on its own, and in due course that company became merged in the larger activities of the Taylor Group as a whole. This is perhaps the most interesting of the Group's activities at the time as it marks their re-entry into Aircraft with which the first Lord Weir and J.G.Weir had been so intimately concerned.

Over the same period the Group acquired all the equity of Peacock Brothers Ltd, an operation which consolidated their Canadian interests, a proceeding necessitated by the fact that the American minority were creating their own separate Canadian company. It had at the time the merit of releasing to the Group a substantial volume of cash.[11]

All these transactions took place before 1965 but two of importance remain to be recorded. In 1962 the Group entered into partnership with Richardsons Westgarth to set up a company known as Weir Westgarth Ltd, for the development of large land distillation plants. This association arose from the fact that while Dr R.S.Silver was engaged on the development of the Multiflash process, Dr A.Frankel of Richardsons Westgarth had been equally engaged and had in fact reached an identical solution. The companies, therefore, found themselves in competition with each other and as the business was almost entirely based on the overseas market, competition between two British firms appeared unnecessary. The association, however, was terminated by the withdrawal of Richardsons Westgarth in 1967, the company thereafter becoming a wholly owned subsidiary of the Group.[12]

The last of the purchases to round off this extensive programme was that of E.Jopling & Sons Ltd, a well-known
Sunderland steel foundry. This represented a logical extension
of the Group's foundry interests into the heavier range of steel
castings. About the same time Weir Housing Corporation,
interested in controlling a source of pre-cast concrete products,
acquired Springbank Pre-cast Concrete Co.[13]

By 1965, therefore, the Group's interests had expanded both
in products and character, thus broadening the base of its
activities. Starting in 1958 under the new Holding Company,
the Group had accomplished the following:

1 They had increased their interest in steel castings.
2 They had embarked more deeply into valve manufacture
and into the air compressor field.
3 They had added an important line of process pumps to the
specialist activities of Weir and Drysdale.
4 They had developed a new concept of large distillation
plants and had entered a wider field of water treatment
generally.
5 They now had important contacts in aircraft equipment.
6 They were producers of a specialist range of packings and
sealings.

All this was accomplished within the period of seven years,
and as a result, the whole pattern of the Group's activities was
materially altered.

These changes could only have been possible because the
Group had a strong financial structure reflecting the past
pattern of prosperity, notably in the forties and fifties, and the
prudent husbanding of its resources: for the changes were all
accomplished without raising new capital or creating prior
charges. Moreover, in addition to the acquisitions, the Group
had borne the substantial losses arising from the Simons-
Lobnitz adventure. The effect, however, on earnings was slow
to emerge and it was not until 1965 that Consolidated Profits
once again topped the figure of £3m.

By 1964 the Chairman was able, in reviewing the Group's

activities, to classify them into four separate product divisions,[14] namely:

Medium and Heavy Engineering
Engineering Supplies and Services
Building
Aircraft Services and Light Metal Working

This concept we shall see emerging in the Group's present structure and at this time gives some indication of the lines along which the Board was thinking.

With the Group's thoughts directed towards a better structure not unnaturally Group pump interests commanded their first attention. We have already noted how specialized were the Weir and Drysdale activities and the first attempt to broaden them through the acquisition of the Pacific licence for process pumps. Much more important, however, was the continuance of Weir and Drysdale as separate companies with the consequent duplication and waste in administrative and manufacturing costs. True, the two companies could be brought together but the emergent unit would still have insufficient market penetration and be too small to be able to compete effectively against such strong American and European companies as Worthington, Ingersoll Rand and KSB.

Indeed, the problem was one not merely affecting the Weir Group but applied with even greater force to the British pump industry as a whole. Much as it was fragmented, even at that stage, Weir and Drysdale together constituted the largest single unit but, as previously noted, their scale of operations was still too small by international standards. What was clearly required was a merging with other firms which would produce a pump organization which could stand on its own and expand.

In this context the Chairman favoured approaches being made to Mather & Platt Ltd, of Manchester, and W.H.Allen Sons & Co. Ltd, of Bedford, with both of whom there had been long established communication. It was true that in certain areas there was active competition between them but on the whole there was a good deal of overlap making many lines of pumping complementary rather than competitive.

Early discussions at chairman level proved rewarding. These began in 1965 and were continued in great depth of detail throughout 1966 with the object of setting up a single pump company in which the tripartite interests would be established, inter alia, on an agreed pattern of assets and past and projected earnings. Although conducted in very great depth covering all phases of corporate activity and in the most friendly manner, by January 1967 an impasse had been reached, one of the major difficulties proving to be the complexity of the problem of separating mixed physical assets without adversely affecting other interests.[15]

By 1967, therefore, Weirs were back where they had started in 1965 but if the talks had achieved nothing else they had been most valuable in emphasizing the importance of size as the basis of a successful pump operation. Indeed the Board were now firmly convinced that they had to establish themselves beyond question as the largest pump manufacturers in the United Kingdom and as amalgamation had failed this could only be achieved by acquisition.[16] In this context the natural candidate appeared to be another Scottish based firm, The Harland Engineering Co. of Alloa, with Worthington Simpson of Newark as an alternative.

The size of the Group as constituted in 1965 began to present a problem in organization and control. As new companies were acquired or created, control and contact was maintained with the main Board through the appointment of senior executive directors as directors of the companies involved, but the profitability of each company remained the direct responsibility of local management, and by 1965 the number of subsidiaries in the Group was well over thirty.

This arrangement, in practice, was found to be weak. Too much autonomy was at the periphery instead of the centre. Control on the part of the Holdings Board was exercised through finance and while the regular reporting of earnings still enabled the Board to judge performance of individual companies, nevertheless the whole system required a complete overhaul.

Accordingly, the advice of a well-known firm of industrial consultants was sought, and in due course their report was presented. Its main recommendations were adopted and in his statement of 1967 the Chairman was able to announce the change in Group organization as having been passed by the Board in June and October of that year, to take effect from 1 January 1968.[17]

The main change in the corporate structure was to group the Company into Divisions in terms of their products and markets, in order to improve coordination among companies with related interests, and to create a new Water Division for those companies concerned with desalination and other water treatment processes. The Divisions created were

Engineering
Building
Foundries and Engineering Supplies
Aircraft Equipment
Water.

The constitution of the Divisions is given in detail in Appendix Three.

In the Engineering Division G. & J. Weir remain as the largest single subsidiary in the Group with a number of smaller companies not all of which at that time were wholly owned. We have already noted, for example, the purchase of Weiritam. Of the smaller companies, Sowit represents a venture in Italy for the exploitation of sales for Weir and Weiritam and Weir Espanola similarly for Spain. Drysdale also controlled a small foundry company, Sharp, but this undertaking has now been closed down. The Weir Drysdale Service (London) Ltd is a valuable asset to give on the spot service in spares and repairs in the South of England.

Dobbie McInnes, makers of fluid monitoring and fluid equipment, were acquired in 1967 but the operation proved unsuccessful and the company was wound up in 1970.

Weir Drysdale (Australia), a small establishment somewhat akin to Peacock in Canada, enables the Group to be more adequately represented in the sub-continent and we shall be referring to Australian activities later in this account. Weir Warmtekracht enables the Group to be directly represented in the Netherlands and at the same time to have another local service base as the company already had a good connection on diesel engine repairs and maintenance. We have already referred to Peacock Bros.

No special comment is called for on the other Divisions, except on one or two minor acquisitions. Of these, the Aircraft Equipment Division expanded its interest in the field of shrink packaging by acquiring in 1967 Adams Powell Packaging Machinery Ltd. The importance of first-class pattern making facilities was obvious to the Foundry Division and this they achieved through the acquisition of G.Perry & Sons Ltd of Leicester in 1968. The Building Division purchased a pre-cast concrete company – Springbank – but its operations proved unsuccessful and it was subsequently liquidated.

Finally, the Water Division comprises, as we have seen, Weir Westgarth Ltd as the principal subsidiary, and a new company acquired during 1967, William Boby & Co. Ltd. This acquisition greatly extended the Division's activities in the more general field of water treatment and water treatment systems, giving it a more comprehensive structure and broadening its base. The Division also took over the G. & J.Weir water activities of Weir Water Treatment Ltd which, in turn, had embraced the County Water Softener Co. and G.S.Tett & Co. Ltd.

Under associated companies, there is shown a holding of 18 per cent in Harland Engineering, this representing the Group's holding in Harland before negotiations which resulted in 100 per cent purchase. The two Spanish companies represent joint ventures in that country by Weir Pacific and Taylor.

The performance and accountability of each Division became the responsibility of a chairman and as the chairmen were all members of the Group Board they had the task of reporting on the performance and policy of the divisions to the Board as a whole.

The second important change was to make certain functions the overall responsibility of the Group Board. These were corporate planning, finance, secretarial services and public relations. Although finance had been already established as a central function the concept of corporate planning was new to the Group and the importance attached to it was such that it was made the special task of an additional deputy chairman.

Further changes were also made. The incorporation of 'G. & J.Weir' in the designation of the Holding Company was held to be somewhat misleading and confusing as it tended to identify the activities of the Weir Group as a whole too closely with those of its largest subsidiary. For this reason the Board proposed that in future the Group should be known as 'The Weir Group Limited' and this change was given effect at the Annual General Meeting in 1968. Also, the Stock was converted into shares.[18] With these changes the Group now emerges in its present form and the new arrangement has worked well.

Since the formation of G. & J.Weir Holdings in 1958, twelve years have elapsed and the Board of the Weir Group Ltd currently reflects not only the effect of time but also the reorganization of control and central management referred to previously. Lord Weir continues as Chairman. J.R.Lang succeeded J.W.W.Drysdale as Deputy Chairman on the latter's retirement in 1965 and was joined as Deputy Chairman in 1968 by W.K.J.Weir who was given special responsibility for planning and development, William Weir being the fourth generation of the family to hold high office. N.M.Niven retired from the Board on the formation of the Weir Group Ltd. He had been closely associated with J.R.Lang and the Chairman in the expansion up to 1967 and in the new organization.

The Divisional Chairmen who form the executive element on the present Board are J.W.Atwell (Engineering) whose first appointment with the Group was as Works Manager of G. & J.Weir in 1954. A.F.Cargill headed the Housing Division with which he had been associated from the earliest days of the founding of the Weir Housing Corporation but unfortunately ill-health compelled his retirement at the end of 1969. S.L. Finch is Chairman of the Foundries and Engineering Supplies Division, having been associated with Catton & Co. as

Managing Director and latterly as Chairman ever since the Group established their steel foundry operation. C.F.Taylor (Aircraft Equipment) joined the Board in 1968 on the formation of the Group. A.C.Smith (Water Division) has a long connection with G. & J.Weir on the sales side and was latterly responsible for the management of Weir Westgarth.

Of the lay directors on the Board of G. & J.Weir Holdings in 1958, Sir Charles Connell, J.A.Lumsden and J.H.Lord continue to give their valuable advisory services to the Board. I.M.Stewart (now Sir Iain Stewart) resigned in 1965 due to pressure of his other interests. His place has been taken by W.D.Coats, a Director of Coats Patons Ltd, with considerable experience in finance and overseas affairs.

Also during the Holdings Board period, J.J.B.Young was appointed a director, filling the joint office of Finance Controller and Group Secretary until his resignation in March 1967.* It was then considered that the dual responsibilities of this post were unduly onerous and the Board decided to separate them. As a result, E.D.Bremner† was appointed Finance Controller in 1967 and F.R.Frame as Group Secretary in 1968.

The Board attaches particular importance to corporate planning based on a long term growth plan for the Group as a whole and within which the Divisions plan their own growth structure. Clearly also, tighter financial control is an essential part not merely of the plan itself but as a strict discipline on the operations of the Divisions. Outside of these the centralized functional services have been left as a basic minimum.

Chronologically we have now entered the concluding years of the decade but already these have acquired great significance in the Group's history and also have profoundly affected its capital structure. In the first place, we have already noted how by 1967 the breakdown in negotiations with Mather & Platt and Allen left unresolved the Group's determination to be the largest pump manufacturer in the United Kingdom. We have also noted that the addition of the Harland Engineering Co. of

* Mr. Young subsequently rejoined the board early in 1971.
† Appointed Director 1971.

Alloa appeared to be the most logical step to give effect to this resolution.

In November 1968 a formal offer was made to the Harland shareholders to acquire the whole Issued Capital of the company. But, perhaps not unexpectedly, the Board of Mather & Platt had been thinking along similar lines and the Weir offer was soon followed by a counterbid. Thereafter began a struggle for possession which was only concluded at the end of 1968, the Chairman being able to report in January 1969 that Harland had become a member of the Weir Group.[19]

With the acquisition of Harland the Group had achieved its objective but during the course of the negotiations it was apparent that they might not necessarily succeed in which case they would face a much more difficult situation. Moreover, although the Harland range of pumps substantially increased the Group's overall market penetration, one important field – that of small standard pumps – was still not adequately covered. Here the largest and most successful company in the United Kingdom was Worthington Simpson Ltd of Newark, who for some years had concentrated their attention on this market with marked success through the production of their well-known Monobloc design. The Board, therefore, in parallel with their operation to acquire Harland, also offered to acquire Worthington Simpson, an announcement being made in the Press on 24 December 1968.

Once again the Group found themselves in competition. This time it was with that large American company, Studebaker-Worthington Inc., who not only possessed substantial resources but had at one time been the owners of Worthington Simpson as the name of that company would imply. Clearly the absorption of an important British pump company by an American Group raised other issues of a national character which could not pass unnoticed by the Industrial Reorganization Corporation who had also followed closely the Mather & Platt/Weir competition for Harland. Studebaker-Worthington had already submitted an offer to the Worthington Simpson shareholders but Weirs' offer bettered it.

This competition had to be considered in the context of what was good for the British pump industry as a whole and here the IRC intervened. They proposed that the two bidders should get together and endeavour to resolve their difficulties, failing which IRC were prepared to adjudicate between the contending parties, the losing offer being allowed to lapse.

After a series of prolonged negotiations both parties were able to reach agreement and under it Weirs withdrew their offer for Worthington Simpson. In return Studebaker-Worthington agreed to make Worthington Simpson an important manufacturing source for their standard pump range, to the creation of a jointly owned selling organization to be known as Worthington-Weir and to transfer to Weirs the manufacture of a substantial number of their product lines at present being manufactured in the United States.

Both parties proceeded with the implementation of the agreement but by the summer of 1969 the arrangement was reconsidered and substantially broadened. Under the terms of the first agreement Weirs were still left free to develop their own line of standard pumps. Such an arrangement undoubtedly conflicted with a friendly agreement between jointly interested parties. Accordingly, it was arranged that Studebaker-Worthington would transfer half their holding in Worthington Simpson to Weirs, in consideration for which Weirs agreed to assume liability for the payment of 55 million Deutsche Marks in 1979.

Following on the acquisition of Harland, these arrangements far increased the extent of Weirs' original plans for their pump business. Under it, wider markets were opened up, notably in the United States, so that their pump business could proceed on much broader and more international lines.

The negotiations first with Harland and then with Studebaker-Worthington had delayed the basic reorganization of the Engineering Division but in 1969 the Chairman was able to report that this Division had been completely restructured.[20] The main feature was the creation of a divisional holding company – Weir Engineering Industries Ltd – which in turn had as its main entity a new company – Weir Pumps Ltd – and the smaller companies of the division. The new company, Weir Pumps Ltd, combined the assets of Drysdale, Harland and G. & J.Weir. The object of the operation was, of course, to coordinate and simplify the administrative structure of the separate units and thereby give effect to the true merging of all the Group's pump interests under one organization.

And now we must retrace our steps a little as we bring this history to a conclusion. If 1969 was a memorable year for the Engineering Division, it produced an even greater expansion in the activities of the Foundries Division. Ever since Catton had become a member of the Weir Group their progress had been of a high order and indeed, judged by all accepted criteria, their earnings performance had been the most successful of the Group's companies. This progress, however, was only possible in terms of a high rate of capital investment, modern foundry techniques being almost entirely in terms of plant and process improvement. It was for this reason that in October 1966 the Board approved a substantial investment in the complete reorganization of the Knowsthorpe foundry. This investment, was originally of the order of £2·5m., but due to rise of costs, by completion, it has been substantially exceeded.

This in itself would have consolidated Catton as certainly one of the most profitable steel founders in the United Kingdom, but during 1969 an opportunity occurred which, unfortunate perhaps in its timing, was one not lightly to be passed up. This was the opportunity to acquire two steel foundries in Sheffield.

In 1967 the long established and well-known steel makers in Sheffield, Samuel Osborn and Hadfields, decided to merge their foundry interests. Accordingly, they set up a jointly owned company, Osborn-Hadfields Steel Founders Ltd, but the results were disappointing. The company encountered serious financial difficulties with the result that it became available for purchase. The opportunity so afforded was a logical extension of the Group's foundry interests, and so during 1969 the company was acquired. It is important to record that the Industrial Reorganization Corporation looked favourably upon this rationalization of the British steel castings industry and did much to ensure the success of the acquisition through a loan of £1·25m. The effect of this has been to make the Foundry Division of the Group the second largest producer of steel castings in the United Kingdom and to make the Weir Foundry Division as strong in the British steel castings market as their colleagues in the Engineering Division in the field of pumps.

Up to and indeed until 1967 the numerous additions to the Group were met from its own resources and without any major adjustments to its capital structure. However, over the last two years of the decade the position was completely changed. Naturally, expansion in trading had placed demands on the Group's liquid resources and when the time came to make the Harland purchase these resources had been heavily committed. To create additional risk capital was clearly out of the question and indeed the Harland purchase corresponded with a period of severe monetary restraint in the United Kingdom, the highest known levels of bank rate affecting borrowings and hence the terms on which funds could be raised. Yet the longer term prospects seemed so favourable that the Board did not hesitate. We have already referred to the Deutsche Mark Loan through which the purchase of the half-interest in Worthington Simpson was effected. For the acquisition of Harland and Osborn Hadfield the Board issued the appropriate volume of Unsecured Loan Stock and further Debentures all of which, of course, become an increasing charge on the Group's earning capacity.

The corporate growth which these pages record is now best illustrated statistically. Taking the period we have been considering, in 1962 the Group's annual turnover was £25·34m. on which profit before loan interest was £521,000. By 1969 turnover had increased to £59·32m. on which profit before loan interest was £3·22m. Profit after taxation attributable to shareholders had correspondingly risen from £225,000 in 1962 to £1·5m. in 1969, representing, as a percentage on issued shares, an increase from 5·4 per cent in 1962 to 34·5 per cent in 1969.

We can now take a final glance at the Group structure as it emerges in 1970 (Appendix Four). It will be seen that the Engineering Division now reflects the streamlining process involved through the creation of Weir Engineering Industries Ltd and Weir Pumps Ltd but not entirely as, at the time, the integration of Harland Engineering Co. into Weir Pumps Ltd was incomplete. It does, however, show the Harland overseas interests in Canada, Australia and South Africa whose future will doubtless be reviewed. The Building Division through the sale of Springbank now comprises one company only, Weir Housing Corporation Ltd. The Foundries and Engineering Supplies Division shows the addition of Osborn-Hadfields Steel Founders Ltd and Osborn Precision Castings Ltd which we have previously noted. The Aircraft Equipment Division and the Water Division remain unchanged.

This chapter has shown how, over the past ten years, the Group has been enlarged, strengthened and reorganized. It is now the largest pump manufacturer in the United Kingdom with an important American connection. It has greatly extended its steel foundry interests so that it has become the second largest producer of steel castings in the United Kingdom. It has led the world in what remains still the most economic process of desalination; revived its interest in the aircraft field; and furthered its contribution to industrialized housing. Finally, it has built up an administrative framework designed to improve central control and to plan future growth.

The expansion over the past decade has therefore been at a greater rate than at any other time in the Group's history although the acquisitions of the last two years have not been achieved without the addition of considerable prior charges on the Group's immediate earning capacity. Nevertheless, the Group now emerges as a significant force in the British engineering industry with substantial earning potential.

Although the Group has become increasingly international in the composition of its constituent companies, it remains, as it did in the days of its founders, based in Scotland and under Scottish direction. As is all too well known, the past forty years have not been happy ones for Scottish engineering in general. Many familiar names have passed into history and the successors are largely the result of external enterprise and control. The Weir Group is proud to be an exception.

Appendix One

Statistical Records of G. & J. Weir Limited and The Weir Group

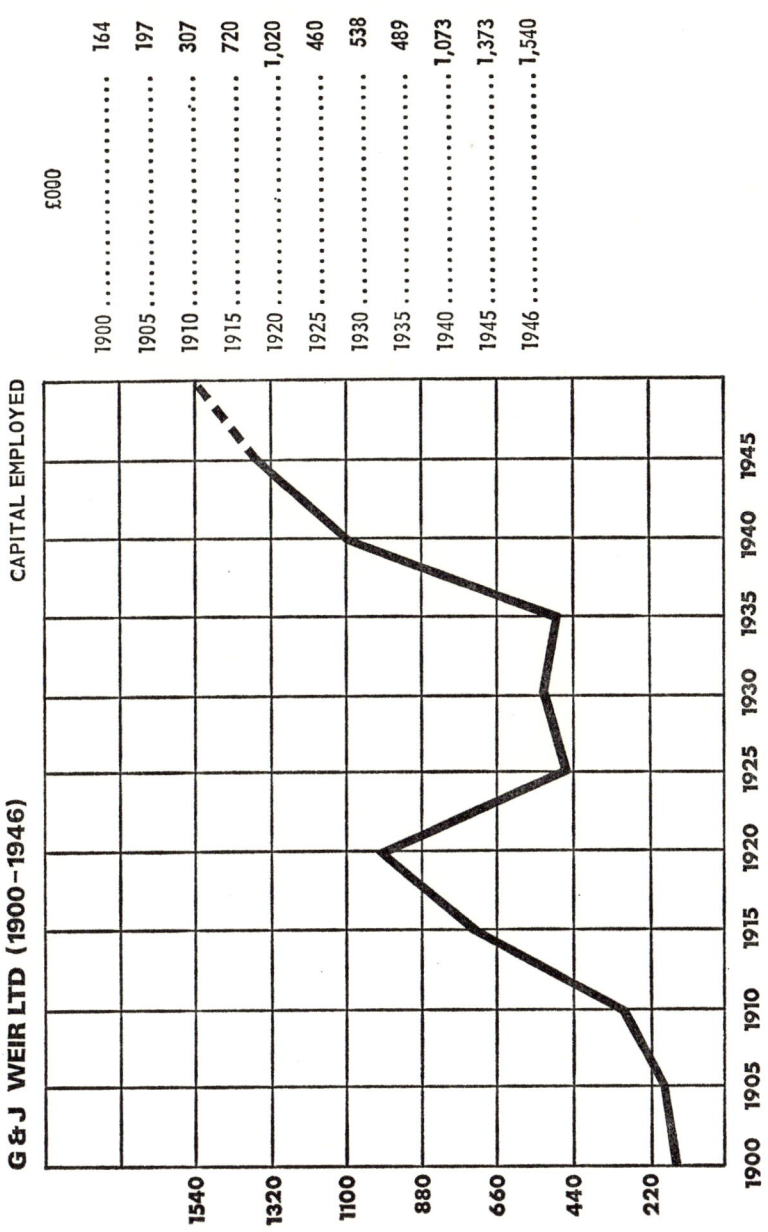

£000

1900	164
1905	197
1910	307
1915	720
1920	1,020
1925	460
1930	538
1935	489
1940	1,073
1945	1,373
1946	1,540

CAPITAL EMPLOYED

G & J WEIR LTD (1900–1946)

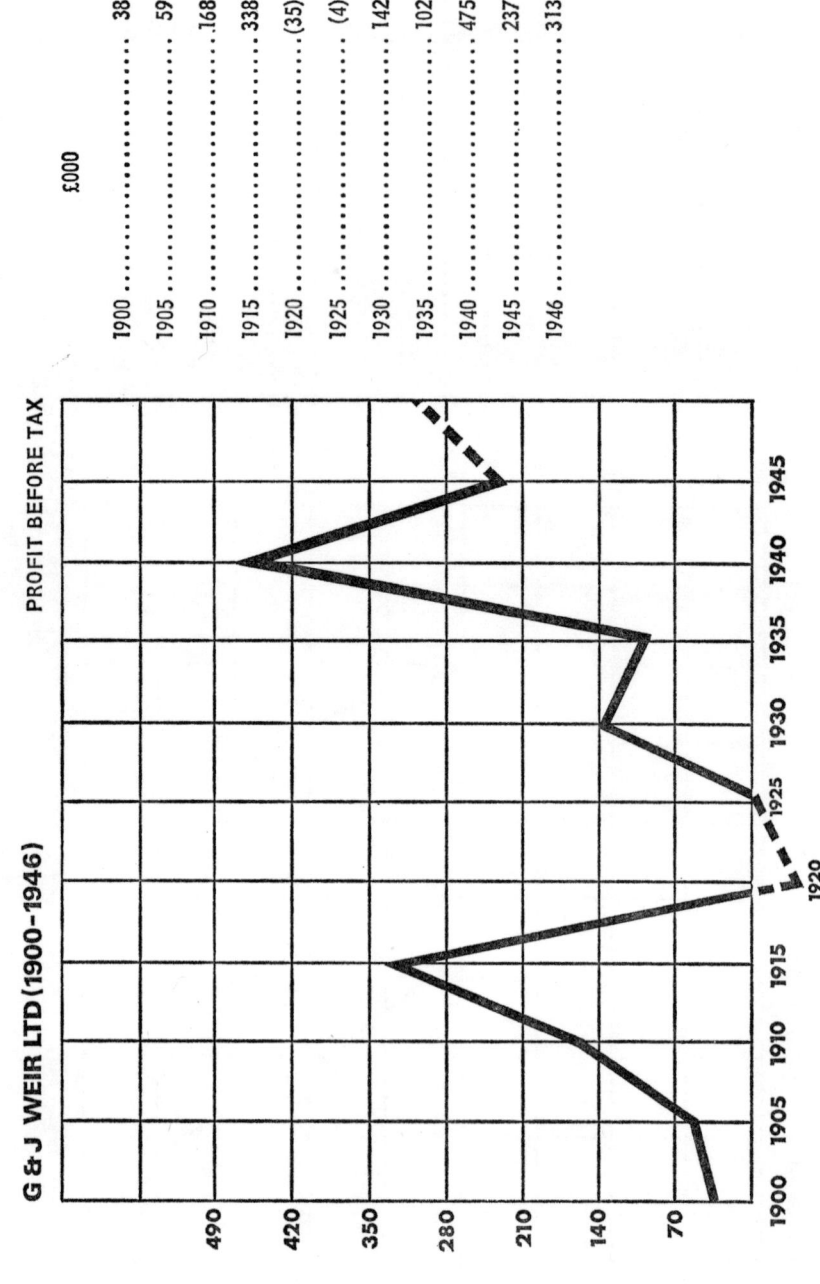

G & J WEIR LTD (1900-1946)

PROFIT BEFORE TAX

£000

1900 38
1905 59
1910 .... .168
1915 338
1920 .... (35)
1925 .... (4)
1930 142
1935 102
1940 475
1945 237
1946 .... 313·

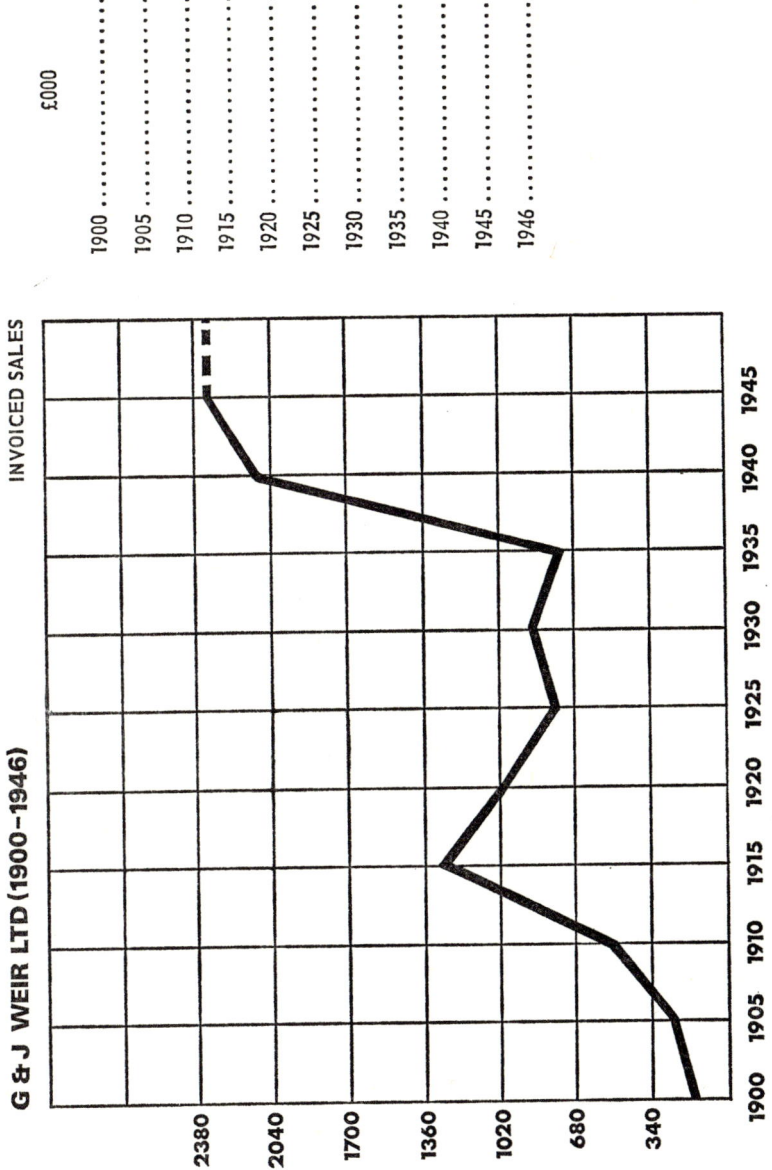

G & J WEIR LTD (1900–1946)

INVOICED SALES

	£000
1900	188
1905	258
1910	534
1915	1,294
1920	1,014
1925	806
1930	880
1935	735
1940	2,108
1945	2,355
1946	2,336

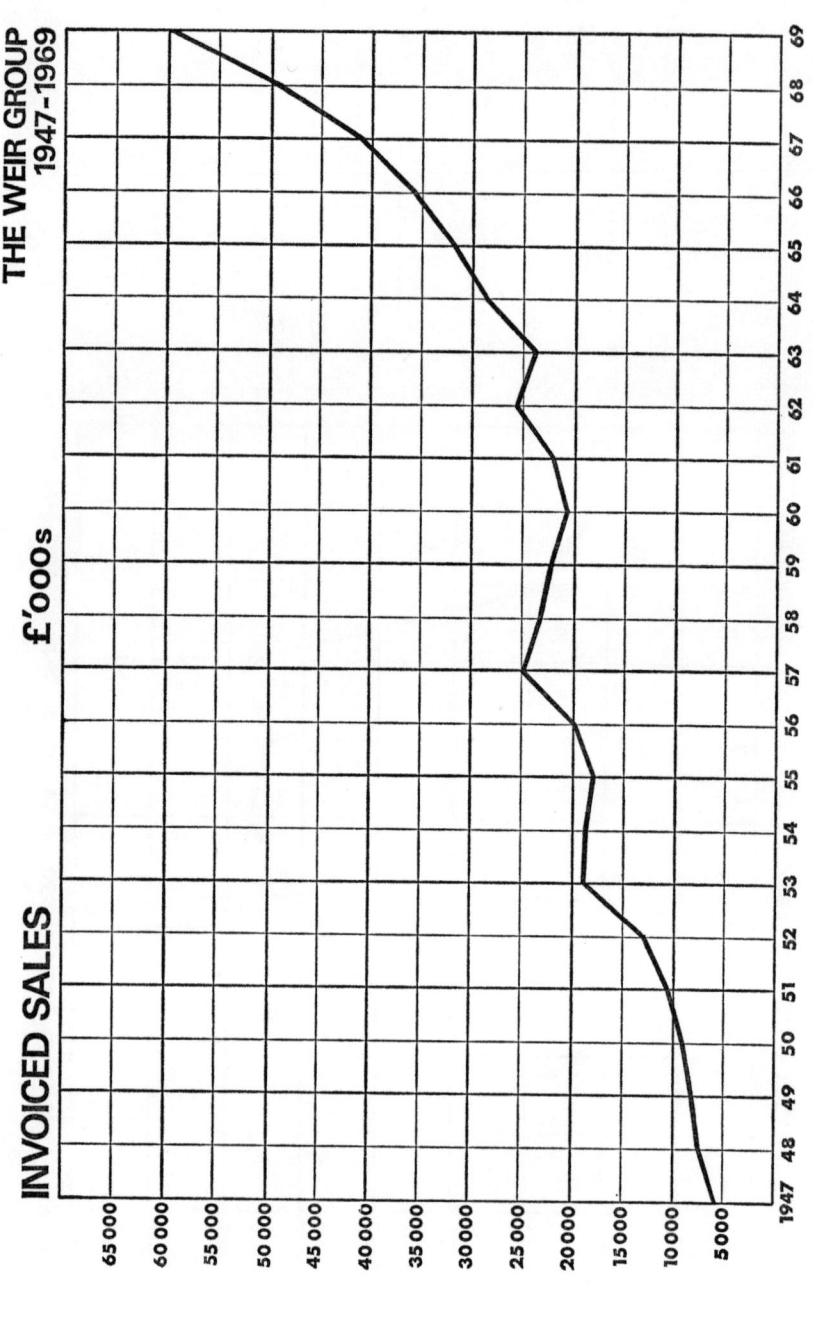

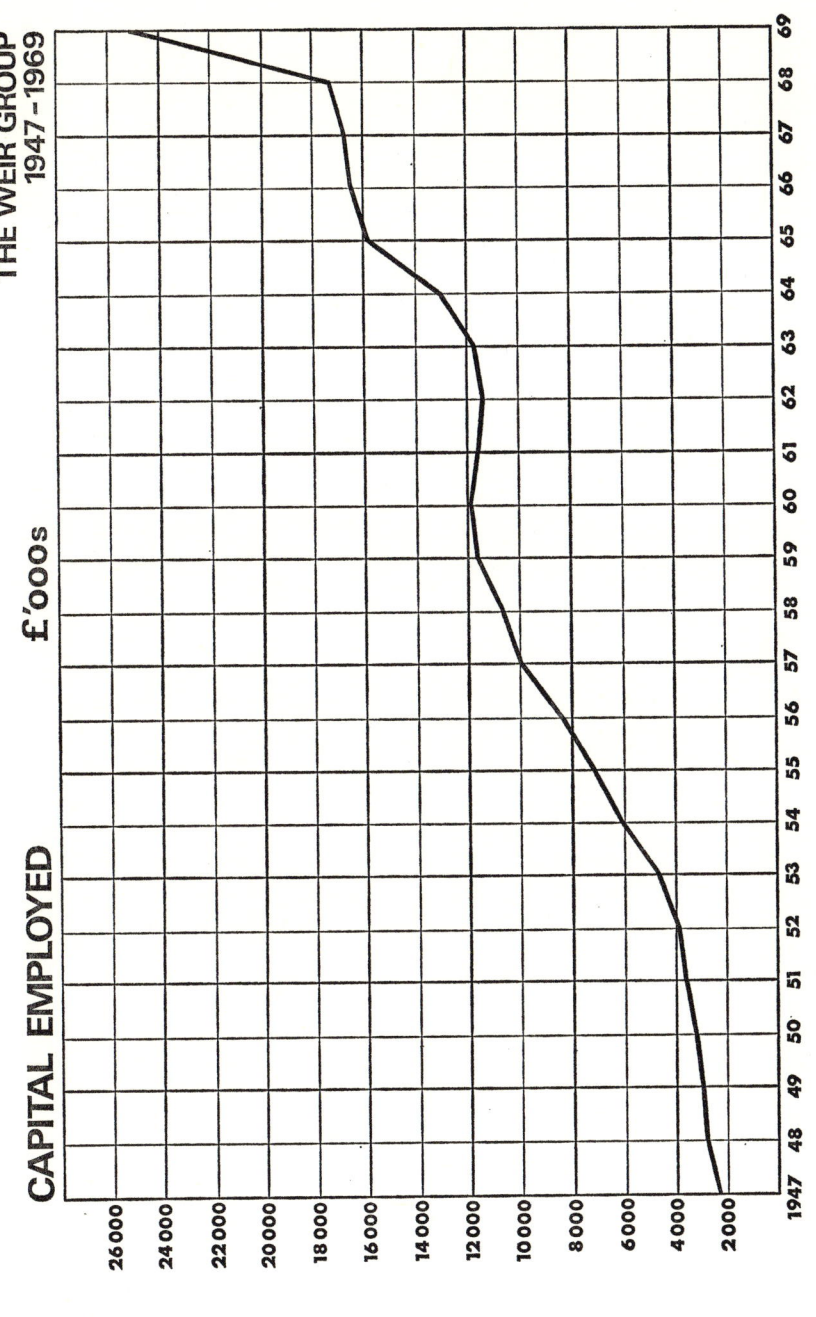

CAPITAL EMPLOYED £'000s

THE WEIR GROUP
1947-1969

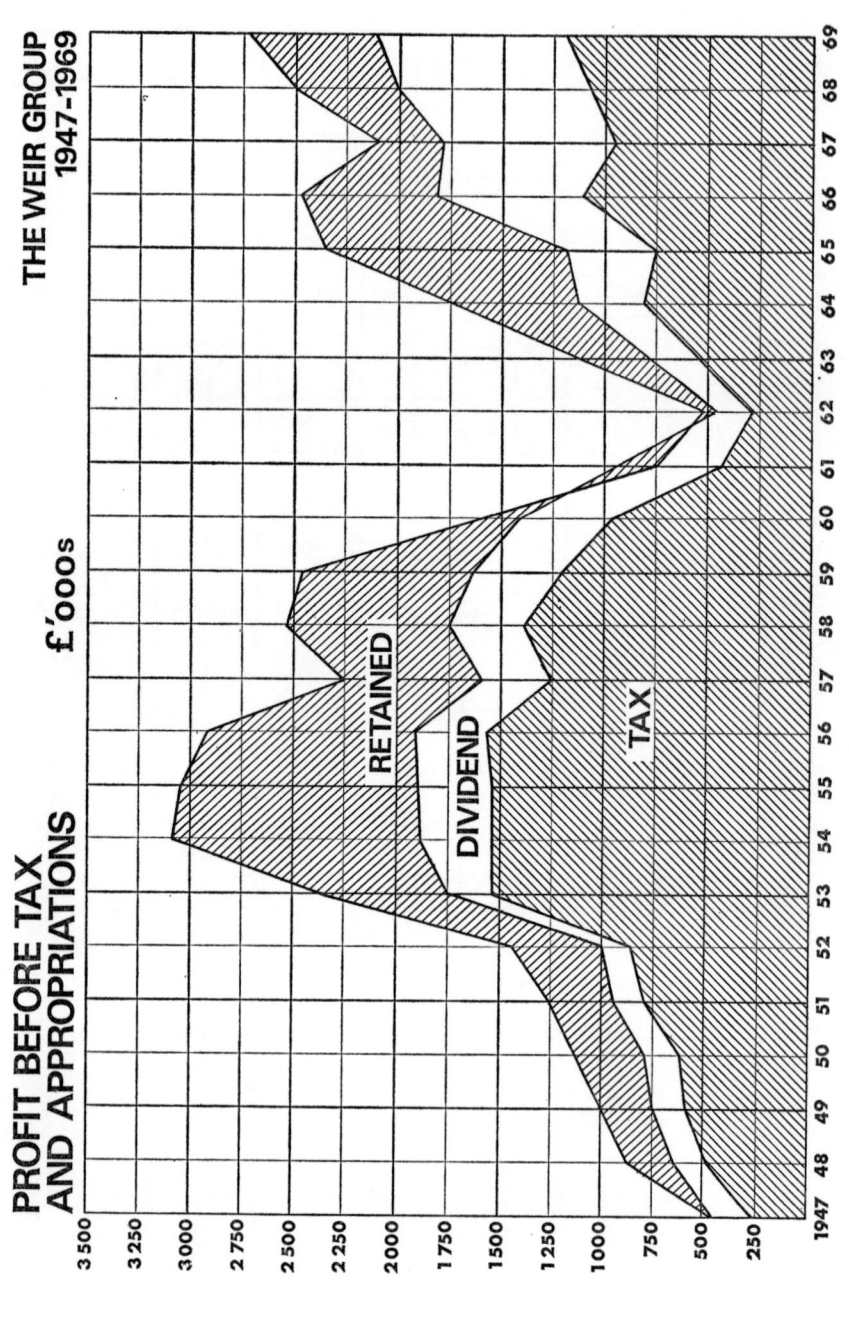

INPUT OF ORDERS TO CATHCART
(G. & J. WEIR)

YEAR	TOTAL	MARINE	LAND	NAVAL	HOME	EXPORT
1898	116,400 100%	86,719 74%	7,833 7%	21,848 19%	103,138 88%	13,262 12%
1903	126,445 100%	48,461 38%	18,716 15%	59,268 47%	111,763 88%	14,682 12%
1908	201,900 100%	110,761 55%	40,818 20%	50,321 25%	170,936 85%	30,964 15%
1913	680,263 100%	158,992 24%	103,781 15%	417,490 61%	468,713 69%	211,550 31%
1921	388,559 100%	231,559 59%	138,000 36%	19,000 5%	336,715 87%	51,844 13%
1925	573,924 100%	274,272 48%	200,346 35%	99,306 17%	473,663 82%	100,261 18%
1928	649,111 100%	350,000 54%	161,111 25%	138,000 21%	524,431 81%	124,680 19%
1929	783,463 100%	422,524 54%	183,105 23%	177,834 23%	650,822 83%	132,641 17%
1930	643,271 100%	324,423 50%	216,178 34%	102,670 16%	508,021 79%	135,250 21%
1931	550,471 100%	153,886 28%	137,375 25%	259,210 47%	469,042 85%	81,429 15%
1932	229,278 100%	53,923 24%	85,152 37%	90,203 39%	186,922 81%	42,356 19%
1933	549,756 100%	123,580 22%	103,198 19%	322,978 59%	513,111 93%	36,645 7%
1934	604,194 100%	159,454 27%	147,598 24%	298,142 49%	543,662 90%	61,532 10%
1935	793,104 100%	168,269 21%	179,089 23%	445,746 56%	722,575 91%	70,529 9%

YEAR	TOTAL	MARINE	LAND	NAVAL	HOME	EXPORT
1936	1,519,910 100%	389,790 26%	185,578 12%	944,542 62%	1,117,593 73%	402,317 27%
1937	2,303,009 100%	1,079,545 47%	278,820 12%	944,644 41%	2,094,988 91%	208,021 9%
1938	1,115,251 100%	412,569 37%	221,496 20%	481,186 43%	996,739 89%	118,512 11%
1939	2,804,560 100%	560,100 20%	311,260 11%	1,933,200 69%	2,687,868 96%	116,692 4%
1940	2,018,238 100%	320,535 16%	271,806 13%	1,425,897 71%	1,686,358 83%	331,880 17%
1941	1,716,931 100%	438,507 25%	201,842 12%	1,076,582 63%	1,400,672 82%	316,259 18%
1942	3,238,395 100%	524,443 17%	305,372 9%	2,408,580 74%	3,109,162 96%	129,233 4%
1943	3,070,310 100%	367,698 12%	121,217 4%	2,581,395 84%	2,955,780 96%	114,530 4%
1944	2,504,164 100%	340,310 14%	352,053 14%	1,811,801 72%	2,448,037 97%	56,127 3%
1945	2,203,568 100%	758,156 34%	539,815 24%	905,597 41%	2,136,697 97%	66,871 3%
1946	2,634,392 100%	1,252,016 47%	1,148,740 44%	233,636 9%	2,505,666 95%	128,726 5%
1947	2,784,824 100%	1,262,368 45%	1,412,513 51%	109,943 4%	2,514,864 90%	269,960 10%
1948	3,049,734 100%	1,254,873 41%	1,587,556 52%	207,305 7%	2,204,418 72%	845,316 28%
1949	2,518,112 100%	1,054,534 42%	994,198 39%	472,380 19%	2,068,812 82%	449,300 18%
1950	3,067,193 100%	1,250,104 41%	1,398,401 46%	418,688 13%	2,421,342 79%	645,841 21%

YEAR	TOTAL	MARINE	LAND	NAVAL	HOME	EXPORT
1951	7,480,698 100%	4,769,374 64%	1,680,533 22%	1,030,791 14%	6,275,295 84%	1,205,403 16%
1952	6,559,822 100%	3,627,984 55%	2,065,306 32%	866,568 13%	5,539,273 84%	1,020,549 16%
1953	5,235,533 100%	2,606,224 50%	1,286,144 25%	1,343,165 25%	4,245,292 81%	990,241 19%
1954	4,202,118 100%	1,788,162 43%	1,676,864 40%	737,092 17%	3,651,460 87%	550,658 13%
1955	4,770,353 100%	2,627,329 55%	1,470,429 31%	672,595 14%	4,030,844 85%	739,509 15%
1956	8,111,488 100%	3,953,548 48%	2,972,240 37%	1,185,700 15%	5,483,218 68%	2,628,270 32%
1957	9,734,679 100%	4,242,759 44%	4,128,824 42%	1,363,096 14%	6,657,861 68%	3,076,818 32%
1958	5,407,488 100%	2,128,630 40%	2,060,569 38%	1,218,289 22%	4,842,565 89%	564,923 11%
1959	4,774,364 100%	1,441,182 30%	2,690,998 57%	642,184 13%	3,680,625 77%	1,093,739 23%
1960	4,343,544 100%	816,167 19%	2,703,330 62%	824,047 19%	3,894,842 89%	448,702 11%
1961	5,895,862 100%	876,547 15%	3,681,445 62%	1,337,870 23%	5,242,591 89%	603,271 11%
1962	8,930,716 100%	663,011 7%	6,977,081 78%	1,290,624 15%	8,494,038 95%	436,678 5%
1963	9,760,465 100%	852,490 9%	5,812,763 60%	3,095,212 31%	9,317,732 95%	442,733 5%
1964	14,599,697 100%	1,213,241 8%	12,050,858 83%	1,335,598 9%	13,931,769 95%	667,928 5%
1965	5,783,485 100%	1,120,818 20%	3,321,064 57%	1,341,603 23%	5,242,259 91%	541,226 9%

YEAR	TOTAL	MARINE	LAND	NAVAL	HOME	EXPORT
1966	9,857,651 100%	499,894 5%	7,195,565 73%	2,162,192 22%	9,407,965 95%	449,686 5%
1967	5,680,071 100%	564,029 10%	3,859,931 68%	1,256,111 22%	4,920,032 87%	760,039 13%
1968	5,243,516 100%	978,170 19%	3,003,084 57%	1,262,262 24%	4,371,369 83%	872,147 17%
1969	6,423,479 100%	1,367,908 21%	4,263,815 67%	971,755 12%	5,481,675 85%	941,804 15%

Appendix Two

Weir Auxiliaries and Drysdale Pumps supplied to HM Ships during the Second World War

WEIR GEAR

Closed feed system machinery, comprising steam turbine-driven extraction pumps, air ejectors, controllers, etc.

Main auxiliary and harbour service boiler feed pumps of the steam turbine-driven centrifugal, and direct-acting types.

Feed water heaters and feed heater drain pumps.

Drain coolers.

Boiler feed regulators.

Oil fuel service pumps.

Harbour deaerating plants.

Gland steam condensers and ejectors.

Steam turbines for driving pumping equipments supplied by Drysdale and Company Ltd.

These were supplied to substantially the greater proportion of the high-powered vessels, from battleships to small destroyers.

Evaporating and distilling plants.

General service air compressors.

High-pressure air compressors.

Steam turbines for driving hydraulic steering gear.

These were supplied to a considerable number of the same ships.

High-pressure air compressors were also installed in a number of submarines.

'Paragon' and 'Monotype' air pumps.

Direct-acting boiler feed, forced lubrication, oil fuel pressure and general service pumps.

Feed water heaters.
Boiler feed regulators.
Evaporating and distilling plants.
These were supplied in large numbers for a high proportion of the lower-powered warships and service vessels, e.g., frigates, corvettes, sloops, minesweepers, trawlers, tugs, depot ships, etc., etc.

DRYSDALE PUMPS

Pumps of Drysdale manufacture are fitted in practically every type of naval vessel – from landing craft to aircraft carriers and battleships – for the following duties:
Main condenser circulating pumps (axial flow and centrifugal types driven either by Weir steam turbines or Drysdale steam engines).
Fire and bilge pumps (turbine and motor driven).
Forced lubrication pumps (turbine and motor driven).
Oil fuel service pumps (turbine and motor driven).
Sanitary pumps.
Fresh and salt water service pumps.
Hull and fire pumps.
Hangar spraying pumps.
Emergency bilge pumps.
Portable bilge pumps.
Evaporating plant pumps.
Oil fuel transfer pumps.
Sullage pumps.
Salvage pumps.
Pumps for refrigeration and magazine cooling plants.
Pumps for air-conditioning plants.
Condensate, circulating and fluid cooler circulating pumps for hydraulic pumping plants.
Feed transfer pumps.
Stern tube water service pumps.
Drain cooler circulating and extraction pumps.

The following pumps were supplied for special use in Submarines:
Sea-water circulating pumps.
Forced lubrication pumps.
Ballast pumps.

Oily bilge pumps.

Circulating and brine pumps for refrigerating plant.

In addition, large numbers of petrol and steam-engine-driven salvage pumps were supplied, together with portable emergency pumping sets for other classes of ship.

Appendix Three

The Principal Companies of the Weir Group and their Activities, 1968

(Direct subsidiaries of the Company are shown in bold type)

	Country of Incorporation	% of Equity owned at 2.1.69
ENGINEERING DIVISION		

Pumps, compressors, marine and power plant auxiliaries, valves, fluid monitoring and control equipment, hydraulic equipment, electric motors, drives and control gear.

	Country of Incorporation	% of Equity owned at 2.1.69
Weir Engineering Industries Limited	Scotland	100
Weir Pumps Limited		
(formerly G. & J. Weir Limited)	Scotland	100
Alley Compressors Limited	Scotland	100
Weiritam, SA	France	80
Societa Italiana Weir & ITAM, SpA	Italy	71
Drysdale & Company Limited	Scotland	100
The Harland Engineering Company Limited	England	100
Simon Electronics Limited		
(now Harland Simon Limited)	England	100
Simon Equipment Limited	England	100
The Harland Engineering Company of Canada Limited	Canada	100
Harland Group Holdings (Australia) PTY. Limited	Australia	100
Harland Group Holdings (South Africa) PTY. Limited	South Africa	100

	Country of Incorporation	% of Equity owned at 2.1.69
Weir-Pacific Valves Limited	Scotland	75
Dobbie McInnes Limited	Scotland	100*
Weir, Drysdale Service (London) Limited	England	100
Weir-Drysdale (Australia) PTY. Limited	Australia	100
Weir-Warmtekracht, NV	Netherlands	100
Peacock Brothers Limited	Canada	100

BUILDING DIVISION

Industrialized and traditional houses, schools and other buildings; private estate development.

Weir Housing Corporation Limited	England	100

FOUNDRIES AND ENGINEERING SUPPLIES DIVISION

Carbon and alloy steel castings, precision moulded packings and oil seals, metal pattern equipment and precision moulds.

Catton & Company Limited	England	100
E.Jopling & Sons Limited	England	100*
Osborn-Hadfields Steel Founders Limited	England	100
Osborn Precision Castings Limited	England	100
BAL Limited	England	100
G.Perry & Sons Limited	England	100*

AIRCRAFT EQUIPMENT DIVISION

Aircraft components and equipment, aircraft refuelling equipment, airport ground servicing equipment, reinforced plastics and packaging machinery.

C.F.Taylor (Holdings) Limited	England	100
C.F.Taylor (Metal Workers) Limited	England	100
C.F.Taylor (Hurn) Limited	England	100

* In addition to Equity, The Weir Group Limited owns all the Preference Shares in these companies.

	Country of Incorporation	% of Equity owned at 2.1.69
C.F.Taylor (Woodworkers) Limited	England	100
Zwicky Limited	England	100
Skyhi Limited	England	100
Servisales Limited	England	100
C.F.Taylor (Industrial) Limited	England	100
C.F.Taylor (Plastics) Limited	England	100
C.F.Taylor (Unity Designs) Limited	England	100
Adams Powell Packaging Machinery Limited	England	100

WATER DIVISION

Industrial and municipal water treatment plant and industrial water softening plant; sea-water distillation plant for use on land.

Weir Westgarth Limited	England	100
William Boby & Company Limited	England	100*
William Boby & Company (Australia) PTY. Limited	Australia	60
G.S.Tett & Company Limited	England	100

ASSOCIATED COMPANIES

Harland Engineering (Australia) PTY. Limited	Australia	50
The Vivian Harland Engineering Company (PTY.) Limited	South Africa	50
Walthon-Weir-Pacific, SA	Spain	19
Taylor Espanola, SA	Spain	50
Hardman-C.F.Taylor Aerospace Inc.	USA	50

* In addition to Equity, The Weir Group Limited owns all the Preference Shares in this company.

Appendix Four
The Weir Group of Companies in 1970

	Country of Incorporation	% of Equity owned at 1.1.71
ENGINEERING DIVISION		
Pumps, compressors, marine and power plant auxiliaries, valves, hydraulic equipment, electric motors, drives and control gear.		
Weir Engineering Industries Limited	Scotland	100
Weir Pumps Limited	Scotland	100
Weiritam, SA	France	80
Societa Italiana Weir & Itam SpA	Italy	71
Alley Compressors Limited	Scotland	100
Weir-Pacific Valves Limited	Scotland	75
Harland Simon Limited	England	100
Harland Group Holdings (Australia) PTY. Limited	Australia	100
Harland Group Holdings (South Africa) PTY. Limited	South Africa	100
Weir-Drysdale (Australia) PTY. Limited	Australia	100
Weir-Warmtekracht NV	Netherlands	100
Peacock Brothers Limited	Canada	100
The Harland Engineering Company of Canada Limited	Canada	100
BUILDING DIVISION		
Industrialized and traditional houses, schools and other buildings; private estate development.		
Weir Housing Corporation Limited	England	100

	Country of Incorporation	% of Equity owned at 1.1.71

FOUNDRIES AND ENGINEERING SUPPLIES DIVISION

Carbon and alloy steel castings, precision moulded packings and oil seals, metal pattern equipment and precision moulds.

Catton & Company Limited	England	100
E. Jopling & Sons Limited	England	100*
Osborn-Hadfields Steel Founders Limited	England	100
Osborn Precision Castings Limited	England	100
B.A.L. Limited	England	100
Polypac SpA	Italy	55
G. Perry & Sons Limited	England	100*

AIRCRAFT EQUIPMENT DIVISION

Aircraft components and equipment, aircraft refuelling equipment, airport ground servicing equipment, reinforced plastics and packaging machinery.

C.F.Taylor (Holdings) Limited	England	100
C.F.Taylor (Metal Workers) Limited	England	100
C.F.Taylor (Hurn) Limited	England	100
C.F.Taylor (Woodworkers) Limited	England	100
Zwicky Limited	England	100
Skyhi Limited	England	100
Servisales Limited	England	100
C. F.Taylor (Industrial) Limited	England	100
C.F.Taylor (Plastics) Limited	England	100
C.F.Taylor (Unity Designs) Limited	England	100
Adams Powell Packaging Machinery Limited	England	100
C.F.Taylor Inc.	U.S.A.	100

* In addition to Equity, The Weir Group Limited owns all the Preference Shares in this company.

	Country of Incorporation	% of Equity owned at 1.1.71

WATER DIVISION

Industrial and municipal water treatment plant and industrial water softening plant; sea-water distillation plant for use on land.

Weir Westgarth Limited	England	100
William Boby & Company Limited	England	100
William Boby & Company (Australia) PTY. Limited	Australia	60
G.S.Tett & Company Limited	England	100

ASSOCIATED COMPANIES

Worthington-Simpson Limited	England	50
Worthington-Weir Limited	Scotland	50
The Vivian Harland Engineering Company (PTY.) Limited	South Africa	50
E.M.G.Harland PTY. Limited	Australia	30
Walthon-Weir-Pacific SA	Spain	19
Taylor Espanola SA	Spain	50
Dart Herald (Support) Limited	England	50
Tyco-Weir Limited	Scotland	50

Appendix Five
Sources of Information

Abbreviations used in References:

LB – Lord Weir's Letter Books

MB – Minute Books of Directors' meetings

WB – *Weir Bulletin*

There is an album of technical diagrams, with explanatory notes, put together by James Weir in 1893 and containing material running back to the 1870s. The Directors' Minute Books of G. & J.Weir Limited run from the formation of the private company in 1895 and there is an unbroken sequence of Weirs' Inward Order Books from 1898 to the present.

From 1902 to 1915 the history of G. & J.Weir is copiously documented in William Weir's letter books, and thereafter, from the same source, much more sparsely. Other surviving correspondence and papers, for the whole period dealt with, are cited in detail in the footnotes.

During the period of the private company Weir's Directors' Minute Books were also used to record Directors' Reports and shareholders' meetings, both annual and extraordinary. From the formation of the public company onward, as well as Directors' Minutes, there is also, of course, a complete series of published accounts, accompanied each year by a Chairman's Review.

A history of Drysdales has been set up in type but not published, and I have also been able to draw on the MS of a projected biography of the first Lord Weir, for which the author was able to consult Sir John Richmond and others now dead.

There is a large collection of photographs dating from about 1900 on.

Privately printed works include catalogues and price lists (the earliest catalogues date from 1895) and also:

G. & J.Weir Ltd. 1886–1936, a 50 years' Retrospect.

G. & J.Weir Ltd. 1939–1945, The War Years.

The Weir Bulletin, 1919 onward – the house magazine of G. & J.Weir and latterly of the Weir Group.

PUBLISHED WORKS PRINCIPALLY CONSULTED

Brie, R.A.C. (Ed), *A History of British Rotorcraft*, Westland Helicopters Limited, 1968.

Checkland, S.G., *The Mines of Tharsis*, London, George Allen and Unwin, 1967.

Edmonds, J.E. & Wyne, G.C., *Military Operations, France and Belgium, 1915*, London, Macmillan, 1927.

Ewing, J.A., *The Steam Engine and other Heat Engines*, Cambridge, CUP, 1st Edn 1894; 2nd Edn 1897; Stereo Edn 1902.

Gablehouse, C., *Helicopters and Autogiros*, London, Frederick Muller, 1968.

Gillies, J.D. and Wood, J.L., *Aviation in Scotland*, Glasgow, Royal Aeronautical Society, 1966.

Haldane, J.W.C., *Steam Ships and their Machinery*, London, Spon, 1893.

Institution of Engineers and Shipbuilders in Scotland, *Transactions*.

Institution of Mechanical Engineers, *Proceedings*.

Jones, H.A., *The War in the Air*, 6 vols, Oxford, Clarendon, vol III, 1931; vol VI 1937.

Mitchell, B.R. & Deane, Phyllis, *Abstract of British Historical Statistics*, Cambridge, CUP, 1962.

Montagu of Beaulieu, Lord, *The Gordon Bennett Races*, London, Cassell, 1963.

Nickols, I. & Karslake, K., *Motoring Entente*, London, Cassell, 1956.

Nockold, H., *The Magic of a Name*, revised edn London, Foulis, n.d.

Periodicals: *Business History, Engineering, Glasgow Herald* (Annual Trade Reviews).

Postan, M.M., *British War Production*, London, HMSO, 1952.

Postan, M.M., Hay, D., Scott J.D., *Design and Development of Weapons*, London, HMSO and Longmans, 1964.

Reader, W.J., *Architect of Air Power*, London, Collins, 1968.

Rowan, F.J., *The Practical Physics of the Modern Steam Boiler*, London, (King) and New York (Van Nostrand), 1903.

Royal Institution of Naval Architects, *Transactions*.

Scott, J.D., *Vickers, a History*, London, Weidenfeld & Nicolson, 1963.

Scott, W.R. & Cunnison, J., *The Industries of the Clyde Valley during the War*, Oxford, Clarendon, 1924.

Smith, E.C., *A Short History of Naval and Marine Engineering*, Cambridge, CUP, 1938.

Wilson, C.H. & Reader, W.J., *Men and Machines*, London, Weidenfeld & Nicolson, 1958.

Appendix Six

by G. F. Arkless

(a) THE WEIR REGENERATIVE CONDENSER

The thermal efficiency of a heat engine is not only directly dependent on the maximum temperature of the cycle on which it operates but also directly dependent on the temperature range over which the engine operates. We now quote directly from the Presidential Address of Mr J.W.Atwell to The Institution of Engineers and Shipbuilders in Scotland, read to that Institution on 7 October 1969.

'Not only is it important to have the maximum temperature as high as possible; it is of equal importance to have the lowest temperature – the temperature of heat rejection – as low as possible. It is surprising how readily this is forgotten – and yet the great contribution of James Watt was the invention of the condenser, external to the engine. In those days steam was supplied at very little above atmospheric pressure and almost all the expansion was in the vacuum range. Even with modern high-pressure turbines, the work done above atmospheric pressure is not very much greater than that done below it. Gains at this end of the cycle can be very important. A good condenser should make the turbine exhaust pressure as low as possible in relation to the vapour pressure corresponding to the temperature of the cooling medium available. The cooling surface, therefore, has to be arranged in such a way that there is a minimum resistance to the flow of steam across it. At the same time, the exhaust steam must come into effective contact with a cooling surface of adequate area and the heat must be efficiently transmitted from the vapour to the circulating water. It is important that this be achieved without the expense of an unnecessarily large cooling surface. Also, air and other non-condensable gases have to be removed. If these gases are present in a condenser they exert partial pressures in addition to the pressure of the vapour, and the pressure at the turbine exhaust is increased by this amount, thereby reducing the available pressure drop across the turbine and reducing the useful work done. Still another point is that the condensate coming out of the condenser should not be appreciably lower in temperature than corresponds to the pressure, or it requires to get this extra heat put back into it, which is wasteful. All of these aspects of condenser design have been subject to progressive development over the years. Different designers have produced solutions which differ in detail, but to many the most familiar design will be the Weir regenerative condenser [shown in Fig. 1 in this appendix]. The wider tube spacing at the top reduces resistance to flow of vapour. The central passage allows a proportion of the vapour to pass straight to the bottom of the condenser where it encounters the drops of condensate falling from the tubes. These drops, like the film of water on the surface of the tubes, are necessarily colder than the exhaust vapour, otherwise there would be no transmission of heat. The vapour which has by-passed the tubes heats up these drops and, at the same time, is condensed by them.

'Air is removed from the condenser by an air ejector. The problem here is that the air and vapour in the condenser are intermixed and the aim is to withdraw the air without drawing too much vapour. So the air and some vapour are drawn across a nest of tubes under a baffle plate in such a way that as the mixture becomes colder vapour is condensed out and the proportion of air to vapour is greatly increased. The air, mixed with little more than its own weight of vapour, is drawn out by an air ejector in which it is compressed and discharged to atmosphere. This separate handling of the air and feed water was the subject of an early patent by James Weir. Hitherto it had been common practice to use a wet air pump whereby extraction of the feed water and air from the condenser was accomplished simultaneously. The introduction of the separate air cooling section was due to J. R. Richmond (later Sir John), a Director of G. & J. Weir Ltd, who patented the concept in 1902.'

(b) THE CLOSED FEED SYSTEM

The primary function of the closed feed system is to convey the condensate from the main condenser to the boiler. As has been noted in the body of this book, as boiler pressures rose, boiler corrosion became a dominant problem, and to overcome it the feed water had to be presented to the boiler as free from dissolved oxygen as possible.

The Weir Regenerative Condenser was itself a first-rate feed water deaerator. The regenerative feature held the condensate close to saturation temperature, thereby preventing absorption of air by the condensate, and together with the good air removal arrangements it was a considerable advance on previous designs.

The condensate was now presented to the feed system with relatively little air dissolved in it, and it was important that the feed system should not subsequently allow air to be absorbed. Indeed,

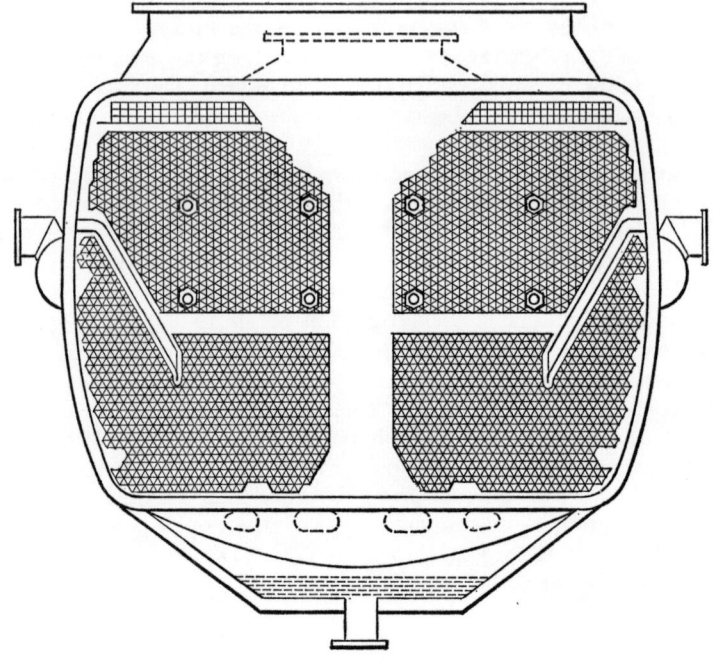

WEIR REGENERATIVE CONDENSER

Fig. 1.

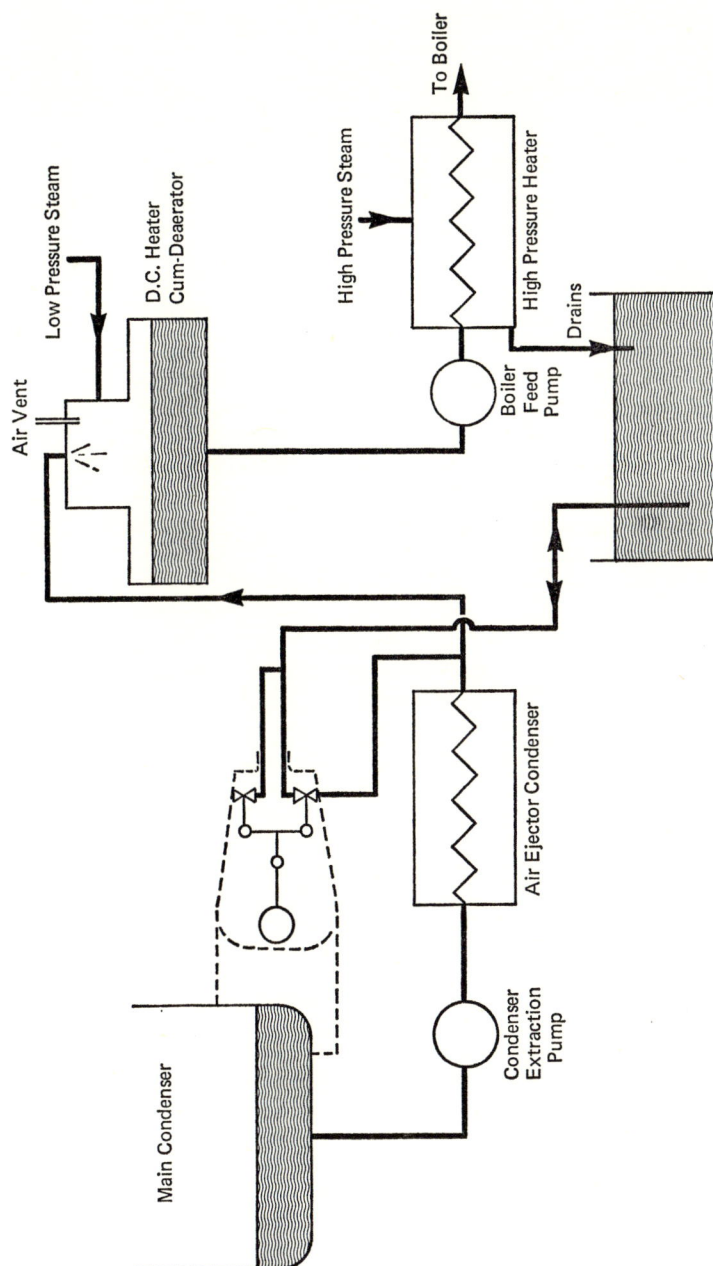

CLOSED FEED SYSTEM WITH DEAERATING DIRECT CONTACT FEED HEATER AND HIGH PRESSURE INDIRECT FEED HEATER

Fig. 2.

213

as boiler pressures continued to rise, the degree of deaeration achieved in the condenser became inadequate and a further stage of deaeration was incorporated within the feed system itself.

This further step, together with James Weir's invention of regenerative feed heating, added two important functions to be performed by the feed system: deaerating and feed heating.

Early feed systems were very simple. A patent, taken out in 1880 by George Weir, stated that the absorption of air into the feed water 'is very much favoured by the mode in which the water is ordinarily removed from the condenser to the boiler, in other words by the action of the air pump, by exposure in the hotwell and by the reciprocating or intermittent action of the feed pumps'.

This statement refers to systems in which a wet air pump simultaneously pumped air and condensate from the condenser, giving plenty of opportunity for the two to combine. Then the condensate was discharged to a hotwell or tank which was open to the atmosphere, so that yet more air was absorbed into the feed before it was pumped into the boiler.

This system was first improved by regenerative feed heating – that is, heating the feed water by direct contact with steam drawn from a point intermediate in its expansion through the engine. The direct contact heater, placed after the open hotwell, got rid of most of the dissolved gases by boiling the feed water before it was pumped into the boiler. Then, in the Weir closed feed system, exposure of the feed water to the atmosphere was avoided altogether, and at the same time provision was made for balancing the boiler demand for feed water against the availability of feed from the condenser.

Firstly the obvious step was taken of directly coupling the condenser extraction pump discharge to the feed pump suction. Thus the feed water had no contact with the atmosphere or any other source of oxygen once it had left the condenser. But this type of direct coupling is only possible if the amount of water to be pumped out of the condenser corresponds to the amount of water required to be pumped into the boiler. Under transient load situations, this coincidence of demand does not exist. The new closed feed system allowed for this by providing for storage capacity between the condenser and boiler. Flow of feed water to or from this storage and the system was governed by a closed feed controller which sensed the level in the condenser hotwell. Thus if the flow of steam to the condenser exceeded the flow of feed demanded by the boiler, the level in the condenser rose and the closed feed controller allowed feed to flow from the system into the storage tank (generally called the feed tank). If boiler demand for feed exceeded the rate at which steam was flowing to the condenser, the level in the condenser hotwell fell and the feed controller allowed water from the feed tank to flow into the condenser to supplement the available supply of condensate.

At first sight it might appear as if this arrangement took us back to a system where because of the open feed tank, the feed water was again exposed to the atmosphere. But it is only that quantity of water equal to the fluctuation in demand between boiler and condenser which is so exposed, and this is tiny compared with the basic steady state feed flow of condensed exhaust steam from the condenser. Thus even if the water flowing into the system from the feed tank is saturated with air, the effect on the total dissolved air in the feed system is relatively small.

It should be noticed that the arrangement described also covers the requirement of the feed system for make-up water, that is the replacement of water lost from the system either in the form of steam (boiler safety valve blow-off, engine and valve gland leaks, etc.) or water – pump gland leaks, boiler blow-down, etc.

Of course, it was relatively easy to add to this simple system either direct contact feed heaters – which also serve as feed water polishers, removing as they do the bulk of the gaseous solutes remaining in the feed water from the condenser, or indirect (tubular) feed heaters. Such feed heating according to whether it is done either before or after the feed pump is known respectively as low or high pressure heating. Fig. 2 illustrates a closed feed system with both low and high pressure feed heating included.

References

I THE INVENTIONS OF A SHIP'S ENGINEER 1870–95

1 B.R.Mitchell and Phyllis Deane, *Abstract of British Historical Statistics*, Cambridge UP, 1962, p. 221.

2 Engineer Captain Edgar C.Smith, *A Short History of Naval and Marine Engineering*, Cambridge UP, 1938, p. 174.

3 *The Statesman's Year Book*, 1895.

4 Smith, p. 174, p. 189.

5 Alfred Blechynden (of the Naval Construction and Armament Works, Barrow-in-Furness), *A Review of Marine Engineering in the past Decade*, Proc. Institute of Mechanical Engineers (IME), 42 (1891), p. 321.

6 For the Weir family see W.J.Reader, *Architect of Air Power*, Collins, London, 1968, ch. 1.

7 On Sir Charles Tennant and his circle, see S.G.Checkland, *The Mines of Tharsis*, Allen & Unwin, Lindon, 1967, ch. 9 and generally.

8 Some of the dates of James Weir's early career can be established from Board of Trade records of his sea service. Others are less certain.

9 J.A.Ewing, *The Steam Engine and other Heat Engines*, Cambridge UP, 1st edn 1894, 2nd edn 1897, stereotyped edition (this reference) 1902, pp. 357–8.

10 Ewing, p. 358. See also T.W.Atwell, Presidential Address to the Institution of Engineers and Shipbuilders in Scotland, 7 October 1969.

11 Blechynden, pp. 320–1. See also Ewing; Frederick J.Rowan, *Modern Steam Boiler*, London, 1903; J.W.C.Haldane, *Steam Ships and their Machinery*, Spon, London, 1893, and others.

12 Haldane, p. 325, p. 327, p. 331. See also Smith, p. 206, on Worthington.

13 Smith, p. 328.

14 Mitchell & Deane, pp. 223–4.

15 Smith, pp. 238–9.

16 David Pollock, *Modern Shipbuilding*, 1884.

17 Chart, 'Fifty Years of Clyde Shipbuilding', *Glasgow Herald Trade Review*, 1934. See also similar chart in *Glasgow Herald Trade Review*, January 1967. Glasgow/German comparison from W.R.Scott and J. Cunnison, *The Industries of the Clyde Valley during the War*, Clarendon Press, Oxford, 1924, p. 74.

18 On Langs, see S.B.Saul, 'The Machine Tool Industry in Britain to 1914', *Business History*, x, 1, p. 29.

19 Engineer Vice-Admiral Sir Henry J.Oram KCB, *Fifty Years' Change in British Warship Machinery*. Transactions of Institution of Naval Architects (INA), LIII (1911), pt 2, p. 96.

2 THE EXPANDING MARKET 1895–1914

1 R.C.K.Ensor, *England 1870–1914*, Oxford UP, 1936, p. 177.

2 *The Statesman's Yearbook*.

3 Ensor, p. 258.

4 Naval figures from *Whitaker's Almanack*, 1914.

5 Andrew Weir (cousin) to William Weir, 13 iii 1908.

6 Lord Weir's Letterbooks – Letter Book VIII, p. 237.

7 R.Hough, *The Big Battleship*, Michael Joseph, London, 1966.

8 *Statesman's Yearbook*, 1913, li.

9 To Thomas Weir, 26 xi 03, LB III, p. 352.

10 E.C.Smith, *Short History of Marine Engineering*, p. 191, p. 251.

11 *Trans*. INA, XXXVIII (1897), p. 154, p. 165.

12 *Proc*. IME, 77 (1909).

13 Smith, p. 253.

14 *Engineering*, 71 (1), (1901), p. 801.

15 Rowan, *Practical Physics of the Steam Boiler*, p. 456.

16 As 14, p. 800.

17 For Weir's public career see W.J.Reader, *Architect of Air Power*, Collins, London, 1968.

18 To Justus, 7 v 06, LB VI, p. 536; J.G.W. to W.W., 1 vii 06 – 1906, Files 20–21.

19 J.G.W. to W.W., 31 x 06 – 1906 Files 22–23.

20 To L. Chereau, 28 viii 12, LB X, p. 207.

21 Figures of orders compiled from Inward Order Books by J.D.Gillies.

22 A.L.Levine, *Industrial Retardation in Britain 1880–1914*, Basic Books, New York, 1967, p. 60.

23 *Engineering*, 71 (1), 21 vi 01.

24 19 xi 01, LB I, p. 328.

25 24 vii 03, LB III, p. 189.

26 LB VIII, p. 752.

27 Dates from Science Museum pamphlet, *Synopsis of Historical Events, Mechanical and Electrical Engineering*, HMSO 1960.

28 Rollo Appleyard, *Charles Parsons*, Constable, London, 1933, p. 173.

29 *Trans.* Institution of Engineers and Shipbuilders in Scotland, LVI (1912–13) – W.Weir, *Development in Auxiliary Units between Exhaust Pipe and Boiler*, 23 x 1912.

30 To M.Jullien, 8 vi 09, LB VII, p. 835.

31 To Andrew Laing, 21 vii 08, LB VII, p. 247.

32 To R.Traill, 25 iii 14, LB XII, p. 137.

33 To E.C.Carnt, 31 iii 14, LB XII, p. 162.

34 To Noltenius, 27 xi 11, LB IX, p. 644.

35 To Croll, Rotterdam, 23 viii 10, LB VIII, p. 789.

36 To Noltenius, 1 ix 13, LB XI, p. 122.

37 To Noltenius, 2 xii 11, LB IX, p. 573.

38 To Noltenius, 29 iv 13, LB X, p. 670.

39 To M.Jullien, 11 vi 02, LB II, p. 56.

40 To M.Jullien, 28 xii 03, LB III, p. 401.

41 To M.Jullien, 8 vi 09, LB VII, p. 835.

42 To Rawlinson, 10 xi 05, LB IV, p. 24.

43 To Eggers, Hamburg Amerika, 26 vi 13, LB XI, p. 45.

44 To Oram, Admiralty, 5 vi 05, LB IV, p. 621.

45 To McLaurin, Admiralty, 13 x 13, LB XI, p. 258.

46 To Lindeke, 8 vii 13, LB XI, p. 76.

47 To Noltenius, 30 iv 14, LB XII, p. 215.

48 To Noltenius, 25 vi 12, LB X, p. 59.

49 To Noltenius, 23 ix 13, LB XI, p. 201.

50 To Latta, Lindeke, 8 vii 13, LB XI, pp. 75–6.

51 To R.W.Allen, Bedford, 3 i 12, LB IX, p. 654.

52 To G.D.Irving, 17 i 12, LB IX, p. 692.

53 W.J.Reader, *Imperial Chemical Industries, a History*, vol. I, Oxford UP, 1970, p. 148.

54 To Fujii, 19 vii 11, LB IX, p. 469; J.D.Scott, *Vickers*, Weidenfeld & Nicolson, London, 1963, p. 252.

55 To Jullien, 8 vi 09, LB VII, p. 835.

56 Weir Files, p. 271.

57 To Patrick T.Caird, Greenock, 19 i 11, LB IX, p. 45.
58 To Thomas Bell of John Brown & Co., 3 xii 11, LB IX, p. 578.
59 To Caird, 21 v 13, LB X, p. 732.
60 To Caird, 30 xi 13, LB XI, p. 376.
61 W.Weir, speech at the Weir Dinner 1907.
62 To George Cumming, Harland & Wolff, 31 i 12, LB IX, p. 732.
63 To Latta, 10 iii 12, LB IX, p. 752.
64 To Fujii, 8 iii 12, LB X, p. 162.
65 As 61.

3 WEIRS AND THE MOTOR INDUSTRY 1902–12

1 C.H.Wilson and W.J.Reader, *Men and Machines*, Weidenfeld & Nicolson, London, 1958, p. 63.
2 W.J.Reader, *Hard Roads and Highways*, Batsford, London, 1969, p. 14.
3 Wilson & Reader, ch. 4.
4 Ian Nickols and Kent Karslake, *Motoring Entente*, Cassell, London, 1956, Part Three ('Darracq to 1920').
5 To Lord Ailsa, 21 ix 04, LB III, p. 929.
6 iii 03, LB II.
7 Nickols & Karslake, p. 122.
8 Nickols & Karslake, Appendix VI ('Darracq Models'); Wilson & Reader, chs 4–5.
9 LB II, p. 361, III, p. 73.
10 LB II, pp. 212–4, p. 307, p. 354, p. 455; Nickols & Karslake, p. 480.
11 LB II, p. 452.
12 To W.H.Kingsbury, Glasgow (a car dealer), 18 v 03, LB III, p. 109.
13 To C.S.Dougall, Dollar Institution, 13 vii 03, III, p. 181.
14 Lord Montagu of Beaulieu, *The Gordon Bennett Races*, Cassell, London, 1963, ch. 1.
15 Montagu of Beaulieu, ch. 5; Nickols & Karslake, ch. V. The two accounts differ slightly in what they say of the Opel-Darracq relationship. I have followed Lord Montagu.
16 To Alfred Rawlinson, 6 i 04, LB III, p. 414.
17 To Rawlinson, 11 i 04, LB III, p. 419.
18 LB III, p. 245.

19 To T.C.Pullinger, 15 iii 04, LB III, p. 578.

20 To Lord Ailsa, 24 iii 04, LB III, p. 536.

21 To James Weir, 17 iii 04, LB III, pp. 596–601.

22 LB III, p. 657.

23 LB III, p. 414, p. 418, p. 461.

24 LB, III, p. 532; Nickols & Karslake, p. 154.

25 Wilson & Reader, p. 73, p. 75.

26 To C.S.Rolls, 1 iv 04, LB III, pp. 634–5.

27 H. Nockold, *The Magic of a Name*, revised edn., Foulis, London, n.d. (1952?), ch. III.

28 To Lord Ailsa, 13 v 04, LB III, pp. 723–5.

29 Nickols & Karslake, p. 156.

30 To Sir W.Avery (of W. & T.Avery, weighing machines), 14 iii 06, LB V, p. 313.

31 To Smith-Winby, 24 iii 06, LB V, p. 353.

32 12 iv 06, LB V, p. 461.

33 LB V, p. 506, p. 519, p. 622.

34 31 v 06, LB V, p. 624.

35 LB V, p. 740, p. 777, p. 781, p. 798, p. 809, p. 813, p. 815, p. 817, p. 830.

36 For Caledonian Railway, see File 24; for G. & S.W., LB VI, p. 681.

37 LB VI, p. 209.

38 T.C.Barker and Michael Robbins, *A History of London Transport*, I, Allen & Unwin, London, 1963. I covers the nineteenth century, II not yet published.

39 LB V, p. 896.

40 To A.Denny, shipbuilder, 13 vi 07, LB VI, p. 796.

41 A.Morris Thomson to W.W., 3 i 08, 1908 File.

42 LB VI, p. 420, p. 798, p. 927.

43 To Lord Ailsa, LB VI, p. 757.

44 16 iv 09, LB VII, p. 663.

45 LB VIII, p. 945, X, p. 74.

46 LB IX, p. 335, p. 372; X, p. 71.

47 Nickols & Karslake, chs VII, VIII.

48 13 ix 06, LB VI, p. 54.

49 23 xii 12, to Smith-Winby, LB X, p. 440.

50 To William Roper, 13 iii 11, LB IX, p. 211.

4 THE GREAT WAR 1914–18

1 To Eng. Vice-Adm Oram, 5 viii 14, LB XII, p. 435.
2 To Eng. Rear-Adm Goodwin, 5 viii 14, LB XII, p. 436.
3 LB XII, p. 107, p. 95 (15 and 13 x 14).
4 LB XIII, p. 90.
5 Weir Board Minutes, 24 v 15.
6 LB XIII, p. 229.
7 LB XIII, p. 380.
8 LB XIII, p. 417. p. 467.
9 LB XIII, p. 247.
10 Reader, *Architect of Air Power*, p. 38.
11 To Northcliffe, 18 iii 15, LB XIII, p. 417.
12 Reader, p. 39.
13 History of the Great War, *Military Operations France and Belgium 1915*, Macmillan, London, 1927.
14 Scott & Cunnison, *The Industries of the Clyde Valley during the War*, Oxford UP, 1924, ch. V.
15 To Eng. Cdr A.R.Emdin, 13 v 15, LB XIV, p. 4.
16 To F.Dudley Docker, 1 vi 15, LB XIV, p. 82; 9 vi 15, p. 111.
17 R.K.Middlemas, *The Clydesiders*, London, Hutchinson, 1965; Reader, *Architect*; autobiographies of various Clydeside MPs.
18 Scott & Cunnison, pp. 98–9, quoting *Labour, Finance and the War*, a Report by J.E. and H.E.R.Highton.
19 Weir Board Minutes, 8 vi and 28 ix 15.
20 G. & J.Weir Ltd 1886–1936, *A 50 Years' Retrospect* (privately printed), p. 12.
21 Minutes, 26 vii 18.
22 G. & J.Weir, Directors' Report for 1917.
23 H.A.Jones, *The War in the Air*, III, Oxford UP, 1931, p. 253 n. 2.
24 J.D.Scott, *Vickers*, Weidenfeld & Nicolson, London, 1963, p. 116.
25 Scott, p. 75.
26 Jones, III, Appendices VI and VII.
27 J.D.Gillies and J.L.Wood, *Aviation in Scotland*, Royal Aeronautical Soc., Glasgow, 1966, p. 61.
28 Jones, III, p. 256.
29 Gillies & Wood, p. 64.
30 Jones, III, p. 255.

31 Jones, VI, p. 31.
32 Gillies & Wood, pp. 61–2.
33 Jones, VI, p. 38.

5 WEIRS IN THE POST-WAR WORLD

1   Wilson, *Unilever* I, p. 244; Reader, *ICI* I,; p.385. On the period generally, W.N.Medlicott, *Contemporary England 1914–1964*, Longmans, London, 1965; A.J.P.Taylor, *English History 1914– 1945*, Clarendon Press, Oxford, 1965.
2   Medlicott, p. 74; *Glasgow Herald Trade Review*, Jan. 1934 and Jan. 1967, p. 148.
3   Medlicott, p. 76.
4   Scott & Cunnison, *Clyde Valley Industries*, pp. 110–11.
5   G. & J.Weir Ltd, Extraord. GM., 9 Sept., 30 Sep., 8 Oct., 1919.
6   *Weir Bulletin* (WB) 5, p. 7.
7   Weir to Sir James Lithgow, 4 ix 34; Weir to McGowan, 18 v 20, LB XVII, p. 549.
8   As 6.
9   WB 3, pp. 4, 6.
10 WB 3, p. 13.
11 WB 5, p. 9, pp. 10–11.
12 G. & J.W. to ASI of Scotland, 30 x 19, printed in WB 3, Suppl., pp. 2–3.
13 WB 3, p. 5.
14 ASI of S. to G. & J.W., 11 i 20, printed in WB 7, p. 1.
15 WB 12, pp. 2–3.
16 LB XX, pp. 527–9.
17 LB XIX, pp. 312–5; XX, pp. 527–9; *50 Years' Retrospect*, p. 14.
18 J.R.R. to W., 19 ii 19, File 68.
19 24 iii 20, LB XVII, p. 250.
20 *Key Statistics 1900–1966*, p. 8.
21 Mitchell & Deane, *Abstract of British Historical Statistics*, p. 67.
22 Mitchell & Deane, pp. 221–2.
23 29 ix 20, LB XVIII, p. 536.
24 8, 13 ii 22, LB XXIII, p. 200, p. 243; CRL to W., 23 vi 22, File 99.
25 Extraordinary General Meetings, 27 xii 23, 11 i 24; Directors' Minutes, 14 iii 24; Ext. GM, 27 vi 29; Minutes, 5 vii 29.

26 AGM 1930; see also Directors' Minutes, generally.
27 Files 99, 101, 102, 105, 106, 131.

6 DIVERSIONS IN THE TWENTIES : HOUSING AND MONEL METAL

1 Medlicott, p. 82.
2 Speech by Lloyd George, 24 xi 18.
3 To Sir John Chancellor. On the whole housing episode, see Reader, *Architect*, ch. 6 (II).
4 To Crawford Greene MP, 14 ix 25, File 120; Reader, p. 124.
5 To Major C.H.T.Parsons, 11 ii 27.
6 LB XIII, p. 173.
7 LB XIII, File 61, pp. 216, 331; JRR/W, 23 ii 15, File 62.
8 To J.Austin, Cunard, 12 xii 23, File 109.
9 To John A.Smeeton, 3 v 20, LB XVII, p. 469.
10 To Sir Charles Parsons, 8 v 23, File 97.
11 As 8.
12 To A.Woodeson (Chapman Clark and Chesterfield Tube Co), 13 v 24, File 109.
13 Eng. Rear-Admiral W.J.Anstey to Weir, with enclosures, 3 i 28, File 136.
14 To Sir J.Biles, 6 xi 25, File 122.
15 J.R.R. to W. (at Monte Carlo), 1 ii 27, File 131.
16 To W.B.Lawson, INCO New York, 5 ii 26, File 124.
17 Directors' Minute Book 2, p. 13, 25 v 26.
18 To J.R.R., 3 iii 28, File 135.
19 Minute Bk 2, pp. 19–21, 12 x 28; G. & J.W.AGM, 26 v 28; Directors' Meeting, 4 ii 29.

7 DEPRESSION, AUTOGIROS AND REARMAMENT, 1929–39

1 Mitchell & Deane, pp. 66–7.
2 *Key Statistics*, 6; M. & D., p. 67.
3 Notice of Extraordinary General Meeting, 15 xi 29.
4 To Dadi Dhunjibhoy Bemanji.
5 36th and 37th AGMs (1930 and 1931).
6 37th and 38th AGMs; Directors' Meeting, 27 vi 32; 39th AGM.
7 Directors' Meeting, 27 ii 33 (Minute Book 2, p. 37).

8   Charles Gablehouse, *Helicopters and Autogiros*, Fredk Muller, London, 1968, generally.

9   To Lord Stonehaven, 21 x 25, File 122.

10   25 xi 28, File 134.

11   R.Kindersley to W., 28 x 25, File 122.

12   K. to W., 18 i 26; W. to K., 19 i 26, File 123.

13   W. to H.F., 25 xi 28, File 134; E.F. to W., 6 ii 29, File 135.

14   Ellington to W., 11 xii 33, and attached memo by W.

15   Minute Book 2, p. 36.

16   Gillies & Wood, *Aviation in Scotland*, pp. 54–9; see also R.A.C.Brie, *A History of British Rotorcraft*, Westland Helicopters Limited, 1968.

17   Minute Book 2, pp. 55–6.

18   Minute Book 2, pp. 65–6.

19   Minute Book 2, p. 73.

20   H.W.Richardson, *Economic Recovery in Britain 1932–39*, Weidenfeld & Nicolson, London, 1967, p. 36 and generally.

21   *Key Statistics*, p. 6.

22   Mitchell & Deane, p. 399, p. 400.

23   Minute Book 2, p. 32, p. 60, p. 65.

24   40th and 41st AGMs.

25   See correspondence with Cadman 1931–2.

26   To W., 17 x 35.

27   W. to Neville Chamberlain, 11 iv 39.

8   THE SECOND WORLD WAR 1939–45

1   Throughout this chapter, I have relied heavily on the 2nd Lord Weir's account of the company's wartime activities, as given in *Six Years of War*, a privately printed work, and in his own notes.

2   Reader, *Architect of Air Power*, p. 235.

3   Report of 52nd AGM, 1946, reprinted in *Weir Bulletin* 41.

4   M.M.Postan, D.Hay and J.D.Scott, *Design and Development of Weapons*, HMSO 1964, p. 261, p. 355, p. 357, generally.

5   Ibid., 255.

6   Reader, p. 237, pp. 249–50.

7   Postan, Hay and Scott, p. 265.

8   Ibid., p. 259, p. 316.

9   Ibid., pp. 315–6.

10 M.M.Postan, *British War Production*, HMSO, 1952 esp. ch. Eight.

11 Postan, Hay and Scott, p. 265.

12 Postan, *BWP*, p. 410.

13 Postan, Hay and Scott, p. 332, p. 333.

14 52nd AGM.

15 *Weir Bulletin*, 16, p. 2; 17, p. 4; 24, p. 1.

16 Reader, p. 310.

17 See, eg., 14 viii, 5 ix, 29 xii 41, Minute Book 2, pp. 71–2.

18 Minute Book 2, p. 82 ff., 10 x 44.

19 *Weir Bulletin*, 39, p. 1.

9 DIRECTION-FINDING IN THE FIFTIES

1 Figures of steamships and motor ships launched in the world from *Whitaker's Almanack* for 1950, 1952, 1957, 1962, 1965, 1969, giving gross tonnage as recorded in Lloyds' Register. No figures for The People's Republic of China, East Germany, Poland, or USSR.

2 *Glasgow Herald Trade Review*, 1934, 1967.

3 As 1.

4 Directors' Minute Book (MB) 2, pp. 140; 3, p. 125.

5 MB 2, p. 112, p. 138, p. 145.

6 *Whitaker*, 1950.

7 Much of the account of Weirs' post-war helicopter activities is based on R.A.C.Brie, *A History of British Rotorcraft 1865–1965* (Westland Helicopters Ltd, 1968). See especially articles by J.Shapiro, *Cierva Autogiro Co. 1943–51* and *Servotec Ltd, 1952–64* and A.McClements, *MCA Review of British Helicopter Activities 1943–46*.

8 MB 3, p. 134, p. 167, p. 176; 4, p. 8.

9 Details of the accident from Shapiro, as note 7.

10 MB 4, p. 77ff. (March 1950), pp. 113–4.

11 MB 4, pp. 113–4, p. 123.

12 MB 4, p. 135.

13 MB 4, p. 140.

14 MB 5, p. 8, p. 219, p. 318.

15 MB 2, p. 88.

16 MB 2, p. 106.

17 MB 3, p. 144.

18 MB 5, p. 7, p. 53, p. 56, p. 101.
19 MB 5, p. 214.
20 *Statesman's Yearbook*, 1962; 1968–9.
21 MB 4, p. 33.
22 *Key Statistics*, p. 6.
23 MB 5, p. 24.
24 Draft History of Drysdales, pp. 53–5.
25 MB 4, p. 104.
26 MB 5, p. 56, p. 60, p. 65.
27 MB 5, p. 106, p. 110, p. 119.
28 MB 5, 4 v 54.
29 MB 3, pp. 4, 5 – 1947–54; Lord Weir's paper (see below).
30 MB 5, p. 152.
    Generally, I have made great use of the paper given by Lord
    Weir at the London School of Economics on 20 November
    1962 – Seminar on Problems in Industrial Administration,
    Paper No. 302, 'Development and Organisation of the G. & J.
    Weir Group.'

10 THE HOLDING COMPANY

1 Directors' Minute Book (MB) 5, p. 115.
2 Annual Reports, 1955 and 1956.
3 Annual Reports, 1958, 1959, 1960. See also R.R.Silver, *Water
   Supply by Distillation*, 2 May 1960 (reprint No. 30, G. & J. Weir
   Ltd, Glasgow).
4 Annual Report, 1959.
5 MB 5, p. 237.
6 Annual Report, 1956.
7 MB 5, p. 312.
8 As (7).
9 Annual Report, 1956.
10 MB 5, p. 12.
11 MB 5, p. 33, p. 82.
12 MB 5, p. 102.
13 MB 5, p. 202.
14 MB 5, p. 269.
15 MB 5, p. 275, p. 305.
16 MB 5, p. 305; Annual Report, 1958.
17 MB 5, p. 305, p. 306, p. 310, p. 321, p. 329.

18 Annual Report, 1961.

19 Internal figures ('Considerations affecting 1959 Interim Dividend'), 2 November 1959.

11 THE WEIR GROUP BY THE VISCOUNT WEIR

1   Annual Report and Chairman's Statement, 1962.
2   Ibid., 1962.
3   Ibid., 1961.
4   Ibid., 1959.
5   Ibid., 1960.
6   Ibid., 1960.
7   Ibid., 1961.
8   Ibid., 1960.
9   Ibid., 1961.
10 Ibid., 1961.
11 Ibid., 1961.
12 Ibid., 1967.
13 Ibid., 1964.
14 Ibid., 1964.
15 Ibid., 1966.
16 Ibid., 1968.
17 Ibid., 1967.
18 Ibid., 1967.
19 Ibid., 1968.
20 Ibid., 1969.

Index